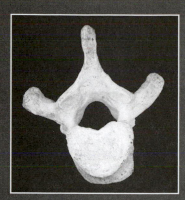

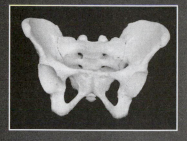

A LAB MANUAL & WORKBOOK

Exploring Physical
Anthropology

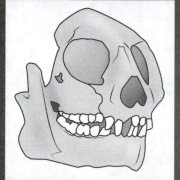

Suzanne E. Walker

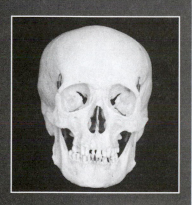

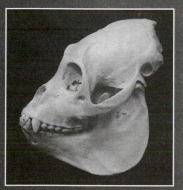

Morton Publishing Company
925 W. Kenyon Avenue, Unit 12
Englewood, Colorado 80110
http://www.morton-pub.com

Book Team

Publisher	Douglas Morton
Project Manager	Dona Mendoza
Copy Editor	Carolyn Acheson
Cover & Design	Bob Schram, Bookends, Inc.
Composition	Ash Street Typecrafters, Inc.

ISBN: 13: 978-0-89582-691-6
ISBN: 10: 0-89582-691-7

10 9 8 7 6 5 4 3 2 1

Printed in the United States of America

Preface

Physical anthropology deals with the use of empirical evidence to place humans in perspective within our historical and biological world: how we came to be human and where we fit among other living creatures. Although the wide array of topics may seem loosely tied together and thus difficult to teach in a cohesive fashion, the topics are tied together by the thread of an underlying evolutionary framework.

In this laboratory manual the evolutionary processes that resulted in humans become understandable to students through examples and hands-on exercises. The manual offers a basic, yet thorough, background in the main areas of an introductory physical anthropology lab course: genetics, evolutionary forces, human osteology, forensic anthropology, comparative/functional skeletal anatomy, primate behavior, and paleoanthropology.

This book is meant to be used primarily as a text for an introductory laboratory course in physical anthropology but also can serve as a supplementary text or workbook for a lecture class, particularly in the absence of a laboratory offering. It can be used with a minimum of laboratory materials.

Features

A lab class typically provides appropriate specimens (skeletal material, fossil casts, and the like), but not all institutions possess a complete collection. This manual can fill in many gaps by providing a full set of graphics and photos to supplement a laboratory collection.

Additional specimens and greater detail can be obtained by also using *A Photographic Atlas for Physical Anthropology*, by Paul F. Whitehead, William K. Sacco, and Susan B. Hochgraf (Morton, 2005) and the brief edition (abbreviated br. ed.) of the atlas (Morton, 2005). Throughout this lab manual, citations for these atlases are identified as (Atlas, p. 000, Figure 000; br. ed., p. 000, Figure 000).

☙ Apart from skeletal and fossil specimens, few laboratory supplies are needed. Most of the experiments and exercises utilize common, everyday materials.

☙ The graphics provided here make it possible to use this manual as a workbook for lecture classes to reinforce the material (Chapter 8 is the only chapter that is primarily dependent upon lab specimens for completion of exercises)

☙ Throughout the book, reference is made to the discussion in earlier chapters, building on previously gained knowledge.

☙ The exercises are planned to be easily completed in the course of a 15-week semester.

☙ Flexibility is built in by the following:

☙ Longer chapters are broken into sub-sections; instructors can choose to include or leave out portions to fit their schedule.

☙ The *Self-Test* section(s) within each chapter may be used either in or out of class.

☙ The online *Instructor's Manual* includes a set of *Additional Exercises* for some chapters; these may also be done in or outside of class.

Organization of the Book

This book is organized into five main topical areas:

1. An introductory section that reviews the meaning and practice of science, introduces evolution as a scientific endeavor, and provides examples about how evolution works.

2. Coverage of the genetic basis for evolution and the forces of evolution, to make the evolutionary process understandable and to learn the path from DNA to organism. Examples, empirical exercises, graphics, and self-tests are used to study genes in individuals and in populations.

3. A primer in skeletal anatomy and anthropometric techniques to analyze human variation in populations. The list of skeletal features is not exhaustive; primarily demonstrated are those that allow for siding bones, sexing skeletal material, and interpreting locomotion from fossil remains.

4. An explanation of functional complexes for diet and locomotion, evolutionary relationships, and comparative mammalian anatomy, with a focus on the nonhuman primates. This information, together with knowledge of skeletal anatomy, provides a basis for interpreting the fossil evidence for human evolution. Knowledge of primate behavior allows us to place humans in a behavioral as well as an evolutionary context, and to model the presumed behavior of early members of the human family. Lab exercises demonstrating primate behavior can be

conducted at any zoo, or may be substituted by videos recommended in the *Instructor's Manual*.

5. A straightforward presentation of the nonhuman and human primate fossil record, despite the complexity of the real-life picture. The emphasis is on the basics of morphology and techniques for interpreting fossil remains rather than on evolutionary relationships.

Organization of the Chapters

Each chapter begins with one or more questions that non-specialists typically ask about each topic (for example: "If humans evolved from apes, why are there still apes?"). The chapters subsequently answer these questions. The chapter begins with basic information to prepare the student for the lab exercises, which are the crux of each chapter. Following the Lab Exercises(s) are Self-Tests, which may be completed either in or out of lab and do not depend upon direct observation of specimens.

Ancillaries

The associated online *Instructor's Manual* (www.morton-pub.com) offers the following features:

- A list of materials required for each lab
- Answers to the Lab Exercises and Self-Tests
- Additional Activities for some chapters, which may be conducted either inside or outside of class
- A set of high-quality photos that correlate with those in the lab manual, which may be printed out (preferably in color, on cardstock) and used by the instructor for practice sessions, lab exercises, or testing purposes.

Physical Anthropology is a fascinating area of study that extends from the roots of humanity to the relatives on the branches of our evolutionary tree. Learning this material should be as hands-on, engaging, and dynamic as possible.

Feedback from instructors and students will improve the quality of this lab manual. for future editions. Your suggestions at www.morton-pub.com will be greatly appreciated.

Skeletal specimens and fossil casts were photographed by the author, using a Canon EOS Digital Rebel XT camera.

Acknowledgments

This lab manual benefited greatly from numerous discussions with Dr. Mary Willis of University of Nebraska at Lincoln, and Dr. Elizabeth Strasser of California State University Sacramento, as well as review by Dr. Margaret Breuchez of Blinn College and Dr. Linda Taylor at the University of Miami. For an encouraging and extensive set of helpful comments and suggestions, I am grateful to Dr. G. Richard Scott of University of Nevada at Reno. Dr. Marilyn Norconk of Kent State University provided a helpful review of Chapter 11.

I thank the generous assistance of Drs. Lesa Davis of Northeastern Illinois University and Mary Willis of the University of Nebraska, each of whom made fossil casts available for photography. I also appreciate the assistance of Dr. Neal Lopinot and Lisa Haney in providing specimens from the Center for Archaeological Research at Missouri State University. Drs. Lisa Sattenspiel and Carol Ward (University of Missouri, Columbia) offered the use of exercises from their laboratory book.

The working environment and moral support of colleagues and students at Missouri State University are greatly appreciated, and I thank the students of the inaugural lab course, wherein much of the manual was written and tested. Nick Evangelista and Scott Jackson supplied specimens for photography, Jason Shepard and Ryan Reusch provided assistance in early stages of the book project, and Lester Lakey aided with the Instructor's Manual.

Several companies graciously allowed me permission to photograph their skeletal and fossil casts: American 3B, Bone Clones, Inc., Carolina Biological Supply Company, Cleveland Museum of Natural History, and Somso. Bone Clones, Inc. also provided a number of specimen photos from its website.

The book team at Morton Publishing has been wonderful to work with. I appreciate Doug Morton's willing support for this project, Julia Havelick for the onerous task of obtaining permissions for specimens to photograph, and especially Dona Mendoza for her patience, attention, and effectiveness at keeping things moving! I also am grateful for the professional skills of Carolyn Acheson for copyediting, Joanne Saliger at Ash Street Typecrafters for typesetting, and Jessica Ridd for the illustrations. John Crawley provided invaluable photographic advice, which will continue to be useful for years to come.

My parents, Warren and Pearl Walker, and my late husband, Jesús (Quique) Pacheco provided continual encouragement for me to follow my interests. The completion of this book would not have been possible without the willing assistance and support of my mother, and the patience and loving smiles of my son Julian.

Suzanne E. Walker, Ph.D.

To my mother, Pearl Walker,
and my son, Julián Enrique Pacheco Walker,
and to the memory of my father, Warren Walker,
and my husband, Jesús Pacheco.

About the Author

Suzanne E. Walker, Ph.D, is Associate Professor of Anthropology in the Department of Sociology, Anthropology, and Criminology at Missouri State University in Springfield. She received her doctorate from the City University of New York, and an undergraduate degree from San Diego State University. Previous to her arrival at Missouri State University in 1999, she taught in northern California. Her primary research has been in the area of primatology, with a focus on primates in Venezuela and Brazil. Since 1997, she has assisted coroners and medical examiners on forensics cases involving skeletal identification. Her current research interests include medical anthropology, with a focus on health issues of Latino immigrants to Southwest Missouri.

Contents

1. Physical Anthropology as a Science

"Have you ever wondered...?"

- If humans evolved from apes, why are there still apes?
- Is "scientific creationism" an alternative theory for evolution?

The Scientific Method: Definition and Steps

Science can be defined as a search for order; it is the activity of seeking out reliable explanations for phenomena that we perceive empirically through one of our five senses. The procedure that is used to investigate questions about phenomena is the **scientific method**. The steps in the scientific method are:

1. **Observation:** Looking at some phenomenon empirically, using the five senses: sight, touch, smell, hearing, taste.

2. **Question:** Asking how the phenomenon came to be? (why, what, how, etc.)

3. **Hypothesis:** Proposing a suggested answer to a question; taking an educated guess at the answer. *A hypothesis must be testable.* It must be formulated so that if it is not true, it may be disproved through experimentation or data collection.

4. **Experimentation/data collection:** Testing the reliability of a hypothesis to corroborate or disprove it.

5. **Theory** or **law:** Based on confirmation of the hypothesis, postulating a theory or law. Both are based upon confirmed hypotheses, but they differ in some fundamental ways.

   a. A theory usually explains a phenomenon in which the explanation is supported by a body of evidence. Many theories are longstanding and well-accepted. Examples are the theory of relativity, gravitational theory, and atomic theory.

   b. A law is often a description of a phenomenon consistently observed under a specific set of conditions. Laws are more common in sciences such as physics and chemistry than the science of biology, and frequently can be described mathematically.

Science strives to explain phenomena and continually search for the most accurate explanation. Thus, theories and even laws are not absolute but, rather, are subject to being disproved in the face of new evidence.

The Process of Evolution

Evolution is best explained from the perspectives of what it is and what it isn't, and how it occurs.

What It Is

Evolution is *a change in gene frequency in a population from generation to generation.* If we consider any trait, in any population, and track the frequency of the genes that determine the trait, we'll find that the gene frequency changes over time. This occurs in nature, in a laboratory, on the farm, and in your garden. The changing nature of a virus as it is transmitted from one species to another, or the bacterial strain that changes to become resistant to antibiotics, or the anatomical and behavioral changes that occur between generations as humans selectively breed for certain features in a dog breed—these are examples of evolution.

What It Isn't

Evolution is *not* simply the changing over time from ape into human! Evolution can *result* in changes that accumulate over time so that organisms are different from their ancestors, but that is not the *definition* of evolution.

Within a population (a group of potentially interbreeding organisms), a certain number of individuals will have, for example, type A blood, type B blood, type O blood, and type AB blood. Also, certain numbers of individuals will have blue eyes, green eyes, or brown eyes.

For any given **trait** (such as blood type or eye color), if you count the number of people with each **form of a trait** (how many with type A blood, green eyes, etc.), your total count is a **frequency** of individuals with each form of a trait. Frequencies are expressed in percentages. For example, in a population of 1,000 people, the frequency of individuals with various eye colors may be: 650 with brown eyes, 250 with blue eyes, 100 with green eyes, and 50 with hazel eyes. In this population, the percentages are 65% with brown eyes, 25% with blue eyes, 10% with green eyes, and 5% with hazel eyes.

Many physical traits (as well as some behavioral traits) have a strong genetic, rather than environmental, influence. You have blood type A or B because of the **genes** you've inherited from your parents. You have green or brown or blue eyes for the same reason. Genes are functional segments of our **deoxyribonucleic acid,** or **DNA.** DNA is the genetic material and, together with certain proteins, makes up the chromosomes in the nucleus of cells. The set of genes on the chromosomes that we inherited from our parents provides the "blueprint" to produce each one of us, and a copy of this blueprint resides in each of our cells.

In any population, we can figure out not only the frequencies for the number of *individuals* with blood type A, B, O, or AB, but we can also determine the number of actual *genes* for a given trait. The number of genes in a population that exists for each form of a trait (for example, blood type A, or brown eyes) is called the **gene frequency.** Again, evolution is defined most accurately as *the change in gene frequency within a population from generation to generation.*

How Evolution Occurs

To illustrate evolution in action, imagine a hypothetical experiment. You will stand at the entrance to your student union for one week, blood-typing kit in hand. You'll take a blood sample from all who pass by (with their permission, of course) to figure out how many people have the blood types A, B, O, and AB. From the frequency of blood types, you can calculate the gene frequency for the A, B, and O genes (alleles, actually) in this sample.

With the results from the current generation of university "inhabitants," you'll wait 20 years for the second part of the experiment. Returning 20 years later to the steps of the student union, you will repeat the experiment, typing the blood of the next generation. The *gene frequency will have changed.* It may be just a little different from the previous generation, but it *will* be different, because the factors that cause evolution are constantly in action. In this case, **migration** has occurred as new people moved in to replace those who leave and, because of chance, they won't have genes in the *exact* same frequencies as those who have left.

A second cause of differences in gene frequency between generations is that only a *sample* of the sperm and egg cells produced in a given generation will combine to form new individuals in the next generation. Thus, it is highly improbable that the next generation will have exactly the same frequencies of blood types as the last generation. This illustrates one form of **genetic drift.** Migration and genetic drift are two types of **evolutionary forces.** A third is **mutation,** and the fourth is **natural selection.** Individuals with features best suited to their specific environment are more likely to pass on their genes in greater numbers. Evolution thus results from this change in gene frequency.

Although discussions regarding evolutionary change had been taking place for many years, not until the mid-1800s was a feasible mechanism for evolution proposed. At that time, Charles Darwin and Alfred Russell Wallace independently established this series of steps by which evolution could work. It is called natural selection.

Steps in Theory of Evolution by Natural Selection

The steps in natural selection are:

1. Within each species, more individuals are produced than can possibly survive.

2. Variation exists within each species, making some individuals better adapted to their environment than others.

3. Members of a population compete for limited resources. (Other factors that limit population growth are also at play here—disease, predation, etc.)

4. Individuals with inherited traits that allow them to be better adapted to their environment will be more likely to survive and reproduce than those with traits that make them less well-adapted.

5. Individuals with the well-adapted traits are likely to reproduce more, passing on their genes to the next generation in higher numbers than those with the less favorable traits, thereby causing a change in gene frequency.

6. If a certain form of a trait continues to have a **selective advantage** in a given environment, it is likely to become more and more common in the population. Accumulated changes in a number of traits over many generations eventually can result in descendants that are sufficiently different from their ancestors to be considered a new species.

These steps are illustrated in the example in Figure 1.1, showing the process of natural selection for short, broad wings over a few generations. In this example, selection favors the bird wing shape that is most efficient for fast take-offs—short and broad. Observe how the variation in wing shape is already present in the population (as a result of inherited features), but because those with the shortest, broadest wings are the most successful at surviving and reproducing, they pass on more of their genes, increasing the frequency of the genes that determine the short, broad wing shape in the next generation. The four evolutionary forces will be discussed further in Chapter 6.

All populations evolve from one generation to the next. Gene frequencies change as a result of individuals moving between populations, random sampling of parental gametes that produce a different combination of individuals making up the next generation, mutations in the genetic material, and natural selection.

Evolutionary Theory as Science

In writing about evolutionary theory, Darwin was aware of two separate tasks:

1. Establishing the fact of evolution; and

2. Proposing a theory to explain the mechanism by which evolution worked ("theory of evolution *by natural selection*").

No set of ideas has been proposed that provides a scientific alternative to evolutionary theory. That is, no alternatives to evolution have been proposed in the form of *testable hypotheses* that explain the genetic and anatomical similarities in groups of organisms, the origin of new species, and the changes occurring within a lineage through time. Although numerous arguments have been advanced to detract from theories of evolution, the arguments against evolutionary ideas are based on a lack of understanding of what evolution is and how the scientific method works. Without going into great detail, two main arguments of detractors of evolution are the following:

1. Evolution is *just* a theory, not a "proven" fact. This statement is unfounded and rests on the confusion of the terms *hypothesis* (an untested idea) and *theory* (an idea that has a basis in a corroborated hypothesis; theories are structures of ideas that explain and interpret facts).

FIGURE 1.1 *Process of Natural Selection for Short, Broad Wings*

The two terms are often mistakenly used interchangeably, which is wrong.

2. Evolutionists themselves disagree as to how evolution works.

In science, it is often said that hypotheses are never *proved*, just *disproved*. We attempt to explain phenomena based on the most reasonable explanations, but theories are always subject to change.

Evolution is a fact. It occurs. Gene frequencies change in each population, even from one generation to the next. That is established, and we can see it all around us. The *theoretical* part is *how* it occurs. For example, natural selection is a *mechanism* for evolution. Scientists may argue about whether natural selection or mutation is what plays the biggest role in producing evolutionary change, but this is *not* an argument over whether evolution does or does not occur.

Gravitational theory describes how gravity is thought to work, but people don't clamor to claim that gravity doesn't exist because it is "just a theory." Keep in mind the key difference between hypotheses and theories: Theories have already been tested and have been stated based upon confirmed/corroborated hypotheses; hypotheses have not yet undergone testing.

Decades (in fact, centuries) of scientific discoveries in the areas of geology, biology, anthropology, paleontology, physics, and chemistry have brought us to the level of knowledge at which we find ourselves now. Questioning, probing, critiquing—these are qualities in the nature of scientists, and we continue to engage in them to better provide explanations for natural phenomena. But *if it's not testable, it's not science!*

Measuring Evolutionary Success

We have established that because gene frequencies change in all populations from one generation to the next, evolution occurs continually in all populations. Evolution is nonprogressive. This means that a species doesn't strive to achieve some specific form by evolving consciously in a particular way. Rather, random factors (such as mutation) and nonrandom factors (such as natural selection) combine to change gene frequencies in a population.

If a species is well-adapted to its environment and the environment remains the same, the species may undergo little or no obvious change. Two excellent examples are sharks (see Figure 1.2), which first evolved about 385 million years ago in the Devonian period of the Paleozoic Era, and cockroaches, which first evolved about 305 million years ago in the Carboniferous period (also in the Paleozoic Era).

A long period of existence is one way to measure evolutionary success. Another is the diversity of species within a taxonomic group. Examples within the Class Mammalia are the more than 2,000 species in the Order Rodentia (rodents) and the approximately 1,100 species in the Order Chiroptera (bats). By contrast, the aardvark order (Order Tubulidentata) has only one species!

Evolution and Human Ancestry

The fossil record and genetic data agree in telling us that the modern African apes (chimpanzee and gorilla) and humans shared a common ancestor between 7 and 8 million years

FIGURE 1.2 *Sharks Have Changed Little Through Time*

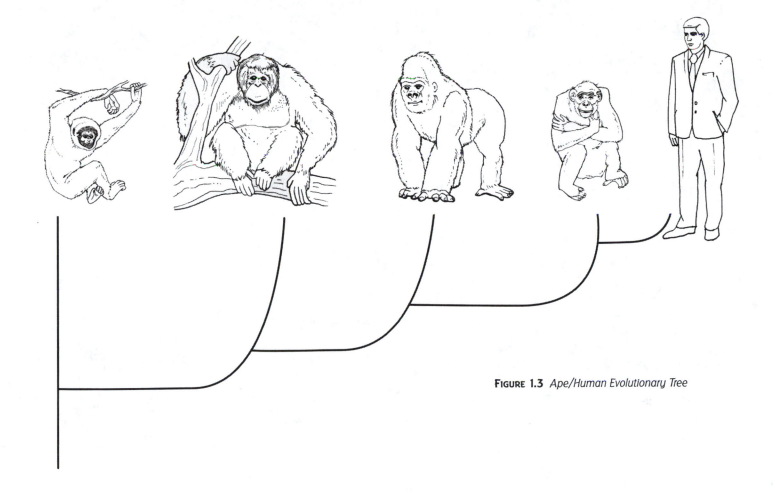

FIGURE 1.3 *Ape/Human Evolutionary Tree*

ago (see Figure 1.3). This common ancestor would have been quite ape-like, and the earliest members of the human family do indeed have many ape-like features (such as a small brain and a forward-jutting jaw).

Keep in mind that evolution continues to occur, depending upon environmental conditions and random changes (mutations) in the DNA. Thus, while both modern apes and humans have evolved since our shared ancestor several million years ago, we have diverged from that ancestor to a much different degree. While the apes have undergone little *obvious* change since that common ancestor, humans have changed a great deal in our appearance and behavior.

LAB EXERCISE 1.1

NAME _____ SECTION _____ DATE _____

Working together in pairs or groups of three:

1. Make up a simple experiment to investigate one of the following phenomena, using all the steps of the scientific method:

   a. Your neighbor's rooster crows every morning at 4:30.

   b. Your cookie dough disappears from the refrigerator every night.

   c. Make up your own phenomenon.

2. Using rulers, calipers, your imagination, or any other tool, document variation in the class population. List three differences (physical or behavioral) exhibited by each student from each other. How might each of these traits be selected for in certain (hypothetical) environments? Write a couple of paragraphs to illustrate how

that variation might be acted upon by natural selection to change gene frequency in this population. In your answer, clearly incorporate all of the steps of evolution by natural selection.

3. As accurately as possible, draw (don't trace) the dog illustrated below. Compare your drawings to those of your classmates. Notice that all drawings look somewhat different from the original. This is analogous to the intraspecific (within-species) variation that all individuals acquire from their parents and contribute to a population. Without variation, natural selection cannot occur!

SELF-TEST 1.1

NAME _____ SECTION _____ DATE _____

By now you should have enough knowledge and information to answer the "Have you ever wondered…?" questions at the beginning of the lab—along with a few additional questions.

1. If humans evolved from apes, why are there still apes?

2. Is "scientific creationism" an alternative theory for evolution? Why or why not?

3. What is the difference between a hypothesis and a theory?

4. What is an example of a "good" (useful) hypothesis?

5. What is an example of a useless hypothesis?

6. What is the definition of evolution?

7. What is gene frequency?

8. How do we know that evolution occurs and is not "just a theory?"

9. What are the four evolutionary forces?

2. The Organism and the Cell

OBJECTIVES

- Understand the levels of organization of the body
- Understand cell structure
- Become familiar with chromosomes, what they're made of, and chromosome structure
- Learn to compose a layout (karyotype) of the human genome

"Have you ever wondered...?"

✋ What are cells made of?

✋ How can you tell if a cell is from a male or a female?

The genetic material of all living organisms is deoxyribonucleic acid, or DNA. Thus, our genetic material is derived from that of our ancestors, from as far back as the first living organism 3.6 billion years ago. Members of the kingdoms Protista, Fungi, Plantae, and Animalia have DNA that is segregated from the rest of the cell by a membrane enclosing it within a nucleus. These are the **eukaryotes** (G *eus*: true, *karyon*: nut, kernel), as opposed to the more primitive **prokaryotes** (G *pro*: before, *karyon*: nut), the latter of which are made up of members of the kingdom Monera (sometimes divided into two kingdoms). These organisms lack a nucleus surrounding the genetic material (see Figure 2.1).

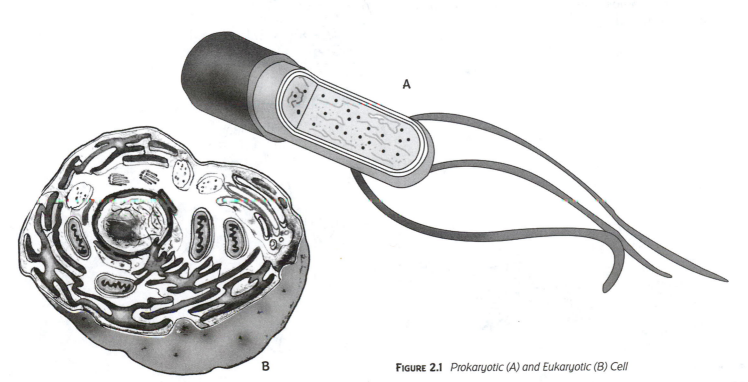

A

B

FIGURE 2.1 *Prokaryotic (A) and Eukaryotic (B) Cell*

The Basic Body Plan

In comparing our body plan with those of other organisms, we find greater similarity to those with whom we share a more recent ancestry. All living vertebrates shared a common ancestor more than 500 million years ago. The genetic material (DNA) passed down from that common ancestor dictates the development of the same features in various groups. We have a femur, humerus, and mandible, as do salamanders, crocodiles, birds, and horses, because our shared common ancestor also had those bones (Figure 2.2). These features we have in common because of our shared ancestry are called **homologous features**.

The human body plan thus shares some basic similarities to other animals, particularly the vertebrates. We all have **cells,** the fundamental units of life. Cells are organized into the **tissues,** which form **organs** (for example, heart and lungs). Organs function together as part of various **organ systems** (for example, cardiovascular system and muscular system), and all of the organ systems are "packaged" into an **organism** (us). In Figure 2.3 observe the relationship of these various levels of organization from the organs to the cells making up the organ tissues.

Over the next few chapters that comprise this section, we'll be "zooming in and out" from looking at entire organisms to the component parts and their functions, then back to the whole organism. In this way, we'll get a look at the whole picture.

Now that you are familiar with the basic body plan, you will learn about the genetic basis for it. First we will discuss the cell, the fundamental unit of living things. Then we will cover the structures that are made up of the genetic material—the **chromosomes**—and conclude the chapter with how they all fit together.

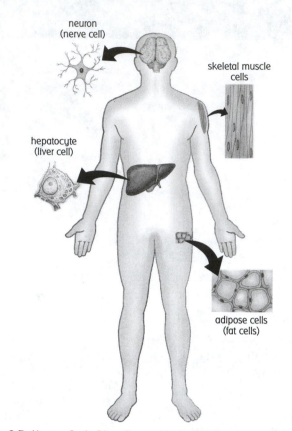

FIGURE 2.3 *Human Body Plan: Organs Made of Cells*

FIGURE 2.2 *Various Vertebrates Demonstrating Same Basic Body Plan*

Cells

Cells are responsible for arranging molecules into living matter. Most plants and animals have millions, or even billions or trillions, of cells, with various types specialized for specific roles in the body. The human body is estimated to have anywhere from 10 trillion to 100 trillion cells, with the number differing from individual to individual and throughout our lifetime. Each cell has a full set of genetic information that directs life and its processes—growth, development, and metabolism. This genetic information is passed from parent to offspring.

Cell Structure

A typical cell is composed of water, salt, proteins, lipids, carbohydrates, and nucleic acids, all held within a permeable membrane. In eukaryotes, a nucleus separates the genetic material from the **cytoplasm.** In the cytoplasm, the various **organelles** each have a function. You should be familiar with the structure and function of the following cell components, most of which are shown in Figure 2.4:

- **plasma membrane** A double-layered membrane, composed of phospholipids and protein molecules, that gives form to the cell and controls passage of material into and out of the cell.

- **nucleus** Contains the genetic material (DNA), separated from the rest of the cell by a **nuclear membrane.**

- **nucleolus** Seen as a dark mass in the nucleus, is made up of proteins and ribosomal RNA and is the site of ribosome production.

- **cytoplasm** Fluid, jelly-like substance, between the cell membrane and the nucleus, in which organelles are suspended.

- **mitochondria** Oblong organelle where adenosine triphosphate (ATP) production occurs for cellular energy; mitochondrial folds provide surface area for chemical reactions.

- **ribosome** Small structures made of proteins and RNA, "reads" RNA strand during protein synthesis; occur free and on endoplasmic reticulum.

- **endoplasmic reticulum (e.r.)** Membranous network of channels in cytoplasm, continuous with nuclear membrane, that forms a pathway for transporting substances within the cell and stores synthesized molecules (intracellular circulatory system).

- **centriole** Pairs of organelles composed of microtubules; organizes the cytoskeleton for cell division.

- **lysosome** Sac-like attachment to cell membrane that digests unneeded molecules; formed from vesicles of Golgi body.

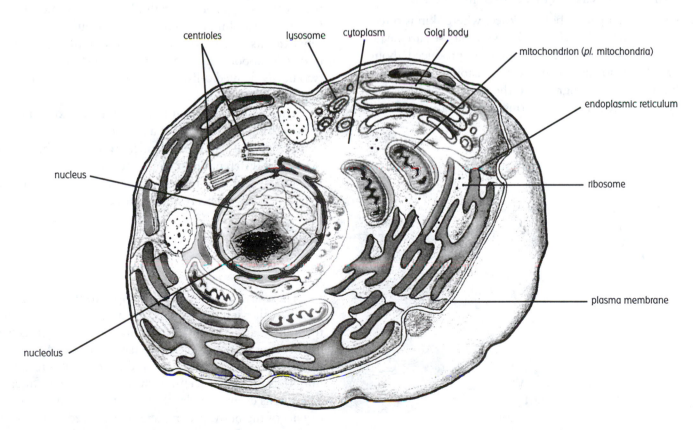

FIGURE 2.4 *Generalized Eukaryotic Cell*

✋**Golgi body and vesicles** Delivery system of cell, which collects, modifies, packages, and distributes **vesicles,** molecules that are synthesized at one location and used at another.

✋**cytoskeleton** Network of microtubules and microfilaments; dispersed in cytoplasm to provide a structural framework for cell division; composed of the proteins tubulin, actin, and myosin.

Classes of Cells

The body has two classes of cells. Figure 2.5 provides some examples.

1. **Somatic cells,** the thousands of types of cells making up our body structure, and

2. **Gametes,** or **sex cells** (**sperm** or **egg** cells), which are of only one type.

Now take a look at two types of somatic cells by following these instructions:

1. Pull out a hair. The expanded base of your hair is embedded in a **hair follicle,** which is like a little sac housed in your skin. The portion of a hair you can see sticking out of your scalp is the hair shaft, which consists of dead cells and proteins. The part of your hair that is buried beneath the surface of your skin is made up of living cells. You can see evidence of this if, when you pluck out a hair, you can see a white covering at the end. This is the hair bulb, which is made up of living cells.

2. Now scratch your elbow or knee, where skin is often relatively dry. The white flakes you may see are dead skin cells (see Figure 2.6). They were produced about a week previously through cell division in the deeper skin layers, then migrated to the surface. The basal cell layer of your epidermis is constantly producing new skin cells.

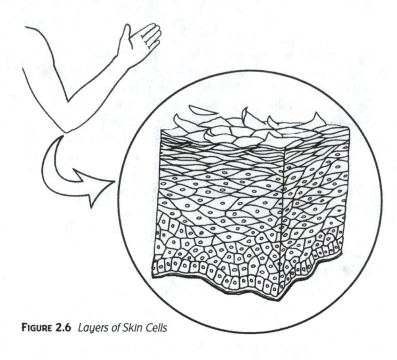

FIGURE 2.6 *Layers of Skin Cells*

Development

All of the cells in an individual are derived from the fertilized egg, the **zygote.** In this single original cell, the hereditary information (DNA) is stored in the nucleus. One-half of this hereditary information (23 chromosomes) has come from the mother's egg, and one-half (23 chromosomes) from the father's sperm. Immediately after fertilization, the zygote first replicates its hereditary material (DNA), then divides into two cells, apportioning one-half of its DNA into each of the two newly formed cells. Each new cell divides in the same way.

This cell division continues until there exists a mass of cells with the appearance of a mulberry. These cells, which up to this point had been identical to one another, begin the process of **differentiation** from one another. That is, after cell division, they suddenly begin to grow and in different ways from each other. This results in three embryonic layers:

1. endoderm,

2. mesoderm, and

3. ectoderm.

These layers eventually develop into the inner primitive gut and other internal organs, the musculoskeletal system and the kidney, and the outside covering of the body together with the nervous system and the eye (see Figure 2.7).

Continued cell division and differentiation results in hundreds of types of cells, each with a different function. These cells eventually develop into the various tissues and organs of the body. A complete set of hereditary information remains stored, intact, in each of the body's somatic cells.

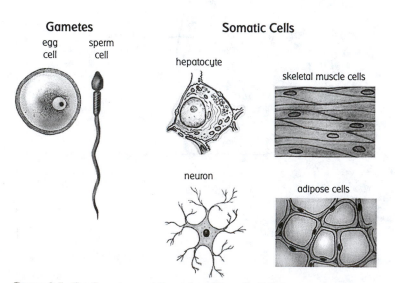

FIGURE 2.5 *The Gametes, and Examples of Somatic Cells*

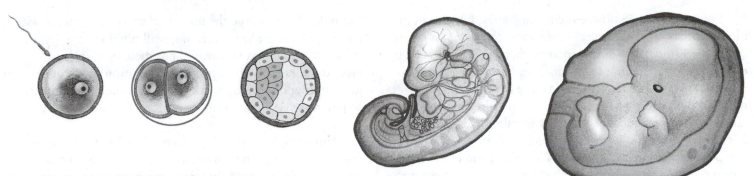

FIGURE 2.7 *Overview of Embryological Development*

The process of cell division in which somatic cells divide to produce more somatic cells is called **mitosis.** Cell division will be discussed in detail in Chapter 4. Keep in mind that, although individuals each have many types of somatic cells, they produce only one type of gamete—eggs or sperm. Sperm originate in the testes of the male, and eggs in the ovaries of females. Both types of gametes arise by **meiosis.** In this process of gamete formation, an individual's genetic information is "reshuffled" to produce the variation that prepares for passing genetic information to the offspring. Each sperm and egg cell that an individual produces is unique in terms of its combination of genetic information.

Chromosomes

We soon will be delving into the molecular world of the actual genetic material, but first we will cover the manner in which the genetic material is packaged. The genetic material, again, is deoxyribonucleic acid, or DNA. Most DNA is found in the nucleus of cells. This nuclear DNA, together with the proteins that it is coiled around, is packaged into **chromosomes** (G *chrome*: color; *soma*: body). Chromosomes are visible in the form shown in Figure 2.8 only during cell division, when the genetic material condenses and contracts. Note the **arms,** the **centromere** (L *centro*: central; *mere*: part), and the **sister chromatids.** When the cell is not in the process of cell division, the chromosomes remain uncoiled and diffuse in a form called **chromatin.**

This chromosome is shown in its doubled state, the way it appears early in the process of cell division. Before cell division begins, the genetic material (DNA) making up the chromosomes is replicated, so the chromosomes will appear first in their doubled state. They will be made up of two identical sister chromatids.

The number of chromosomes, and thus the amount of genetic material, is the same for all members of a species. For example, a goldfish has 92 chromosomes in each of its somatic cells, a chicken and a dog each have 78, a rat has 42, and a fruit fly has 4. A baboon has 42 chromosomes, a chimpanzee 48, and a human 46. The number of chromosomes does not correlate with "complexity" or place within

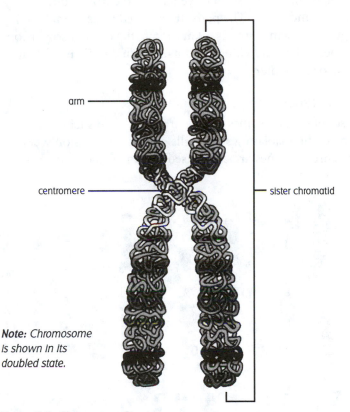

arm

centromere

sister chromatid

Note: Chromosome is shown in its doubled state.

FIGURE 2.8 *Chromosome Structure*

the biological classification system, as chromosomes of different species are of varying sizes, with different proportions of active regions.

Chromosomes in Humans

In humans, the chromosome number of 46 refers to the number in *somatic cells.* Remember that all of these cells originally were derived, via continual mitosis, from the zygote, which consisted of one set of 23 chromosomes from the mother's egg and 23 from the father's sperm. These two sets of 23 chromosomes make up the full complement of 46 chromosomes, referred to as the **diploid** number. The single set of 23 chromosomes contained within each *gamete* (egg or sperm cell) is referred to as the **haploid** number. When a haploid sperm and egg combine, the zygote they form will have the full (diploid) complement of 46 chromosomes.

Humans have 23 different chromosomes, which can be identified based on their *size*, *centromere location*, and *banding pattern* (the bands show up after chemical staining). With one exception, resulting from mistakes before microscopes were as powerful as they are today, the chromosomes are numbered according to their size, with number 1 being the largest. Chromosome 21 is actually smaller than 22. The 23rd chromosome is a sex chromosome, X or Y.

Because each person inherits 23 chromosomes from the mother and 23 from the father, we have two sets of chromosomes in each cell. All of the 23 members of a set can be arranged into pairs so that we have two chromosome 1s, two 2s, and so on. The pairs are referred to as **homologous**. Figure 2.9 demonstrates a **karyotype**, the chromosomal complement of an individual. Is the individual in Figure 2.9 a male or a female?

Karyotypes

A set of chromosomes can be organized into such a karyotype by first isolating some cells during cell division when the chromosomes are condensed and in visible form. For example, if you scrape the inner surface of your cheek with a toothpick, you almost certainly will obtain some dividing cells. After staining, you would put these on a slide to be viewed under a microscope and photograph the image. From the resulting photograph, you would arrange the chromosomes into matching (homologous) pairs based on the criteria listed.

This completes your karyotype. The 23 chromosomes fall into several groups, based on their size and centromere location. Keep in mind that these same 46 chromosomes are found in the nucleus of *each* somatic cell and are identical copies of those in the nucleus of *you* back when you were just a zygote (Figure 2.10).

One use of a karyotype is to evaluate the health of a developing fetus by examining its chromosomes. During pregnancy, a karyotype is made with cells taken from the amniotic fluid surrounding the fetus. Chromosomal anomalies, or abnormalities, usually are fatal; these will be discussed further in Chapter 4.

Chromosome pairs numbered 1 through 22 are called **autosomes**, and pair number 23 consists of the **sex**

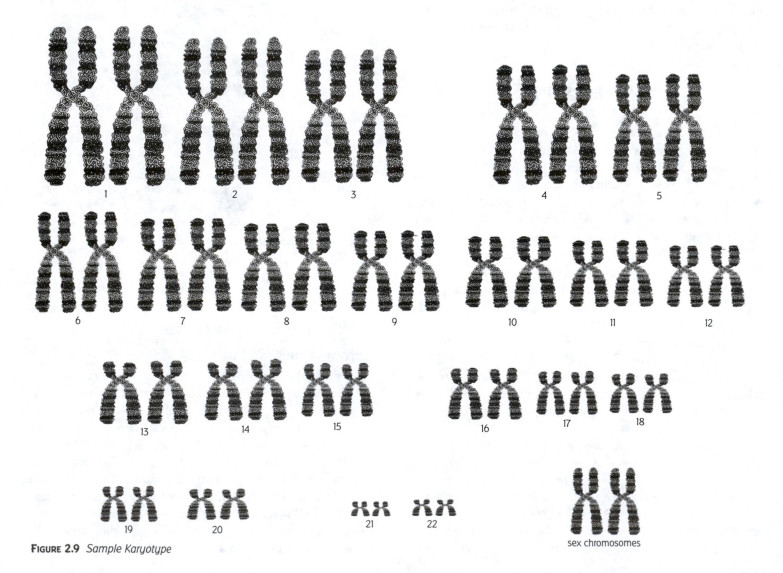

FIGURE 2.9 *Sample Karyotype*

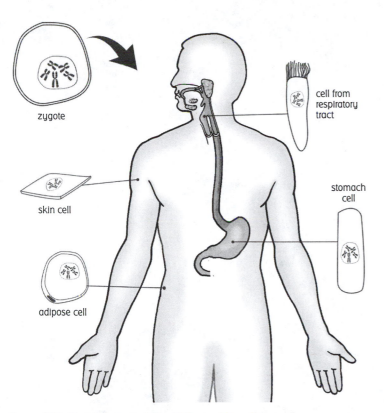

FIGURE 2.10 *Body's Somatic Cells, All Derived From Zygote*

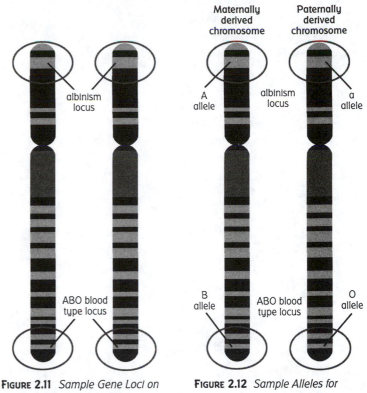

FIGURE 2.11 *Sample Gene Loci on Chromosome 9*

FIGURE 2.12 *Sample Alleles for Genes on Chromosome 9*

chromosomes, **X** and **Y**. The sex chromosomes determine an individual's sex. Each female has two X chromosomes along with the 22 pairs of autosomes in each somatic cell. Each male has one X and one Y chromosome. The much larger X chromosome has more than 1,100 genes, and the Y chromosome has only about 250 genes.

Homologous Chromosomes

What makes a chromosome pair homologous? Although the size, shape, and banding pattern can help identify which members of a pair go together to form a pair and which of the 23 types they are, what makes a pair homologous is *what is on the chromosomes*. A **gene** is a segment of DNA that codes for a specific polypeptide or protein (which eventually determines one's traits). The position a gene occupies on a chromosome is called a **locus** (*pl.* loci). A locus is analogous to a street address, with many loci on each chromosome. Larger chromosomes have more loci and more genes than do smaller chromosomes.

Two chromosomes are **homologous** when the genes occurring at a given locus code for the same trait on both chromosomes. Figure 2.11 gives examples of genes on chromosomes. We'll learn more about genes in Chapter 3.

Because the karyotype represented within each somatic cell of an individual consists of two sets of chromosomes

(one set from the mother's egg and another set from the father's sperm), different "versions" of a gene may appear on each member of a pair of homologous chromosomes. For example, at the locus for ABO blood type, the mother's egg may have carried a gene coding for type A blood (see Figure 2.12). The corresponding locus on the chromosome contributed from the father's sperm may have a gene coding for type O blood. These alternative versions of a gene are called **alleles** (in the example, B allele, O allele).

Organisms, Cells, and Chromosomes

Chromosomes are made up of our genetic material, DNA. DNA controls all cell processes, and thus dictates the development, metabolism, and repair of the body in case of illness or injury. Chromosomes are replicated to allow for the production of new cells for two purposes: to make new somatic cells that maintain the body, and to make gametes that combine in a new individual and carry our genetic information to the next generation. The reshuffling of genetic material that occurs during the process of gamete formation, together with the combining of parental genes in sexually reproducing species leads to incredible variation within each species. This variation is what provides the raw material upon which natural selection can act.

LAB EXERCISE 2.1

NAME _____ SECTION _____ DATE _____

Pretend that you've just scraped the inside of your cheek with a toothpick to get a cell sample. You put your inner cheek "extract" on a microscope slide, observe it under magnification, then take a black and white photo of the magnified slide. The result is shown below.

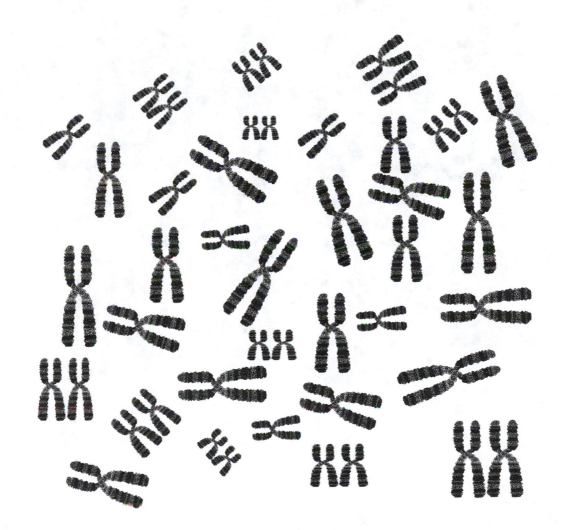

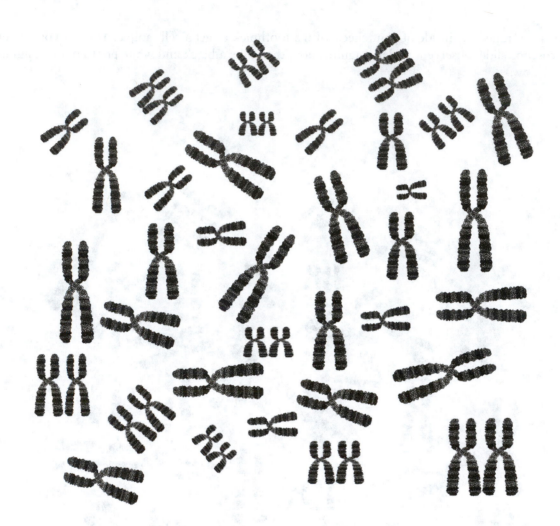

1.   Which of the two karyotypes would more closely match your own? Why?

2.   To avoid confusion, scribble out the side that does not match your own.

3.   Cut out the chromosomes.

4.   Match up the homologous pairs and put in the proper order according to size and banding pattern. Remember that Chromosome 21 is smaller than 22 (the only exception to the size-numbering rule). Use the karyotype form below to categorize them into the seven groups (plus the sex chromosomes) listed.

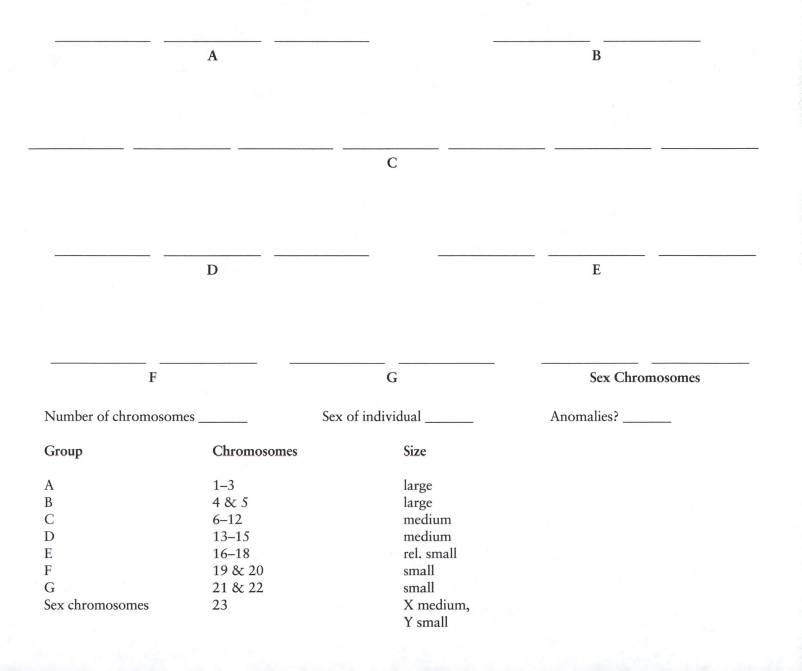

Group	Chromosomes	Size
A	1–3	large
B	4 & 5	large
C	6–12	medium
D	13–15	medium
E	16–18	rel. small
F	19 & 20	small
G	21 & 22	small
Sex chromosomes	23	X medium, Y small

SELF-TEST 2.1

NAME _____ SECTION _____ DATE _____

1. What are cells made of?

2. How can you tell if a cell is from a male or a female?

3. Fill in the blanks to label the structures in the cell.

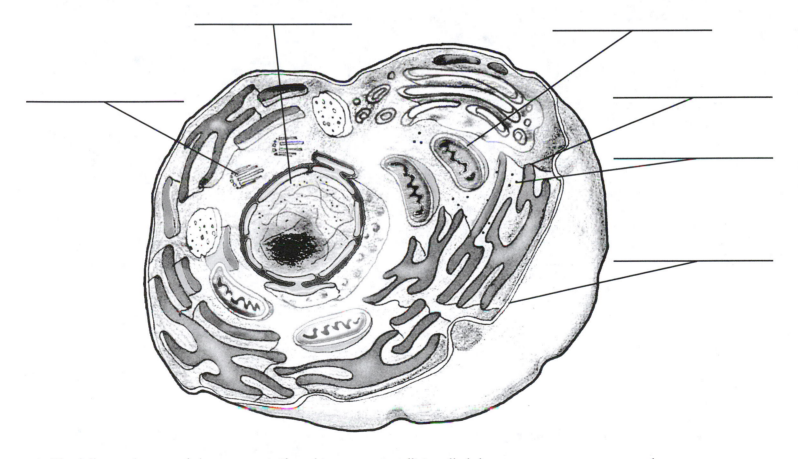

4. The full complement of chromosomes (found in a somatic cell) is called the _____ number.

5. Regarding the previous question, what is this number for humans?

6. Pretend that you are observing a skin cell from a chicken under a microscope.

    a. What is the *class* of cell you're looking at?

b. If the nucleus of this cell has 78 chromosomes, how many chromosomes would the chicken's sperm cell have?

7. What are gametes, and how many chromosomes do they each contain in humans?

8. What is a zygote?

9. How many chromosomes does a zygote have, and where did these chromosomes come from originally?

10. What is a gene?

11. What makes homologous chromosomes homologous?

12. What are alleles? What are examples of two alleles for a given gene?

13. a. Draw a chromosome in its doubled (replicated) state, and label the parts: arms, centromere, and sister chromatids.

    b. Draw three different chromosomes, and show how they can differ in terms of size, centromere location, and banding pattern.

    c. Draw a pair of chromosomes, and demonstrate one hypothetical locus for a gene on each. Choose (or make up) a trait and two possible alleles. Label these similar to Figure 2.12.

14. What are autosomes? What is a chromosome if it is not an autosome?

3. The Double Helix

OBJECTIVES

- Understand the genetic material, its structure and function
- Understand processes dictated by DNA—DNA replication and protein synthesis
- Know how DNA replication allows for cell division
- Know how DNA sequence determines protein production
- Extract and observe the DNA from an organism (a banana)

"Have you ever wondered...?"

✋ I've heard of DNA, but *how* is DNA our genetic material?

✋ What exactly *are* genes anyway?

✋ How do you get from DNA to a person? Or an eel? Or a nectarine tree?

✋ Why is *all* of my DNA in each of my cells?

Now that you are familiar with the cell—the fundamental unit of living things—and the genetic material of which chromosomes are composed, we'll learn about the genetic material itself.

The Genetic Material

The structure of **deoxyribonucleic acid,** or **DNA,** was unknown until 1953, although the component parts had been identified. Several scientists were engaged in a race to discover DNA's structure; the race was won by James Watson and Francis Crick, who published their results in a 1953 issue of Nature and shared the Nobel Prize in 1962 with Maurice Wilkins. Rosalind Franklin, who worked in Wilkins' lab and whose X-ray diffraction photo provided the final piece to the puzzle, died before the prize was awarded.

DNA is a large molecule in the nucleus of all eukaryotic cells and, together with several types of proteins, is "packaged" into chromosomes that are contained in the nucleus of every cell in the body (see Figure 3.1). DNA is an extremely long molecule, but very thin. In fact, approximately 6 feet of DNA are coiled and crowded into *each cell!* DNA is responsible for two vital processes:

1. **replication** (making a copy of itself), and

2. **protein synthesis** (the manufacture of proteins).

The structure enables it to carry out these processes, which allow for growth and development, and for genetic information to be passed from generation to generation.

Why should we care about a *molecule?* What is its relevance or interest to us? Knowledge of the

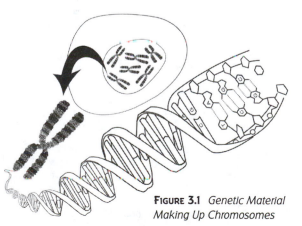

FIGURE 3.1 *Genetic Material Making Up Chromosomes*

structure and function of DNA, and how DNA sequences are inherited, allows us to:

🖐 Be aware of the risks of transmitting genetic diseases to our children, based upon the genetic makeup of both biological parents.

🖐 Identify perpetrators of various crimes.

🖐 Identify biological relationships among individuals and among species.

🖐 Track historical events in our species, as the story of our ancestry lies in our DNA sequence.

Nucleic Acids

Within the nucleus of all eukaryotic cells are two types of **nucleic acids**. They are referred to as nucleic because they are found in the nucleus, and acidic because they release H+ ions when they disassociate in water. Those molecules that release OH− or accept H+ are basic. The two variants of nucleic acids are DNA (deoxyribonucleic acid) and **RNA (ribonucleic acid)**. DNA is the actual genetic material, and RNA is a similar substance that can be thought of as a vital "helper" for some DNA functions.

The "building blocks" of the nucleic acids are called **nucleotides** (see Figure 3.2). A nucleotide is the most basic unit of both DNA and RNA. Each nucleotide has three components:

1. A **sugar** molecule. DNA has a type of sugar called **deoxyribose**, and RNA has a sugar called **ribose**. These sugars differ from one another only slightly in chemical structure, with deoxyribose having one fewer oxygen atom than ribose.

2. A **phosphate molecule**, and

3. A **base.**

Bases are one of four chemical substances, each of which is made of simple atoms of hydrogen, carbon, oxygen, and nitrogen. Three of the four bases of DNA and RNA are the same: **adenine (A)**, **guanine (G)**, and **cytosine (C)**. The fourth base differs, with **thymine (T)** found only in DNA and the chemically similar **uracil (U)**, found only in RNA.

Because nucleotides are composed of simple atoms such as carbon, hydrogen, oxygen, and nitrogen, the nucleus of cells has a constant supply of free DNA and RNA nucleotides. These are used in DNA replication and protein synthesis.

The Structure of DNA

A number of nucleotides strung together are referred to as a **polynucleotide** (*poly:* many) **chain.** DNA consists of two polynucleotide chains, or strands. The DNA molecule is called the **double helix** because of its helical (twisted) structure and because it has two strands. Its overall appearance is that of a twisted ladder. The "backbone" of DNA, or sides of the ladder, is composed of alternating molecules of phosphates and sugars. The pairs of bases, or **base pairs**, make up the "rungs" of the ladder (see Figure 3.3). The human genome has nearly 3 billion base pairs, and the rat has about 2.75 billion (Rat Genome Sequencing Project Consortium, 2004). By comparison, a fruit fly has 1.2 billion base pairs and an *Escherichia coli* bacterium has 4.6 million (Blattner et al., 1997; Adams et al., 2000).

On each strand, the phosphates and sugars of adjacent nucleotides and those between sugars and the bases are held together by strong chemical bonds. The bonds holding the base pairs together, however, are weak bonds, called **hydrogen bonds**, which can be easily broken by enzymes.

The pairing of bases in DNA has specific "rules," based upon the size of the four different bases and their available

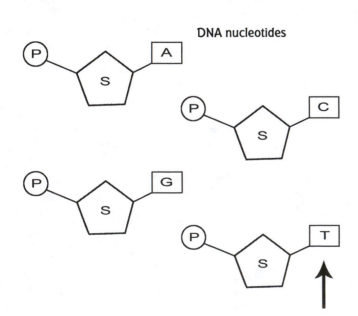

DNA nucleotides

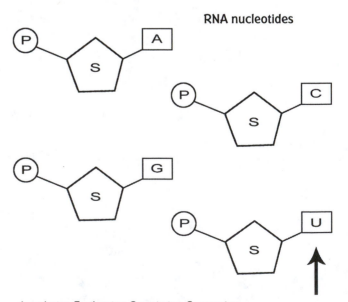

RNA nucleotides

A = adenine; T = thymine; C = cytosine; G = guanine; U = uracil; P = phosphate; S = sugar

FIGURE 3.2 *Nucleotides of DNA and RNA*

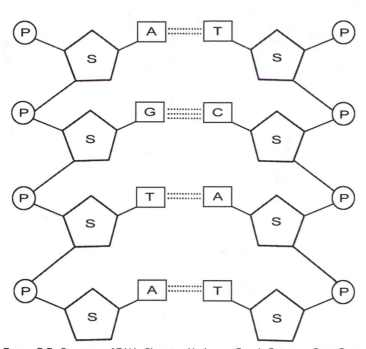

FIGURE 3.3 *Structure of DNA, Showing Hydrogen Bonds Between Base Pairs*

sites for bonding with one another. Adenine and thymine consistently bond together, as do cytosine with guanine (see Figure 3.3).

Important to understanding DNA structure is that the two strands (polynucleotide chains) are *complementary*, not identical, to one another. Thus, by knowing the sequence of one strand, you can easily infer the sequence of the other strand. This complementarity in its structure allows for the two vital processes of replication and protein synthesis that are directed by the DNA.

Summary of Genetic Material

To summarize—DNA is a nucleic acid whose double helix (twisted ladder) structure is based upon sugar and phosphate molecules comprising the "backbone," and paired combinations of the four types of bases (A,C,T,G) making up the "rungs" of the ladder. The smallest unit of DNA, a nucleotide, consists of one sugar molecule, one phosphate, and one base. The two polynucleotide chains in DNA are linked by weak hydrogen bonds between the bases.

In Watson and Crick's famous 1953 publication announcing the discovery of the structure of DNA, the ending reads, "It has not escaped notice that the specific pairing we have postulated immediately suggests a possible copying mechanism for the genetic material." We will deal with these functions next, but before you go on—and preferably without looking at the previous discussion—answer the questions in Self-Test #1.

SELF-TEST 3.1

NAME _____ SECTION _____ DATE _____

1. How many nucleotides are represented below?

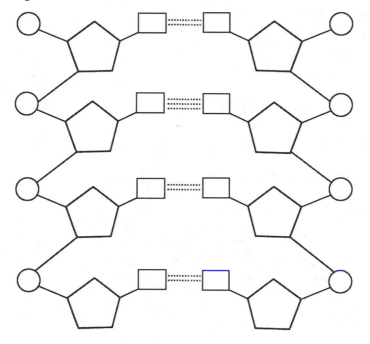

2. The "backbone" of DNA is made up of _____ and _____ molecules.

3. The four bases in DNA are:

   _____   _____

   _____   _____

4. In the DNA molecule, the base adenine always forms a complementary pair with _____.

5. Which of the following is *not* a base found in DNA?
   a. uracil
   b. guanine
   c. thymine
   d. adenine

   Where *is* it found? _____

6. What would the complementary strand of the DNA section A G T G A T T C C be?
   a. A G T G A T T C C
   b. A G U G A U U C C
   c. T C A C T A A G G
   d. T C A C T A A C C

7. The DNA molecule can be described as a:

    a. single-stranded chain

    b. double helix

    c. rung of a ladder

    d. sphere

8. A DNA nucleotide:

    a. is composed of a base, a sugar, and a phosphate molecule.

    b. is the same thing as an RNA molecule.

    c. codes for the production of an amino acid.

    d. can include the base uracil.

9. DNA is found in the _____ of all cells.

10. The two processes for which DNA is responsible are: _____ and _____.

11. How many polynucleotide chains are in each DNA molecule? _____

12. Fill in the blanks in the illustration below.

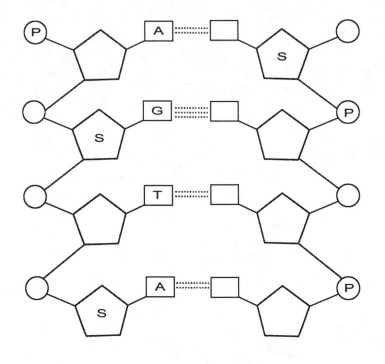

DNA Function: Replication

DNA replication is a vital process that *always* occurs just before cell division, so that a full set of genetic information is passed on to the daughter cells. Thus, *the DNA making up the chromosomes is identical in the nucleus of all somatic cells within an individual's body*. DNA replication is the process that enables cell division to occur successfully and allows for hereditary information to be passed from parent to offspring.

The replication process is controlled by **enzymes**, which are a class of proteins in the body that carry out metabolic activity in cells. For DNA replication, two important enzymes are DNA polymerase and DNA ligase. The steps by which the DNA in each cell replicates itself before it divides (see Figure 3.4) are listed below.

1. Enzymes cause the double helix to unwind by breaking the hydrogen bonds between the bases.

2. The two DNA strands separate from each other as they are unwinding, leaving the bases exposed on each strand.

3. These exposed bases attract free DNA nucleotides that are in the cell's nucleus, and these free nucleotides bond to the appropriate (A with T, and C with G) exposed bases on both of the original (and now separated) DNA strands.

4. The DNA nucleotides that have just arrived to bond with the exposed bases on each of the original DNA strands now bond together by their phosphates and sugars, forming a new strand (polynucleotide chain) on each side.

5. This process now has resulted in two double-stranded DNA molecules (each is one sister chromatid, connected via the centromere), which are identical to each other and consist of one original and one new strand. These newly forming molecules begin to wind up into double helices, even as the original strands are still unwinding and separating along their length (see Figure 3.5).

6. Remember the idea of complementarity? This allows each original strand to serve as a "template" for the production of a new strand.

7. The newly replicated DNA molecule coils and condenses into the recognizable form of the chromosome prior to cell division in its doubled (replicated) state (see Figure 3.6).

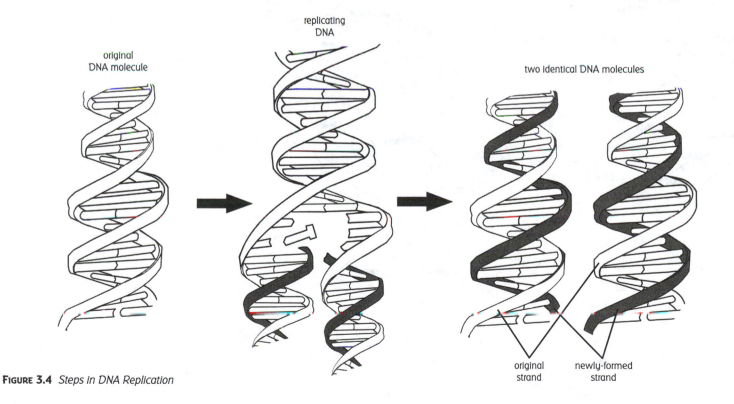

FIGURE 3.4 *Steps in DNA Replication*

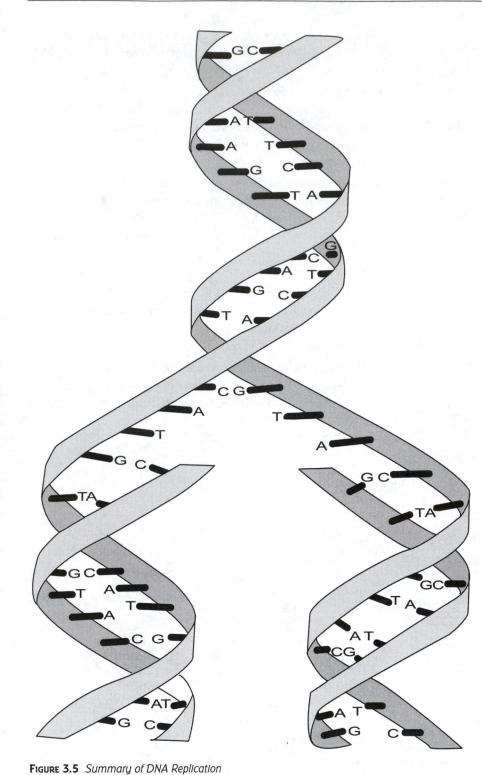

FIGURE 3.5 *Summary of DNA Replication*

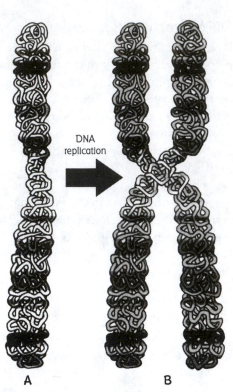

FIGURE 3.6 *Chromosome Form in Single (A) and Doubled (B), or Replicated, State.*

DNA replication

A

B

LAB EXERCISE 3.1

NAME _____ SECTION _____ DATE _____

The goal of today's exercise is to isolate the nucleic acids in a banana and see firsthand what DNA looks like. You will break open the cells of a banana, letting the cells' molecules spill into a solution. This solution at first will contain proteins, lipids, and carbohydrates in addition to the DNA and RNA, but you'll bind up the proteins with detergent to separate the DNA.

Supplies Needed

one or two bananas
sharp knife and cutting surface
blender
meat tenderizer
2 small glasses
several coffee filters (recommended) or strainer
liquid dish detergent
box of toothpicks
a teaspoon
isopropyl (91% alcohol) (recommended) or regular rubbing alcohol (better if cooled in refrigerator overnight beforehand)
paper towels for cleanup

Method

Step 1. Peel and slice banana into thin disks.

Step 2. Place sliced banana into blender, and add a little water to dampen the banana.

Step 3. Blend until a semi-thick paste forms in the blender (about 10 seconds blend time). Blending will break up the banana tissue; the goal is a solution of proteins and DNA.

Step 4. Add two dashes of meat tenderizer on top of the banana slices. The meat tenderizer contains papain, which is a mixture of enzymes that cleave proteins, serving to help isolate the DNA and catalyze (speed up) chemical reactions in the cell. Papain is derived from unripe papaya juice.

Step 5. Place coffee filters around the rim of the glasses. If you dampen the coffee filters, they will grip the glasses around the edges so you won't have to hold them on by hand.

Step 6. Pour contents of blender proportionally into the coffee filter-topped glasses.

Step 7. Filter to separate the DNA and proteins from the other cell components. If filtering occurs too slowly, gently use a toothpick to poke small holes into the coffee filters to quicken the drainage time. Avoid making large tears in the filters. (Filtration time usually is 5–10 minutes). After fluid drainage begins to slow, hasten the filtering process by gently lifting the coffee filter (being careful not to spill the contents) up over the glass, and then gently squeeze the filter by hand. (This can be messy, so have towels handy to wipe off your hands.) If a few banana chunks accumulate in the glass in this way, it shouldn't harm the outcome.

Step 8. Add small amounts of detergent into opposite sides of the glasses in three or four spots. This serves to dissolve the lipids and proteins of the cell by disrupting the bonds that hold the cell membrane together. Breaking open the plasma and nuclear membranes releases DNA into the solution. The detergent then binds to the lipid–protein layers, forming complexes with them so they can be separated from the DNA.

Step 9. Gently mix the contents of the glass with a toothpick, and continue stirring for a few minutes. Do not stir too roughly, as this can break up the DNA into fragments (this is bad). A gentle diagonal pattern of stirring usually yields the best results.

Step 10. Place a teaspoon gently on top of the banana–detergent mixture (as if you were about to eat it). Be careful not to dip the spoon into the banana mixture itself.

Step 11. Carefully pour the isopropyl alcohol so it runs down the spoon into the banana–detergent mixture (rather than dumping the alcohol directly in the banana mixture). The alcohol will form a layer on top of the banana mixture because it is less dense than the solution under it. *Note*: Fill the glass with alcohol proportional to the amount of banana fluid in the glass (should be 50/50). Alcohol serves as a gradient for the DNA to precipitate up through.

Step 12. In a successful experiment, the DNA should rise to the surface of the mixture in only a few seconds; it will appear as a cotton-like material forming where the banana mixture meets the alcohol layer.

Step 13. You now should be able to spool the DNA up, using a toothpick. The clumped DNA is a white-ish substance with a mucous-like consistency. Although this method extracts RNA as well as DNA, much of the RNA is cut by ribonucleases (a type of enzyme) that are released when the cells are broken open. Thus, most of what you spool up will be DNA. Keep in mind that your DNA is the same "stuff" as the banana's DNA, as well as that of all organisms.

SELF-TEST 3.2

NAME _____ SECTION _____ DATE _____

1. The steps of DNA replication are as follows:

The _____ bonds between the bases break, and the two DNA strands unwind and _____.

_____ _____ are brought in, and they attach to _____. Bonds

form between the _____ and _____ molecules of the free DNA nucleotides, forming a new

strand. The result of DNA replication is two DNA double helices, each composed of one _____ and

one _____ strand. The new DNA is _____ to each other and to the original DNA.

2. Why is DNA replication so important?

3. Fill in the blanks in
   the illustration.

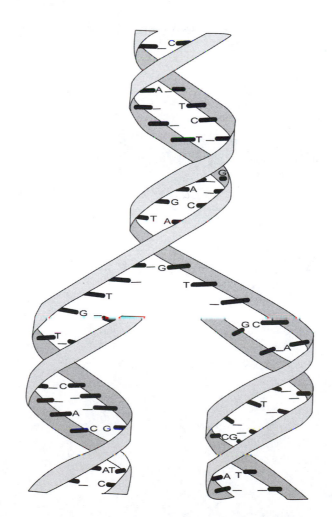

4. Draw and label the components of a segment of DNA (include all four bases, phosphates, and sugars). Be sure to bond the correct molecules together. Make your segment at least eight base pairs long.

5. Draw this same segment undergoing the process of DNA replication. Show the original strands separating and the new strands forming. Label all parts.

Protein Synthesis:
How Genes are Expressed

Before describing the process of protein synthesis, we'll briefly discuss what a protein is, and why proteins are so vitally important in the body. Keep in mind that the sequence of bases in our DNA is what ultimately determines the proteins we produce.

Proteins

Proteins make up about 50% of the weight of each cell, after the water is squeezed out. The human body has approximately 250 kinds of proteins, with up to 10,000 proteins in a single human cell! Many proteins are structural proteins, which make up body structures such as tendons and ligaments, cores of bones and teeth, hair filaments, and nails. Functions of other proteins include facilitating the transport of molecules into and out of cells, regulating metabolism, performing mechanical work such as that involved in muscle contraction, or participating in the immune system.

If proteins are heated, or are degraded by stomach acids, they break down into subunits. These "building blocks" of proteins are **amino acids**. Strings of amino acids combine to form the various proteins. Twenty common types of amino acids are found in most proteins. Although a few other types exist, they are relatively rare and occur in few proteins. About half of the twenty primary amino acids are produced by the body, derived from carbohydrates or fat, and the others are called **essential amino acids**, which must be taken in as food.

Thus, when you take in proteins from foods, they are broken down by digestive enzymes and the amino acids are released into your bloodstream. The amino acids then circulate, ready and available to be taken up by any cell in your body that needs them for manufacturing a specific kind of protein.

Amino acids are joined end to end by **peptide bonds**, and a string of amino acids is called a **polypeptide, or polypeptide chain** (see Figure 3.7). Polypeptides vary in length (they average approximately 100 amino acids) and the amino acid sequence. After a polypeptide chain has been formed, it may join up with another such chain to form a protein.

Keep in mind that the *protein is the functional unit*, not the polypeptide. One or more polypeptides together make up a protein. The complex shape of a protein determines its function in the body, and its shape is determined by the amino acid sequence and by the number and kinds of polypeptides comprising it. Proteins have "nooks and crannies" to fit specific molecules whose chemical reactions they are controlling.

Let's use as an example a protein familiar to us all: **hemoglobin.** Hemoglobin is the molecule in our red blood cells that carries oxygen to our tissues, and it also removes carbon dioxide from tissues to be carried back to the lungs and exhaled. The iron-containing portion gives the molecule its red color. Hemoglobin is made of four polypeptide chains; two "alpha" chains and two "beta" chains. The alpha chains are each made of 141 amino acids, and the beta chains are 146 amino acids long. We'll now see how proteins such as hemoglobin are manufactured in the process dictated by the sequence of bases in the DNA.

Although *all* of our cells contain the "blueprint" to synthesize *all* of the proteins that the body produces, each type of protein is produced in cells of only particular parts of the body (Figure 3.8).

An overview of protein synthesis demonstrates how we get from a gene (a segment of DNA on a chromosome) to a protein. The general flow of genetic information from the DNA to a protein is:

DNA → mRNA → amino acid → polypeptide → protein
sequence sequence   sequence

The blueprint used to make an individual's proteins (and thus comprise their physical traits) remains in the DNA in the nucleus of cells. Proteins, however, are actually constructed outside the nucleus—in the cytoplasm of cells, where the "workbench" for protein synthesis is found. To form a protein, *information* contained in the nuclear DNA somehow *must* be *taken out to the cytoplasm*, where proteins are put together. This process is analogous to the information you may need from a book in the Reserve Book Room of your library (the nucleus). You can't check out and remove the book (the DNA) from the library, but you can make a copy (transcription into mRNA) so the information can leave the library with you (go out into the cytoplasm).

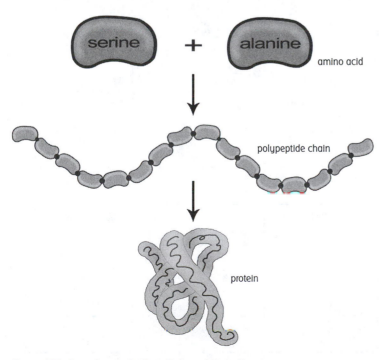

FIGURE 3.7 *From Amino Acids to Polypeptide to Protein*

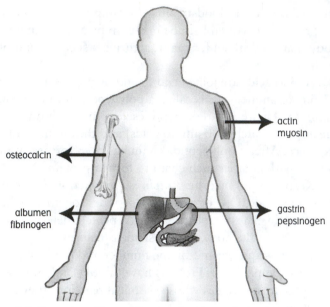

FIGURE 3.8 *Examples of Proteins Produced in Various Parts of the Body*

Cell Components Involved in Protein Synthesis

In protein synthesis, the component parts of a protein are put together, based upon the sequence ("code") that ultimately is dictated by the DNA. The components of the cell that are involved in synthesizing proteins are primarily the following:

- ✋ ribosomes,
- ✋ the three kinds of RNA,
- ✋ DNA,
- ✋ amino acids,
- ✋ various enzymes, and
- ✋ an energy source (ATP).

Again, the two types of nucleic acids are RNA and DNA. The actual genetic material is DNA, and RNA is a vital "assistant" in protein synthesis. The basic differences in structure between the two are as shown in Figure 3.9.

There are three types of RNA, which differ from one another in structure and in their function during protein synthesis (see Figure 3.10) despite the fact that all have, as their most basic unit, the RNA nucleotide. All are essential in the manufacture of protein.

Steps in Protein Synthesis

The complex process of protein synthesis has *two main steps.*

1. The first step occurs in the cell nucleus where the DNA resides, and *results in the formation of a strand of mRNA.*

2. The second step *carries the message of the DNA sequence* to the cell's cytoplasm, and "translates" it into a specific order of amino acids that will form a polypeptide.

First Step: Transcription Picture a DNA double helix, and zoom in on it in your mind. "Highlight" a portion of the DNA on just one side, or strand. This portion represents a **gene**. The human genome, it was discovered recently, is made up of about 25,000 genes. A gene is a functional unit, not a structural one. A gene begins and ends at the nucleotides that comprise the beginning and end of a sequence that will "code for" a specific polypeptide. The gene coding for

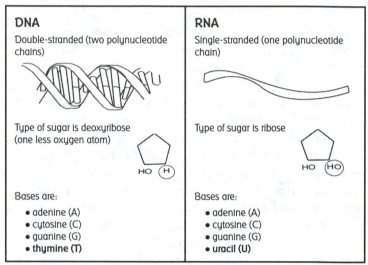

DNA	RNA
Double-stranded (two polynucleotide chains)	Single-stranded (one polynucleotide chain)
Type of sugar is deoxyribose (one less oxygen atom)	Type of sugar is ribose
Bases are: • adenine (A) • cytosine (C) • guanine (G) • **thymine (T)**	Bases are: • adenine (A) • cytosine (C) • guanine (G) • **uracil (U)**

FIGURE 3.9 *Differences Between DNA and RNA*

	Messenger RNA (mRNA)	Transfer RNA (tRNA)	Ribosomal RNA (rRNA)
Idealized drawing		2 — amino acid binding site / 1 — anticodon	Shown: ribosome
Function	Carries the message of the sequence of DNA bases for a gene	Brings amino acids to appropriate place along the mRNA strand in the formation of a polypeptide chain	Together with proteins, makes up the *ribosomes*, where the mRNA strand is read and decoded
Proportion of RNA in cells	Between 80 and 90%	Between 5 and 10%	Between 5 and 10%
Form	A simple single strand	Single stranded; folds back on itself so parts are double-stranded. Important functional parts: 1) the three exposed bases at one end—the **anticodon**; 2) amino acid binding site	Ribosomes are the site at which amino acids are bonded together to form polypeptides; comprised of a large and small subunit that together clamp onto the mRNA strand for decoding
Length	Between 300 and 10,000 nucleotides	Between 75 and 90 nucleotides	Between 120 and 4800 nucleotides

FIGURE 3.10 *Differences Among the Three Types of RNA*

hemoglobin's alpha chain is on chromosome 16, and a gene on chromosome 11 codes for the beta chain. Hemoglobin synthesis occurs in the stem cells that divide to develop into red blood cells, so the hemoglobin is produced as the cells that house them are developing.

Remember that the first step of protein synthesis results in the *formation of a strand of mRNA*. This part of the process is called **transcription** (see Figure 3.11):

1. The process begins in a manner similar to that of DNA replication. The two DNA strands begin to separate and unwind, the result of enzyme action. But in protein synthesis the strands separate along only a small portion: along the gene. Bases now are exposed on both DNA strands. Remember that a gene is a segment of DNA along only one side (one strand).

2. This is where RNA comes into the picture. Numerous free RNA nucleotides are present in the nucleus. The

exposed bases along the DNA gene will attract these free RNA nucleotides. As the RNA nucleotides line up along the DNA gene, they bond together to form a strand. They line up with the DNA bases following the same base pairing rules as for DNA, but with one exception: There is no thymine (T) in RNA; instead, uracil (U) of RNA acts as a substitute for T, and bonds with A (Figure 3.11a). Thus, the portion of the DNA gene that reads:

CACGTGGACTGAGGACTC

would attract the following RNA nucleotides:

GUGCACCUGACUCCUGAG.

Again, this occurs only along the *gene side* (the exposed bases along the corresponding segment on the other DNA strand merely wait patiently for transcription to be done). The RNA nucleotides will continue to line

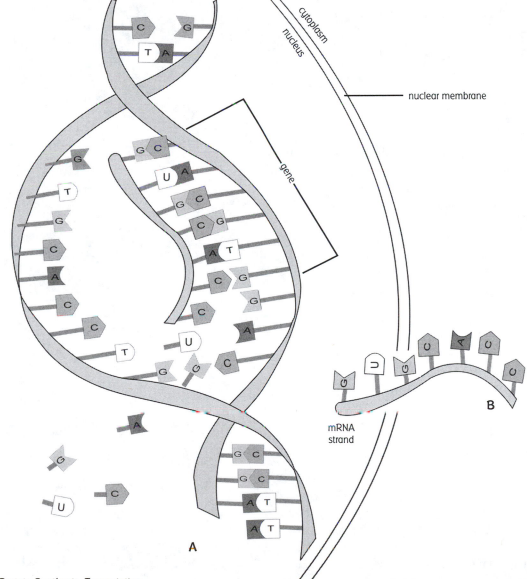

FIGURE 3.11 *First Step in Protein Synthesis: Transcription*

up and bond with the appropriate DNA base and with each other, forming an RNA strand, until no more exposed DNA bases remain with which to bond. This will correspond to the end of the DNA gene.

3. The RNA strand forms quickly (30–50 nucleotides are added per second!), then breaks away immediately from the DNA. Now it has what it needs: It has formed itself on the basis of the DNA sequence of a specific gene, so in its very form carries the message of the code for the production of a particular protein. (Before continuing on to the next step of protein synthesis, the RNA strand goes through "processing," in which parts of the strand are removed while still in the nucleus.) The strand now is referred to as mRNA. The mRNA leaves the nucleus, passing through the nuclear membrane into the cytoplasm, for the process of translation (Figure 3.11B).

4. The final product of transcription is

✋ a single-stranded RNA molecule, complementary to the sequence of bases of the original DNA gene (DNA was used as a blueprint) an average of 5,000 nucleotides long

✋ called mRNA (messenger RNA), because it now is carrying the message of the sequence of the DNA bases

Second Step: Translation In the second step of protein synthesis, the message of the DNA sequence will be "translated" into a specific order of amino acids, which will be joined end to end to form a polypeptide (remember, a chain of amino acids). A protein is made of one or more polypeptides. The specific protein that is formed depends upon the order of the amino acids that comprise it. Thus, the DNA sequence of a gene determines the amino acid sequence, which in turn determines the protein that will be produced.

Translation involves the newly formed *mRNA, tRNA, ribosomes, amino acids,* and more *enzymes.*

1. After passing through the nuclear membrane into the cytoplasm, the mRNA goes to a ribosome and is clasped between its two subunits (Figure 3.12A). The ribosome, in effect, "reads" the mRNA strand three bases at a time. These "words" made of triplets of mRNA bases are called **codons**. Each codon corresponds to a specific amino acid.

2. Next, the corresponding amino acids are brought into place along the mRNA strand. This is accomplished by the tRNA. As each codon is "read" by the ribosome, a tRNA is "called over," carrying with it the correct amino acid for each codon (Figure 3.12B). The tRNA must have some way to briefly "dock" onto the mRNA to transfer its cargo. This is accomplished by chemical bonds that are formed briefly between the bases making

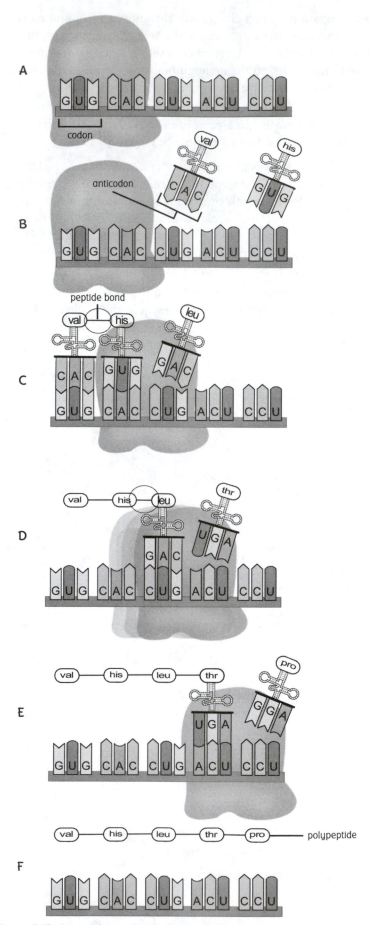

FIGURE 3.12 *Second Step in Protein Synthesis: Translation*

up a codon and the three exposed bases at the end of the tRNA. These three bases comprise the **anticodon**. Each anticodon of tRNA is complementary to the codon's bases. Thus, each codon of mRNA (for example, AAU) has a counterpart of tRNA (UUA).

3. As each amino acid is brought into place by its tRNA, it immediately forms a chemical bond (a peptide bond) with the previously transferred amino acid (Figure 3.12C, D, E). The chain of amino acids grows as the ribosomes read the mRNA strand. As in the building of the mRNA strand in transcription, the amino acid chain grows quickly, with the growing polypeptide chain adding about 10 to 15 amino acids per second. A beta chain of hemoglobin takes only about 10 seconds for its 146 amino acids to be brought together into a polypeptide.

4. Eventually a ribosome reads a mRNA codon for which there is no tRNA anticodon. This will be the **stop codon**, or **terminating triplet** (not shown in Figure 3.12). The codons UAA, UAG, and UGA are all stop codons. At that point, the ribosome dissociates, its parts separate, and the newly formed polypeptide (chain of amino acids) floats free (Figure 3.12F).

5. When a polypeptide chain has been formed, it may join up with another such chain to form a protein, and protein synthesis is complete. For example, remember that a gene on chromosome 16 and a gene on chromosome 11 determine the four polypeptide chains (alpha and beta) contributing to the protein hemoglobin. The *protein* (not the polypeptide) is the actual functional unit, and its complex shape determines its function in the body.

The Genetic Code

The 20 amino acids each correspond to a specific sequence of three bases (a codon) on the mRNA strand, consistent in all species. There are 64 combinations of the three bases (64 different codons) but only about 20 amino acids, so some amino acids have more than one codon coding for them (some have up to six). For example, the codons that code for phenylalanine are UUU or UUC. This is what is referred to as the **genetic code** (see Table 3.1).

Summary of Protein Synthesis

1. *Transcription:* Occurs in the nucleus; a complementary copy (blueprint) of DNA is made and transcribed

		U		C		A		G
U	UUU UUC	phenalalynine	UCU UCC UCA UCG	serine	UAU UAC	tyrosine	UGU UGC	cysteine
	UUA UUG	leucine			UAA UAG	Stop codon Stop codon	UGA UGG	Stop codon tryptophan
C	CUU CUC CUA CUG	leucine	CCU CCC CCA CCG	proline	CAU CAC CAA CAG	histidine glutamine	CGU CGC CGA CGG	arginine
A	AUU AUC AUA	isoleucine	ACU ACC ACA ACG	threonine	AAU AAC AAA AAG	asparagine lysine	AGU AGC AGA AGG	serine arginine
	AUG	methionine Start codon						
G	GUU GUC GUA GUG	valine	GCU CCC GCA GCG	alanine	GAU GAC GAA GAG	aspartic acid glutamic acid	GGU GGC GGA GGG	glycine

TABLE 3.1: The Genetic Code

onto an mRNA strand, which leaves the nucleus to the cytoplasm.

2. *Translation:* The mRNA carries its message of the sequence of DNA bases out to the cytoplasm. With the aid of ribosomes "reading" the mRNA bases three at a time (codon by codon), tRNA brings the appropriate amino acids into place along the mRNA strand to form a polypeptide.

3. Thus, the DNA has been transcribed into RNA, then translated into amino acids, then synthesized (put together) into a polypeptide, one or more of which comprise a protein.

Note: Because in prokaryotes (like bacteria) the nucleus is not separated from the cytoplasm, transcription and translation can occur at the same time!

Mutations

As you are well aware, genetics processes sometimes go awry, or the genetic material can be affected by an external source (for example, radiation). An inherited change in the DNA is called a **mutation**. Mutations can occur at various levels, from an extra or missing set of chromosomes, an extra or missing single chromosome or piece of one, to an extra or missing base or bases.

We will discuss mutations at the level of the chromosome, or chunks of chromosome, in Chapter 4. A mutation involving only a single nucleotide out of place can have devastating effects on an individual's development and survivability. Such a mutation can be inherited from a parent's

DNA, or it may occur in an individual during early DNA replication or protein synthesis. Three main types of such mutations are **single base substitution (point mutation)**, **insertion**, and **deletion**.

In a single-base substitution mutation, one nucleotide is replaced mistakenly by another. For example, a C may be inserted in DNA where a T should be. If the same amino acid is coded for after the mutation, it is known as a **silent mutation** and results in successful production of the correct protein. For example, look at the genetic code chart (Table 3.1), at the mRNA codon CCU. It codes for the amino acid proline. A substitution that results in another C instead of the U would also code for proline, thereby producing the same protein as if no mutation had occurred. If the second C were replaced by a U, however, this new codon CUU would code for leucine. This is a **missense mutation**, with the mutated codon coding for a different amino acid. If the mutation causes a change in the codon such that it becomes a stop codon, it is known as a **nonsense mutation**. This causes premature halting of translation, and thus a truncated polypeptide length and almost certainly a malformed protein.

Insertions add one or more nucleotides to the DNA, while deletions remove them. Because codons are composed of groups of three bases, inserting or deleting a base from a codon changes the reading of all of the rest of the codons on the mRNA strand. This difference in the way the ribosome will now read the mRNA strand is referred to as a **frameshift mutation**, and this affects the final production of the protein.

As mentioned in Chapter 1, mutation is one of the four evolutionary forces. It is the only evolutionary force to produce *new* variation to introduce into a population, which is vital for the action of natural selection. The evolutionary forces will be covered more in Chapter 6.

L A B   E X E R C I S E   3 . 2

NAME _____ SECTION _____ DATE _____

1. The illustration below represents a portion of the DNA strand for production of hemoglobin's beta chain. The strands are
    in the process of separating for transcription. Transcribe and translate the entire shaded portion into an mRNA strand,
    and using the genetic code chart (Table 3.1), translate it into a part of the hemoglobin protein.

DNA Strand   ____ ____ ____   ____ ____ ____   ____ ____ ____   ____ ____ ____   ____ ____ ____

mRNA Strand ____ ____ ____   ____ ____ ____   ____ ____ ____   ____ ____ ____   ____ ____ ____

Amino Acids _____   _____   _____   _____   _____

2. There are numerous known mutations of the genes that dictate
   hemoglobin production. In this exercise you will trace the route
   from DNA to a faulty type of hemoglobin.

   a. Draw a double helix.

   b. Highlight (or circle) a portion
      that will represent a segment of
      DNA on one strand (your gene).

   c. Now re-draw this segment of DNA,
      making it large enough to see the
      DNA bases. Use the DNA sequence
      from question 1 above for your gene,
      but change the 17th base from T to A.

   d. You have just caused a mutation. Transcribe and translate your strand as you did in #1.
      Is your amino acid sequence the same or different?

      DNA Strand   ___ ___ ___   ___ ___ ___   ___ ___ ___   ___ ___ ___   ___ ___ ___   ___ ___ ___

      mRNA Strand   ___ ___ ___   ___ ___ ___   ___ ___ ___   ___ ___ ___   ___ ___ ___   ___ ___ ___

      Amino Acids   _____   _____   _____   _____   _____   _____

   e. This mutation results in abnormal hemoglobin production, and if an individual receives this mutated gene from both
      parents, he or she will have sickle-cell anemia.

3. Diagram the steps of protein synthesis, labeling these parts: *nucleus, DNA, RNA, ribosomes, mRNA, tRNA,* and *amino
   acids.*

SELF-TEST 3.3

NAME _____ SECTION _____ DATE _____

1. Proteins are made of _____.

2. DNA and RNA are both _____, found in the _____ of cells.

3. Which is the actual genetic material, DNA or RNA? _____

4. What are three structural differences between DNA and RNA?

   a. _____

   b. _____

   c. _____

5. Answer the following questions about the molecule illustrated below.

   a. What is this molecule (the entire thing)? _____

   b. What is its function? _____

   c. Identify A _____

   d. Identify B _____

6. Hereditary information (in the form of the sequence of DNA bases) is taken from the nucleus to the cytoplasm by:

   a. the nucleotides

   b. mRNA

   c. ribosomes

   d. tRNA

7. A segment of DNA that codes for the synthesis of a particular protein (or polypeptide) is a _____.

8. In protein synthesis, the process called translation is the:

   a. manufacture of transfer RNA

   b. assembly of polypeptide chains

   c. manufacture of messenger RNA

   d. production of amino acids

9. Which of the following sequences is correct?

   a. DNA → mRNA → tRNA → protein

   b. mRNA → DNA → tRNA → protein

   c. DNA → tRNA → mRNA → protein

   d. tRNA → DNA → mRNA → protein

10. Proteins are manufactured within the cell at structures called:

    a. mitochondria

    b. nuclei

    c. nucleoli

    d. ribosomes

11. What is a mutation?

    Why is it so important for evolution?

12. The amino acids used by the cell to manufacture proteins are:

    a. manufactured by the body

    b. derived from ingested protein food

    c. both a and b

    d. found on the DNA molecule

13. Describe the basic structure and main functions of mRNA.

14. What is a polypeptide?

15. What is the name for a triplet of mRNA bases? _____

    Of tRNA bases? _____

16. Where does transcription occur?

    Translation?

17. What process, and what portion of this process, is represented here?

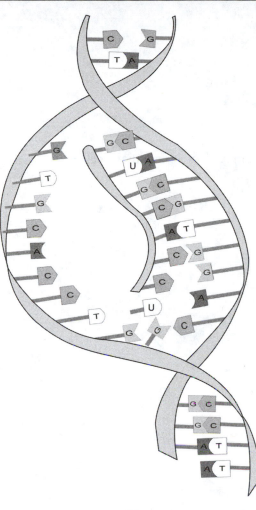

18. What process, and what portion of this process, is represented in the illustration?

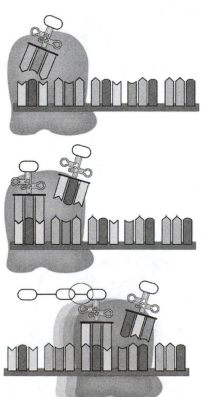

19. What is an important difference in the potential outcome of a *single base substitution mutation* and the other two types of point mutations, *insertions and deletions*?

20. Why is *all* of your DNA in *each* of your somatic cells?

4. How Cells Are Made

- Know the two main classes of cells and their main characteristics
- Understand the process of somatic cell production
- Understand the process of gamete production, and how variability is introduced into the gene pool
- Be familiar with somatic cell function
- Be familiar with gamete function
- Understand how mistakes in cell division can occur, and how these mistakes affect further development
- Recognize some of the common syndromes (chromosomal anomalies) that result from mistakes in cell division
- Understand the differences between mistakes in autosomes and sex chromosomes

"Have you ever wondered...?"

✋ How did the genetic material from my parents combine to form me?

✋ Why doesn't the DNA get reduced by half every time a cell divides?

✋ How long does it take a cell to divide?

Cell Division

As you recall, the cells making up the structural composition of your body—the majority of cells you have—are **somatic cells**. Because all of the somatic cells in your body were originally derived from the zygote, the nucleus of each has 46 chromosomes—a set of 23 chromosomes from each of your biological parents. Somatic cells arise by the process of **mitosis,** whereby one cell divides to produce two identical daughter cells. **Gametes,** or sex cells, have but one set of the 23 chromosomes. These egg or sperm cells potentially can join together with another gamete at fertilization to produce a zygote with the full complement of 46 chromosomes. Gametes are produced by the type of cell division called **meiosis,** a more complex process. Gametes do not divide. *Somatic cells are the cells that divide*, whether by mitosis to produce more somatic cells, or by meiosis to produce gametes.

Keep in mind that just *prior to* either type of cell division, *the DNA in the nucleus* (in the chromatin) *replicates itself*, so when the chromatin condenses and becomes visible, the chromosomes are first observed in their doubled state (made up of two sister chromatids). You may want to review the discussions of cell classes and chromosomes in Chapter 2.

Mitosis

Mitosis begins early—immediately after fertilization. The zygote divides to produce two embryonic cells, each of which divides in turn. The developing embryo continues to divide many times into many identical cells until cells begin to undergo differential development and become specialized for different functions. Each of these more specialized cells then divides into two identical daughter cells.

All of your somatic cells are produced in this way. Mitosis occurs often throughout life, during growth and for healing. Many types of cells are replaced almost constantly by new ones, such as skin cells. Others, such as nerve cells and liver cells, are rarely, if ever, replaced once cells are mature. In mammals, the entire cell cycle (cell growth, DNA replication, chromosome division, and cytoplasm division) takes 18 to 24 hours. The actual mitosis portion, however, usually lasts only an hour at most.

Mitosis begins with a somatic cell whose nucleus contains 46 chromosomes (in humans). *The end result is two identical daughter cells, each also with 46 chromosomes.* Keep in mind that each somatic cell maintains a *complete DNA blueprint* of an individual: All of the DNA that makes up the chromosomes is present in each cell.

We can observe a series of phases when cells divide, as these phases are visible under a microscope. Figure 4.1 illustrates the phases of mitosis and what happens to the chromosomes in each phase. It is less important to memorize these phases in detail than to understand the overall process, how chromosomes come to be distributed equally in the daughter cells, and the end result of cell division. The portion of the cell cycle in which cell division is *not* occurring is called the **interphase**. At this time, the cell is anything but inactive. For example, replication of DNA is in progress, and organelles are replicating themselves.

Follow along with Figure 4.1 as the process of mitosis is demonstrated for a cell with only four chromosomes (the diploid number for fruit flies, for example). Remember that if this somatic cell were from a human, it would have 46 chromosomes.

Meiosis

The term *meiosis* derives from the Greek *diminution*, meaning to make smaller, or reduce, which roughly translates to "reduction division." Meiosis is the production of gametes (sperm in males and eggs in females). Meiosis is a more complex process than mitosis and produces cells with a different function. The end result of meiosis is the production of haploid gametes that carry genetic information and introduce genetic variability among the daughter cells. This ensures that each individual is different from any other individual, thereby causing variability in populations.

The meiotic process begins with a somatic cell specialized to divide and produce another kind of cell. The specific type of cell to undergo meiosis and produce egg cells is the **primary oocyte**, and **primary spermatocytes** divide to produce sperm. Primary oocytes are found in the ovaries of females, and primary spermatocytes in the testes of males. Because *these are somatic cells*, each has 46 chromosomes. After the process of meiosis is complete and gametes have been produced, no more cell division occurs in the resulting cells. Again, the *gametes themselves do not undergo cell division*!

In males, the production of sperm cells begins at puberty. Sperm are produced regularly and stored in the epididymis for 10 to 20 days, on the off chance that during that time one of these sperm will enter the female reproductive tract and fertilize an egg. In females, the process of meiosis begins in the ovaries before birth (beginning at about the 12th week), and the precursor egg cells are held in "suspended animation" until puberty. At that time, they begin to mature

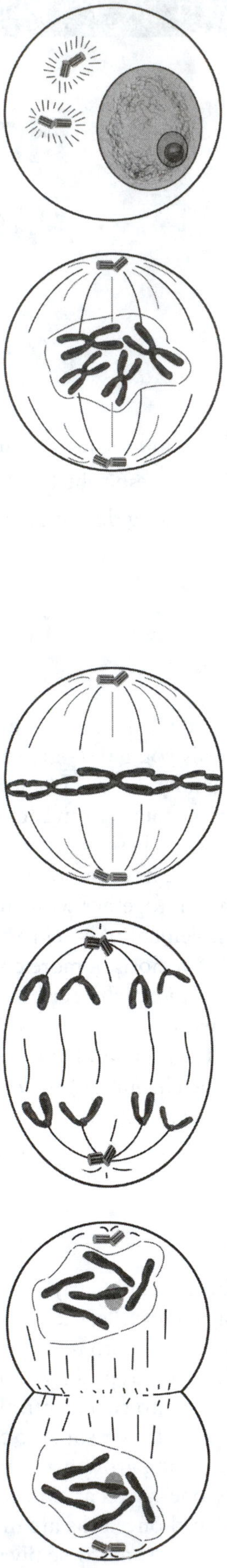

Interphase
- DNA is replicating.
- DNA is in the form of chromatin, so the chromosomes are not visible.
- Mitochondrial DNA is replicating.
- Organelles are replicating, preparing to be split into two different cells when the original cell divides.

Prophase
- Nuclear membrane of phospholipids is breaking down into small vesicles, or sacs.
- Chromatin has condensed and contracted into visible chromosomes, which are in their doubled state after DNA replication.
- The cytoskeleton is organizing into a spindle apparatus, making a framework for chromosome movement in the cell.
- The cell's two centrosomes (each composed of a pair of centrioles) are separating and moving to opposite poles of the cell.
- Spindle fibers coming from centrioles at opposite poles of the cell are attaching to the protein complexes on *both sides* of the chromosomes' centromeres.

Metaphase
- Chromosomes are being pulled into place along the equator of the cell by a "tug-of-war" between spindle fibers from centrioles at opposite poles of the cell.

Anaphase
- Continued tugging by the spindle fibers is resulting in the chromosomes being pulled apart at the centromeres, resulting in the separation of the sister chromatids of each chromosome—known as disjunction.
- These are now referred to as chromosomes; temporarily, the cell has eight chromosomes.
- The two groups of chromosomes are gathering at opposite poles of the cell.

Telophase
- Nuclear membrane is re-forming around the chromosomes grouped at each pole.
- The cell wall is pinching in, eventually causing the original cell to separate into two daughter cells; this process is called cytokinesis.

FIGURE 4.1 *Phases of Mitosis: Somatic Cell Production*

and are released from the ovary, one per month, until menopause.

Until recently, each female was thought to be born with the full complement of precursor egg cells that she will produce in her lifetime, while males continue to produce sperm throughout their lifetime (see Figure 4.2). Recent work on mice and humans, however, suggests that egg production continues into adulthood (Bukovsky et al., 2005; Johnson et al., 2006). The differences between meiosis in males and females are summarized in Table 4.1.

The stages are named the same as in mitosis, but to accomplish the goals of producing four haploid cells that differ in their genetic makeup, there are two meiotic divisions, **Meiosis I** and **Meiosis II.** The first of these reduces the number of chromosomes from 46 in the parent cell to 23 in the daughter cells, and the second division cleaves the sister chromatids apart so the chromosomes in the final daughter cells are in their single state.

The most important thing to remember is the end result of each part of the process, as well as the phenomenon that enables genetic variability. As you will see from the process outlined in Figure 4.3, homologous pairs of chromosomes will exchange pieces of one another to "reshuffle" genes, and the distribution of chromosomes into the daughter cells is a random process. These factors increase the potential genetic combinations that can result in the gametes.

Follow along with Figure 4.3 as it illustrates the process of meiosis for gamete production in a species (again, such as the fruit fly) with only four chromosomes in its somatic cells (the diploid number is four). If this were a human, the cell we would start with would have 46 chromosomes, and each of the four daughter cells would have 23 chromosomes.

The key to learning the process of meiosis is being aware of:

1. *Where the chromosomes originally came from.* The 46 chromosomes in the specialized somatic cell that is about to divide (a cell in the ovary or testis) were originally derived from the zygote, which formed from the 23 chromosomes of the mother's egg cell and the 23 chromosomes of the father's sperm. Remember that each somatic cell now in your body contains an exact replica of those original chromosomes, 23 maternally and 23 paternally derived.

2. *What happens to those maternally and paternally derived chromosomes during this process.* Their "behavior" is what makes meiosis such a unique and important process and introduces the genetic variability that typifies sexual reproduction.

TABLE 4.1: Differences in Meiosis Between Males and Females

Difference	Males	Females
Meiosis begins	At puberty	Before birth (~12 weeks)
Meiosis ends	At death	At menopause
Location of gamete production	Testes	Ovaries
Number of functional gametes produced	Four sperm	One egg

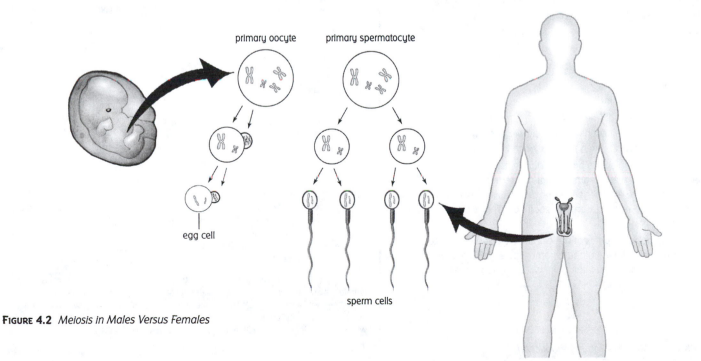

primary oocyte   primary spermatocyte

egg cell

sperm cells

FIGURE 4.2 *Meiosis in Males Versus Females*

What's Happening?

Meiosis 1

Interphase

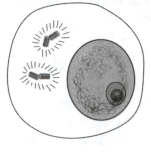

- DNA replication is occurring.
- DNA is in the form of chromatin, so the chromosomes are not visible.
- Mitochondrial DNA is replicating.
- Organelles are replicating, preparing to be split into two different cells when the original cell divides.

Prophase 1

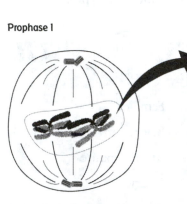

As in mitosis, the following events occur:

- Nuclear membrane of phospholipids breaks down into small vesicles, or sacs.
- Chromatin has condensed and contracted into visible chromosomes, now in their doubled state after DNA replication.
- Cytoskeleton organizes into a spindle apparatus, making a framework for chromosome movement in the cell. (This is the longest stage and contributes to meiosis taking days to complete!)
- Centrioles separate and move to opposite poles of the cell.

A vital event unique to meiosis is:

- The homologous pairs of chromosomes join together, lining up next to each other with point-by-point precision.
- Because the chromosomes occur in pairs, and are each in their doubled state (with sister chromatids), each pair is referred to as a **tetrad**.
- The members of the homologous pairs *exchange portions of each other* where they touch along their length, so that pieces of the maternally derived chromosome are exchanged with exact precision with pieces of the paternally derived chromosome in each pair! This is **crossing over,** or recombination of genes.
- Spindle fibers from opposite poles of the cell attach to the protein complex on the centromere of each of the chromosomes of the homologous pair, so that when the fibers pull, the pairs will be pulled apart.

Metaphase 1

- Chromosome pairs are pulled into place along the equator of the cell by the spindle fibers, like couples lined up opposite their partners at a barn dance.
- The sister chromatids of each chromosome are no longer identical, because crossing over has occurred.
- Within each tetrad, there is a random assignment of sides (so either maternally or paternally derived chromosome could end up on either side; this is **independent assortment** of chromosomes).

Anaphase 1

- Continued tugging by the spindle fibers results in pulling apart of the homologous pairs so that the *maternally and paternally derived chromosomes are separated*; disjunction.
- These two groups of 23 chromosomes, each still consisting of two sister chromatids, collect at opposite poles of the cell.

Telophase 1

- As the chromosomes are grouped at each pole of the cell, the cell wall constricts (cytokinesis), which causes separation of the original cell into two daughter cells.

The end result of Meiosis I is:

1. Two haploid daughter cells (23 chromosomes each), chromosomes still in doubled state.
2. Homologous pairs have been separated (so chromosome number drops from 46 to 23).
3. Daughter cells now are different from each other in their chromosomal makeup, because pieces of the maternally and paternally derived chromosomes have been interchanged (crossing over), with a random distribution of maternally and paternally derived chromosomes in the daughter cells during cell division (independent assortment).

In a male, the two daughter cells resulting from Meiosis I are the same size. In a female, one of the two daughter cells keeps most of the cytoplasm so it is much larger than the other (see Figure 4.2). The smaller cell is called a polar body, which is left with its 23 chromosomes, but little else. This polar body may or may not divide again, but it will never develop into a functional egg, and is reabsorbed by the body.

FIGURE 4.3 *Phases of Meiosis: Gamete Production*

Continued

Meiosis II

Prophase II

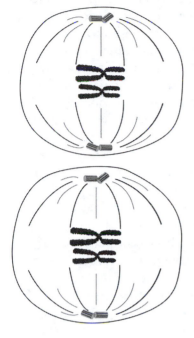

- Begins with the end products of Meiosis I: two daughter cells whose homologous pairs have been separated, so that now each cell has only one set of the 23 chromosomes in each cell; chromosomes are still in their doubled state.
- Spindle apparatus begins to form in each of the two new cells.
- Spindle fibers coming from centrioles at opposite poles of the cell attach to the protein complexes on both sides of each chromosome's centromeres.

Metaphase II

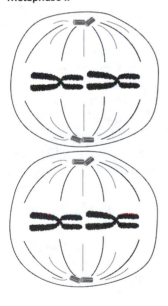

- As in mitosis, all of the chromosomes in each cell are pulled by the spindle fibers into lining up on the equator of the cell.

Anaphase II

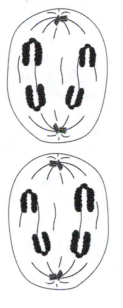

- Continued tugging by the spindle fibers results in the pulling apart, or disjunction, of the chromosomes at the centromeres, so that the *sister chromatids of each chromosome are separated*.
- The two groups of 23 chromosomes, now in their single state, gather at opposite poles of the two cells.

Telophase II

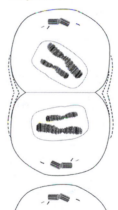

- Nuclear membrane re-forms around the 23 chromosomes grouped at each pole.
- The chromosomes are uncoiling and taking the form of chromatin.
- Cytokinesis occurs, eventually causing separation of each of the two original cells into two daughter cells, for a total of four haploid cells.

The end result of Meiosis II is:
Four haploid cells (each with 23 chromosomes), now in their single state because the sister chromatids of each chromosome have been separated. In a male, a total of four sperm eventually develop.

In a female, the second division also results in one big cell with most of the cytoplasm from the parent cell, and one polar body. Only the larger daughter cell continues to develop into an egg cell (see Figure 4.2).

3. *How many chromosomes are present* in the parent and daughter cells before and after each of the two meiotic divisions, and whether they are in their single or doubled state.

In addition to females' beginning to produce egg cells while still in the womb, the chromosomes actually begin crossing over. In this state, the precursor eggs are held in "limbo" until puberty, when the meiotic process continues at the rate of only one cell per month.

Summary of Meiosis

Meiosis I Homologous pairs are separated into different daughter cells, immediately reducing the number of chromosomes from 46 in the parent cell to 23 in daughter cells (crossing over has occurred, so the pairs are no longer identical).

Meiosis II Sister chromatids of each chromosome are separated from each other.

Variation Each gamete is now unique as a result of crossing over, and the independent assortment that occurs during meiosis. These events are vital in producing variation, and ensuring that gametes are produced that are different from one another!

Mitosis Versus Meiosis The differences between somatic cell production (mitosis) and gamete production (meiosis) are summarized in Table 4.2. Again, keep in mind that mitosis is the division of an existing somatic cell into two daughter somatic cells, whereas meiosis is the division of a specialized kind of somatic cell into first two, then four cells, which mature into gametes and never will undergo cell division.

Chromosomal Aberrations

Fortunately, cell division most often proceeds smoothly, but mistakes do occur. Mistakes that result in an extra or missing piece of chromosome, an entire chromosome, or even a set of chromosomes are called **chromosomal mutations**. Having too many or too few chromosomes is a **chromosomal anomaly** or **chromosomal aberration** and can cause an early miscarriage in pregnancy (often before a woman even knows she is pregnant), or can lead to serious or fatal conditions.

Chromosomal mutations can occur in various ways. A common cause is failure of chromosomes to separate properly from one another during cell division. The separation of chromosomes to move toward opposite poles of the cell during anaphase is called **disjunction**; failure to separate is **nondisjunction** (see Figure 4.4).

If nondisjunction occurs during mitosis of the embryo in very early development, all subsequent cells deriving from that cell will have the wrong number of chromosomes. If nondisjunction occurs during meiosis, gametes with the improper number of chromosomes will be produced. A zygote (or later, an embryo) without some of the genes necessary for development, or a zygote that possesses too many genes, will develop either improperly or not at all. Nondisjunction during Meiosis I results in all daughter cells having the wrong number of chromosomes, and in Meiosis II one-half of the daughter cells will be normal and one-half will have chromosomal anomalies (see Figure 4.5).

In addition to nondisjunction, mutations can result in the wrong number of chromosomes, called **aneuploidy**; diploid rather than haploid gametes; or fertilization of an egg with more than one sperm. The correct number of chromosomes is referred to as **euploidy** (G *eu*: good, *ploid*: set).

Normally, the set of chromosomes in a human zygote includes 23 homologous pairs, consisting of two chromosomes of each "type" (two chromosome number 1s, two number

TABLE 4.2: Differences Between Mitosis and Meiosis		
Difference	**Mitosis**	**Meiosis**
End result of process	Division of somatic cell to produce more somatic cells for growth and tissue repair	Division of specialized somatic cell to produce haploid gametes that can combine with another gamete to form a new individual
Number of divisions	One	Two
Chromosome number in daughter cells	Chromosome number of 46 is maintained from parent cell to daughter cells	Chromosome number is *reduced* from 46 in the parent cell to 23 in each of the resulting daughter cells (gametes)
Similarity of DNA of daughter cells to that in parent cells	Identical	Each gamete unique in its genetic makeup
Location in body	Throughout body	Ovaries or testes only

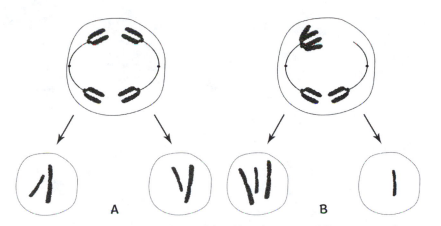

FIGURE 4.4 *Anaphase of Normal Mitosis (A) and Nondisjunction of Chromosomes During Anaphase (B)*

2s, two sex chromosomes, etc.). This normal condition is called **disomy** (referring to the two chromosomes that make up each pair). When one of a pair is missing, it is called a **monosomy**, and when there is an extra, it is a **trisomy**.

For most chromosomes, missing one of a pair or having an extra is a fatal condition. One important exception is **Trisomy 21**, which produces the condition known as **Down syndrome**. Because chromosome 21 is the smallest chromosome, less damage occurs by having three copies of its genes than with trisomy of larger chromosomes.

Anomalies in number of sex chromosomes are less damaging. Because survivability is not affected, sex chromosomal aberrations are observed more commonly in living individuals. An individual may have an extra of one of the sex chromosomes, or have only one, but at least one X chromosome must be present because survival without any X chromosome is incompatible with life. The conditions caused by this type of mutation are outlined in Table 4.3.

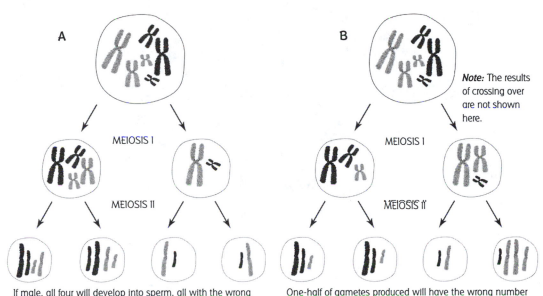

Note: The results of crossing over are not shown here.

If male, all four will develop into sperm, all with the wrong number of chromosomes. If female, only one egg matures, with the wrong chromosome number.

One-half of gametes produced will have the wrong number of chromosomes, and one-half will have the correct number.

FIGURE 4.5 *Nondisjunction During Gamete Formation: In Meiosis I (A) and In Meiosis II (B)*

TABLE 4.3: Examples of Sex Chromosomal Anomalies			
Sex Chromosomes	**Name of condition**	**Symptoms**	**Incidence**
XO	Turner syndrome	Underdeveloped breasts, infertile, rudimentary ovaries, lack of menstruation, short stature, neck webbing, heart problems, skeletal abnormalities[1]	1 in 2,000 female births[2]
XXY	Klinefelter syndrome	Malformed and/or small testes, lack of sperm development, some with breast development, low fertility, some with mild retardation[1]	1 in 500 to 1,000 male births[2]
XYY	XYY syndrome	Poorly known	1 in 1,000 male births[1]
XXX	XXX syndrome	Tall, thin, some with menstrual difficulties and mental retardation[1]	1 in 1,000 to 1 in 2,000 female births[1]

[1]Mange and Mange, 1990).
[2]National Institute of Child Health and Human Development, 2004.

LAB EXERCISE 4.1

NAME _____ SECTION _____ DATE _____

1. Before completing this question, review the process of mitosis so you can fill out the diagrams and answer the questions without looking at the preceding information.

   MITOSIS

   Interphase:

   a. In the cell provided, draw the form the DNA takes in the nucleus at this stage.

   b. What is the "main event" occurring in the nucleus *before* cell division?

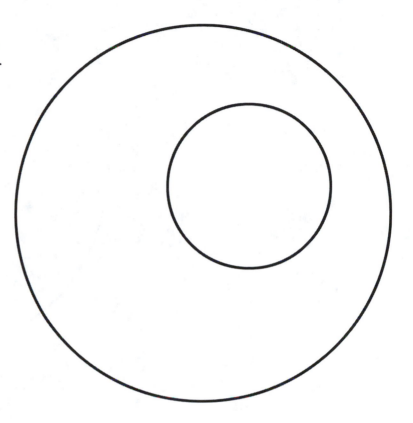

   Prophase:

   a. Draw four chromosomes in the blank cell. Think about the state in which they will appear (single or doubled).

   b. If this were a human, how many chromosomes would appear?

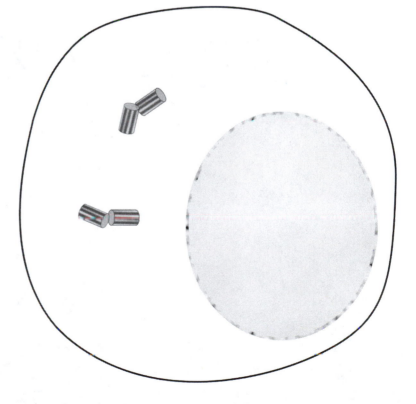

Metaphase:

a. Draw the chromosomes along the equator of the cell.

b. Draw the pairs of centrioles at opposite poles of the cell, and add spindle fibers connecting them to the centromeres of the chromosomes.

Anaphase:

a. Draw the chromosomes. In what form are they now?

b. What exactly is happening to the chromosomes?

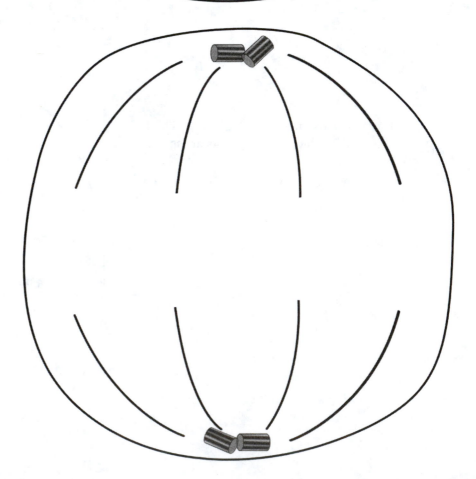

Telophase:

a. Draw the chromosomes at each pole, surrounded by their newly formed nuclear membranes.

b. In this example, how many chromosomes are in each nucleus?

c. If this were a human, how many chromosomes would be in each nucleus?

d. Note the cell walls at the sides of the cell pinching in. This is accomplished by a ring of elastic proteins around the cell, constricting much the way a rubber band tightening around a balloon would appear. What is the term for this process of separating the one cell into two?

2. You will re-create the process of meiosis in an individual whose diploid chromosome number is six. From the sample of chromosomes given in Appendix 1, choose and cut out the appropriate ones to fill in the stages of meiosis. All of the sample chromosomes should be used; none should be left over.

Look at the chromosomes in Appendix 1. What do the two different colors of chromosome represent?

Would this example be more representative of the meiotic process in males or in females? Why?

MEIOSIS I

MEIOSIS II

3. In Figure 4.1 you saw a diagram of normal anaphase of mitosis occurring, and nondisjunction in Figure 4.4. Take another look at these figures. In the illustration, anaphase is in progress. Draw the remaining four chromosomes (in the right half of the cell) as though nondisjunction were occurring for the chromosome indicated by the arrow (and anaphase proceeding normally for the other three chromosomes). Then draw the outcome in the daughter cells.

4. Determine from the karyotype below whether the individual represented is chromosomally normal or abnormal. If abnormal, which syndrome do you see, from the information you were given in this chapter? What is the sex of this individual?

SELF-TEST 4.1

NAME _____ SECTION _____ DATE _____

1. a. What process is represented here?

   b. How do you know?

   c. What kind of cell is being produced?

   d. If you find out that the diploid number of chromosomes for this species is eight, will that change your answers to 1.a and 1.c?

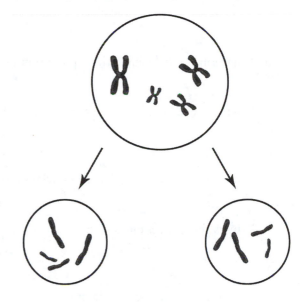

2. a. What process is represented here?

   b. How do you know? (Give two reasons.)

   c. The original cell that is dividing is what kind?

   d. What is the end result of this process?

   How similar or different are the daughter cells?

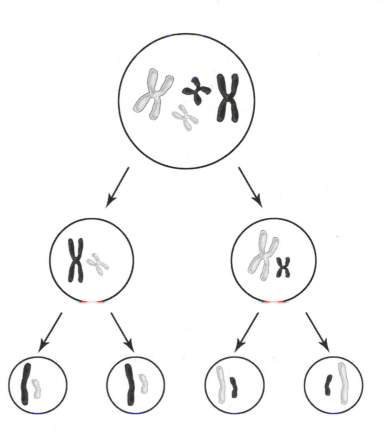

3. a. What kind of cells have the haploid number of chromosomes?

   b. Why do these cells have the haploid number?

   c. What is the haploid chromosome number for humans?

4. a. What kind of cells have the diploid number of chromosomes?

   b. What is the diploid chromosome number for humans?

5. a. What process occurs in the cell nucleus *before* cell division begins?

   b. Why is this process necessary?

6. What are chromosomes made of?

7. Explain how the genetic material from your parents combined to form you as a zygote.

8. Why doesn't the DNA get reduced by half every time cell division occurs?

9. How long does it take a cell to divide?

5. Inheritance

"Have you ever wondered...?"

✋ Why do I look so much more like my father than my mother, if each contributed 50% of my genes?

✋ How can a set of parents with brown eyes produce a child with blue eyes?

Gregor Mendel

Although Darwin and Wallace knew that variation was vital for natural selection to occur, they didn't know how that variation came to be. The mystery of how traits were passed from parent to offspring was solved by Johann Mendel (he took the name Gregor later while at a monastery) in the 1860s. Mendel's breeding experiments with pea plants led to his discovery of the laws of inheritance, which later were verified with knowledge of chromosomal behavior during meiosis.

Mendel was successful partly through luck but mainly because of carefully planned experiments, a large sample size (about 28,000 individual plants!), use of a statistical approach (probability), and his fortuitous choice of genetically **simple traits** (those controlled by only one gene). These traits are now called **Mendelian traits**.

Mendel's experiments included observing the transmission of a single trait at a time and also observing two traits at a time. From these experiments, he concluded these two "laws" of inheritance:

1. For any given trait, members of a pair of "characters" separate (segregate) from each other during the formation of gametes, so only one copy (one gene) is passed on from each parent. This is his **principle of segregation.** We now know that this explains the separation of members of a gene pair from each other during the formation of gametes (when homologous pairs separate).

2. Genes on one set of homologous chromosomes don't influence the distribution of gene pairs on other chromosomes (for example, the chance for a pea seed to be round or wrinkled is independent of its chance of being yellow or green). This is because genes from homologous chromosomes separate independently from each other during meiosis and are randomly assorted in the gametes. This is the **principle of independent assortment.**

Recall from Chapter 2 that a **gene** is a segment of a chromosome's DNA coding for a specific protein, and an **allele** (G *allelo*: one another, parallel) is an alternative form of a gene. For any trait, an individual inherits one allele from each parent so each individual always has two alleles for each trait. The two alleles at a given locus make up an individual's **genotype**. The alleles are represented by letters (see Figure 5.1). As shown in Chapter 2, chromosome 9 has genes for melanin production and for blood type for the ABO blood group.

If an individual inherits two alleles coding for the same form of the trait, they are said to be **homozygous** for that trait. If the alleles code for different forms of the trait, the genotype is **heterozygous**. Thus, for example, if someone inherits one allele that does not result in normal melanin production and the other allele that does code for melanin production, what determines which form the trait will take? Will the person produce melanin or not?

Many traits have a consistent pattern of expression such that one allele may be expressed whenever it is present and the other allele is expressed only if it has been passed on by both parents. If an allele is always expressed when present, this allele codes for the dominant form of the trait. The **recessive** form of a trait is expressed only when both "recessive" alleles are present and there is no allele for the **dominant** form of the trait present. Genotypes can be **homozygous dominant**, **heterozygous**, or **homozygous recessive**.

The physical expression of a trait is the **phenotype** (G *pheno*: show, seem, appear). Thus, the *genotype* consists

of the genes (alleles) present at a particular locus on a homologous pair of chromosomes, and the *phenotype* is the resulting observable form of the trait.

If a specific trait is coded for by a gene on a chromosome numbered 1–22 (the autosomes), it is an **autosomal trait**. A trait coded for by a gene on the 23rd pair (the sex chromosomes) is a **sex-linked trait**.

Autosomal Traits

In the following discussion, we will first consider transmission of one trait, then two traits.

Consideration of One Trait

It is straightforward to follow the transmission of *one* autosomal trait from parents to offspring. We'll use albinism as an example.

Albinism (lack of production of the pigment melanin) is coded for by a recessive autosomal gene. This gene has two alternative alleles: *A* (the dominant allele) and *a* (the recessive allele). Therefore, using the letters *A* and *a* to represent the dominant and recessive alleles, the genotypes *AA* and *Aa* (homozygous dominant and heterozygous, respectively) would result in normal melanin production, and therefore in phenotypes with normally pigmented coloration. The genotype *aa*, by contrast, would result in the recessive form and thus an albino phenotype.

The following explains how to predict the probability of offspring from a cross between an *albino woman* and a *man heterozygous for albinism*.

1. List the genotype of the mother as *aa* and the father as *Aa*.

2. Figure out what alleles for this trait will be carried by the gametes in individuals with the above genotypes. Remember that during meiosis the homologous chromosome pairs are separated from each other during the first division (review in Chapter 4, if necessary, and see Figure 5.2). Although an individual has two alleles for each trait in each somatic cell (one maternally and one paternally derived), when they produce gametes, each gamete will have only *one* allele representing each trait (to potentially combine with an allele from an individual of the opposite sex).

   In our example, the mother has only *a* alleles, so all of her eggs will carry one of these recessive alleles (see Figure 5.2A). The father is heterozygous, so he will produce sperm carrying dominant and recessive alleles in approximately equal numbers. Therefore, half of his sperm will carry an *A*, and half an *a* (see Figure 5.2B). In this process, alleles are passed on to daughter cells, which develop into gametes.

3. Set up a **Punnett square**. This is a simple tool, developed in the early 1900s by geneticist Reginald Punnett, to

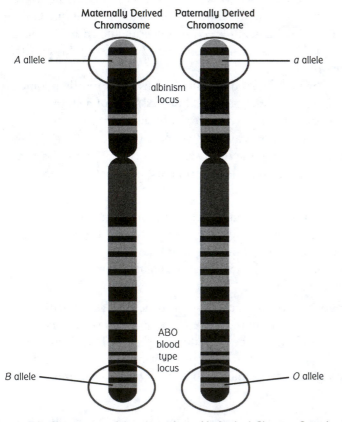

FIGURE 5.1 *Chromosome 9 for a Hypothetical Individual, Showing Samples of Loci for Two Traits*

Meiosis in Mother (aa)

Meiosis in Father (Aa)

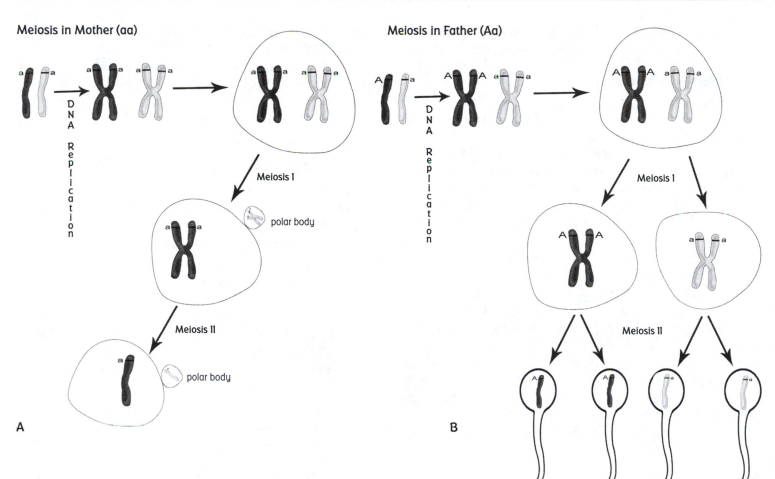

FIGURE 5.2 *Process of Meiosis in Mother (A) and Father (B)*

predict offspring outcomes depending upon the parental genotypes.

List the alleles possessed by one parent along the top of the square and those of the other parent along the left side of the square—in our example, we'll list the mother's alleles along the top. Thus, these will represent the kinds of alleles present in the eggs of the mother and the sperm cells of the father (see Figure 5.3). Keep in mind that we are only focusing on one trait—actually, in each gamete there will be alleles present for *all* traits.

4. Fill in your Punnett square. The results represent possible outcomes of allele combinations (genotypes) in the zygote (see Figure 5.4).

5. List the possible genotypes and phenotypes of the offspring, as well as the probability of each type.

genotypes	phenotypes	probability
Aa	nonalbino	1/2 (50%)
aa	albino	1/2 (50%)

6. List the ratio of the phenotypes and the genotypes, in terms of probabilities:

a. **genotypic ratio**—number of homozygous dominant to heterozygous to homozygous recessive: 0:2:2

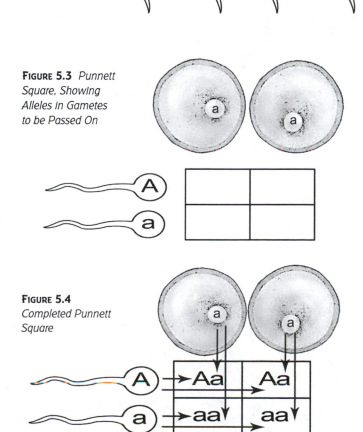

FIGURE 5.3 *Punnett Square, Showing Alleles in Gametes to be Passed On*

FIGURE 5.4 *Completed Punnett Square*

b. **phenotypic ratio**—number expressing dominant form of trait to number expressing the recessive form: 1:1

Consideration of Two Traits

If we consider *two traits* at once, Mendel's principle of segregation becomes important in demonstrating that the chances of inheriting one trait has no effect on the chances of inheriting the other. That is because, during gamete formation, the alleles (on their respective chromosomes) segregate/assort independently from one another and are assorted randomly in the gametes. Thus, the chances for someone's bloodtype to be A or B is independent of his or her chances of being an albino or not.

The Punnett square also can be used to determine the probabilities of outcomes of more than one trait considered together. We'll use the traits of tongue-rolling and albinism in this example. Remember that albinism is inherited recessively by a gene on one of the autosomes. Tongue-rolling is inherited as an autosomal dominant trait. That is, the ability to tongue-roll is dominant, so someone who is heterozygous (*Rr*) for the trait can roll the tongue, and someone who is homozygous recessive (*rr*) does not have the musculature to tongue-roll. Actually, tongue-rolling may be controlled by genes at more than one locus, and it has some environmental

component as well (e.g., Martin, 1975). Still, the trait serves as a useful example.

Work through this example of a woman who cannot roll her tongue and is not an albino (she's homozygous dominant for albinism) who marries a man who can roll his tongue (he's heterozygous for tongue-rolling) and is an albino.

1. List the genotypes of the parents for both traits:

   Mother: *rrAA*   Father: *Rraa*

2. Next, figure out what alleles are present in the gametes of the mother and father. *This is a crucial step! Do it carefully, and ask your instructor if you do not understand!* See Figure 5.5. The process of meiosis will result in the following:

   a. In the mother's eggs, the tongue-rolling trait will be represented only by the *r* allele (the mother's genotype is *rr*), and the albinism trait will be represented only by the *A* allele (the mother's genotype is *AA*). Thus, all eggs she produces will have an *r* and an *A* to represent those two traits. This can be written as *rA* (see Figure 5.5A).

   b. The father's sperm will have two possible combinations of alleles. Because he is heterozygous for tongue-rolling, half of his sperm will have the *R* allele and

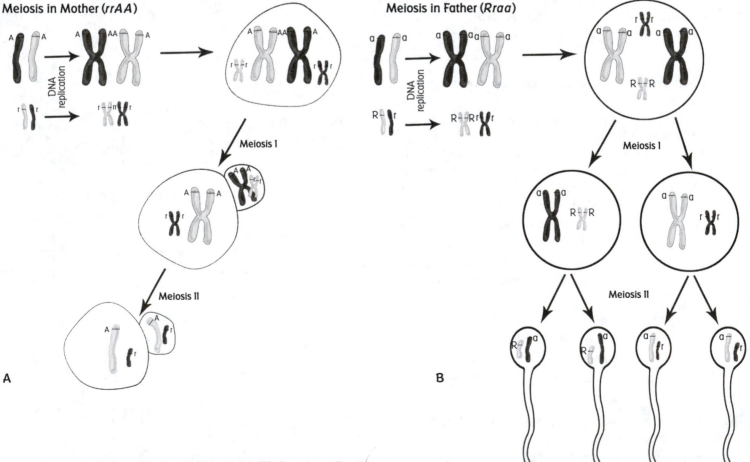

FIGURE 5.5 *Process of Meiosis in Female (A) and Male (B), Considering Two Traits*

half the *r* allele. All of his sperm will be produced carrying the *a* allele for albinism. Thus, half his sperm will have *Ra* and half will have *ra* (see Figure 5.5B).

3. Set up your Punnett square. The number of columns and rows will be dependent upon the number of possible combinations in the parents' gametes. Because there is only one possible type of egg, the mother will produce (*rA*), and the father will have two types of sperm (*Ra* and *ra*). The Punnett "square" can be as small as a 1 × 2 table (see Figure 5.6).

4. Fill in the Punnett square with the expected types of offspring (Figure 5.7).

5. List the possible genotypes and phenotypes of the offspring, as well as the probability of each type.

genotype	phenotype	probability
RrAa	tongue-roller, non-albino	½ (50%)
rrAa	non tongue-roller, non-albino	½ (50%)

We have focused on traits that are coded for by only one gene—called **monogenic,** or simple traits. Although many traits are coded for by more than one gene—called **polygenic**—and also may have an environmental contribution, we continue to use as examples these simple, or Mendelian, traits for the purpose of illustrating patterns of inheritance.

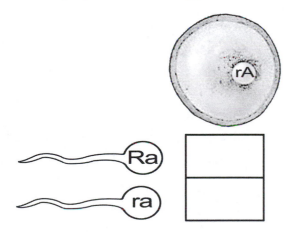

FIGURE 5.6 *Punnett Square, Showing Alleles in Gametes to be Passed On for Two Traits*

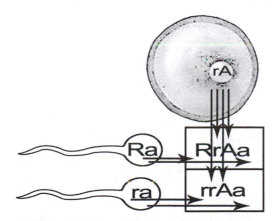

FIGURE 5.7 *Completed Punnett Square for Two Traits*

Blood Typing

Although one usually hears about type A, B, O, and AB, as well as positive and negative blood, we each actually have not two, but about 24 blood types! Each different blood type is coded for by genes at different loci on our chromosomes. A blood type is determined by the kind of antigen present on the surface of our red blood cells. Blood types are useful for tracking genetic traits within and between populations, investigating their biomedical effects, and learning about inheritance.

ABO Blood Group

In the blood serum, each person has **antibodies** against foreign blood antigens. By determining the type of antibodies in the blood, you can determine the individual's blood type. The simplest way to test for the type of antibody present is to add **antigens**. If the antibodies attack the antigens, the result is a clumping affect, called **agglutination**. The surface of the red blood cells has antigens with the same common name on their surface as the person's type of blood (A or B).

The **ABO blood group** is coded for at a locus on chromosome 9; alleles called I^A, I^B, and I^O (hereafter referred to simply as A, B, and O alleles) determine enzymes that are responsible for the type of antigens that are produced and reside on the surface of red blood cells. These antigens are composed of a chain of simple sugar molecules and differ just slightly from each other depending upon the alleles present. The difference between A and B antigens (determined by A or B alleles) is that each has an extra sugar molecule (different from each other) on the end of the chain, which is lacking in the chain produced by someone with only O alleles.

The various genotypes for this trait are: AA, AO, AB, BO, OO, and BB. A and B alleles are both dominant over O but are **codominant** with regard to each other. Thus, if both an A and a B allele are present, both A-type and B-type antigens are produced (and the genotype is type AB). O alleles are expressed only if they occur without an A or a B allele to "mask" their appearance in the phenotype: An OO genotype (type O blood) is the only one to produce a sugar chain with no end sugar as in blood types A, B, and AB. Table 5.1 lists the genotypes, phenotypes (blood types), antigens, and antibodies for each blood type in the ABO group.

Blood types for the ABO blood group must match if blood from one person (a donor) is to be used for another (a recipient), as a result of the reaction of anti-A and anti-B antibodies against the A and B antigens, respectively, on the surface of the red blood cells. Because type O blood has neither A nor B antigens on its cell surface, it has both anti-A and anti-B antibodies in its serum. For that very reason (lack of A or B antigens), however, type O blood does not provoke a reaction (**agglutinate**) with type A, B, or AB blood. Therefore, individuals with type O blood are known as **universal**

TABLE 5.1: Characteristics of ABO Blood Group			
Genotype	Blood type	Type of Antigens on Red Blood Cell Surface	Type of Antibodies in Serum
AA or AO	Type A blood	A antigens	Anti-B
BB or BO	Type B blood	B antigens	Anti-A
OO	Type O blood	None	Anti-A and anti-B
AB	Type AB blood	A and B antigens	None

donors. Type AB blood has neither anti-A nor anti-B antibodies with which to attack incoming blood cells, so it can receive any blood—type A, type B, type AB, or type O. Thus, type AB individuals are referred to as **universal recipients.**

Rh Blood Group

The blood types associated with the **Rh blood group** are Rh+ and Rh− (A+, B−, etc. really represent blood types from two different blood groups, ABO and Rh). There are actually several alleles coding for Rh blood types, determined by simple dominant/recessive inheritance. If an individual is homozygous dominant or heterozygous, he or she is Rh+; the individual is Rh− if homozygous recessive. A person who is Rh+ has antigens on the surface of the red blood cells that can provoke the production of antibodies in the serum of someone without those antigens (an Rh− person).

The Rh blood group has great significance medically, because of potential problems with **Rh incompatibility** between a mother and her developing fetus. If the antibodies are produced by a (Rh−) mother's immune system in response to antigens on her (Rh+) fetus' red blood cells, the mother's antibodies can attack the fetal cells and break them open, releasing the hemoglobin within and resulting in severe **anemia** in the infant around the time of its birth. If the mother receives prenatal care, medical advances have virtually eliminated the problem in our society today.

LAB EXERCISE 5.1

NAME _____ SECTION _____ DATE _____

1. Can you roll your tongue? Can you tell what your genotype is? What are the possibilities for your genotype for this trait? Make a Punnett square for the following exercise to answer these questions.

    a. If you can roll your tongue, let's (for the purposes of this exercise) assume that you're heterozygous. If you produce offspring with another heterozygote, what are the possible genotypes of these offspring? Their phenotypes? (Remember, use the letter R and r to represent the dominant and recessive alleles.)

    b. If you cannot roll your tongue, and you produce offspring with someone who is heterozygous for tongue-rolling, what are the possible genotypes of these offspring? Their phenotypes?

2. Represented in the illustration on the next page is chromosome 11 (it hypothetically shows several Mendelian traits to illustrate; the actual genes present on chromosome 11 are different from these). This chromosome pair is taken from the karyotype of three different individuals—Individuals 1, 2, and 3.

    Using the information given in the chart below and previously in this chapter, you will create genotypes for each chromosome pair for four traits: ABO blood type, cleft chin, earwax form, and PTC tasting.

Trait	Description	Dominant form of trait	Alleles
Cleft chin	Dimple in center of chin	Possession of cleft chin	D, d
Earwax (cerumen) form	Sticky yellow/brown vs. dry grayish earwax	Sticky earwax	C, c
PTC (phenylthiocarbamide) tasting	Ability to taste bitterness	Ability to taste PTC	T, t

a. Fill in the alleles on the chromosomes illustrated below, using whatever combination of dominant and recessive alleles you wish. (One example is filled in for you; you may change them if you wish.)

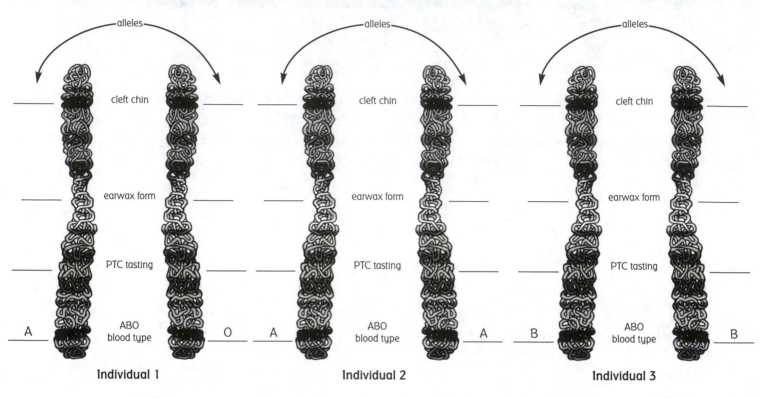

Individual 1   Individual 2   Individual 3

b. Fill in the chart below, making the genotype for each trait different for individuals 1, 2, and 3.

	Individual 1		Individual 2		Individual 3	
	Genotype	Phenotype	Genotype	Phenotype	Genotype	Phenotype
ABO blood type	AO	Type A	AA	Type A	BB	Type B
Cleft chin						
Dwarfism						
PTC tasting						

c. Compare the genotypes and phenotypes for your three individuals with a classmate's results. Are your results the same?

This demonstrates the variation that can result from the different combinations of alleles produced by the parents and randomly passed on to the next generation (Mendel's principles). There are several hundred thousand possible combinations of genotypes for these four traits for any group of three individuals randomly chosen from the population! Imagine the possible allelic combinations if we consider all approximately 25,000 traits represented by the genes on all 23 chromosomes!

3. At DuPont Company in 1931, a chemist instigated an accident, in which some synthesized compound phenylthiocarbamide (PTC) exploded into the air (*Gadsby*, 2000). Some of the workers actually could taste bitterness in the air and others couldn't. This led to the "taste test" for PTC. When the compound was handed out as crystals at the 1932 American Academy for the Advancement of Sciences (AAAS) conference, about a quarter of the people could not taste it ("non-tasters"), and the others ("tasters") said it was incredibly bitter.

It was quickly noted that the ability to taste was determined genetically, and it was transmitted in a simple Mendelian fashion. Phenotypes were divided into non-tasters and tasters. The ability to taste is dominant to the inability, so a non-taster would be homozygous recessive.

a. Taste the PTC paper, and note your:

phenotype   **genotype (or at least any known alleles—use the letters *T,t*)**

More recently, human taste specialist Linda Bartoshuk (1994), found a third level of tasters, and thus divided people into super-tasters, tasters, and non-tasters. These may correlate with homozygous dominant, heterozygous, and homozygous recessive genotypes.

We have four types of **papillae** on the tongue. The papillae house the receptor cells (taste buds). Molecules with sweet, salty, sour, or bitter tastes stimulate the receptors, which stimulate nerve endings inside the tongue, and the message of the type of taste is carried along the nerve cells to the brain. The number of taste buds embedded in the tips of the tongue are controlled by our genes. The types of papillae are **circumvallate, foliate, filiform,** and **fungiform** (the mushroom-shaped bumps concentrated more at the tongue's tip), as illustrated.

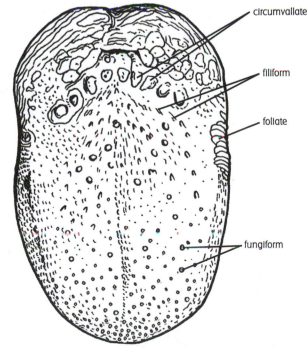

circumvallate

filiform

foliate

fungiform

b. Drip a small drop of food coloring (green or blue works best) onto a thin strip of paper, then use it to paint the tip of your tongue (Scientific American Frontiers Archives, 1999).

c. Punch a hole in an index card and place the hole over the tip of your tongue. This small area of your tongue will serve as your sample of taste buds (Shahbake et al., 2005). The edge of the hole should be on the tip of the tongue, in the center.

d. Have someone else count (using a magnifying glass, if available) the fungiform papillae (these should appear pale against the food-colored tongue background). *Super-tasters* may have up to 50 fungiform papillae. *Tasters* usually have 15 to 30, and *non-tasters* may have as few as 10 (Bartoshuk et al., 1994, 1998; *Discover* magazine, 2000).

e. Are you a PTC taster? According to fungiform-counting, what is your tasting level? Do your taste preferences match the results of PTC tasting and fungiform papillae-counting? Super-tasters often avoid black coffee, grapefruit, and very sweet desserts. (More females than males tend to be super-tasters.)

f. Take a count of the phenotypes of all of your classmates so you have a total number of supertasters, tasters and non-tasters.

Supertasters: _____   Tasters: _____   Non-tasters: _____

SELF-TEST 5.1

NAME _____ SECTION _____ DATE _____

1. Two normally pigmented parents have an albino child. What are the parents' genotypes? The child grows up and marries another albino. What is the probability of their having an albino child?

2. A zebra population has a mutant allele for spots. The spot trait (S) is dominant to the striped allele (s).

   a. A spotted male mates with a striped female. Assuming that he is homozygous, what is the probability that they will have striped offspring?

   b. If one of their daughters mates with a spotted (heterozygous) male, what is the probability the offspring will be striped?

3. If a male who is Rh⁻ mates with a female who is Rh⁺ (heterozygous), what are the possible genotypes and phenotypes of their offspring? (Use the letters D and d to represent the dominant and recessive alleles, respectively; use a Punnett square.)

4. A normally pigmented woman and an albino man have nine normally pigmented children and one albino child. What is the woman's genotype?

5. The ability to taste the chemical PTC is transmitted as a dominant allele, represented by T; the recessive allele is t. Two normally pigmented taster parents have an albino son and a non-taster daughter with normal pigmentation.

   a. What are the genotypes of the parents?

   b. What is the chance that the albino son is a taster?

   c. What is the chance that the non-taster daughter is heterozygous for the gene controlling albinism?

   d. The non-taster, non-albino daughter marries a taster man with normal pigmentation; his mother was a non-taster albino. What is his genotype?

   e. What is the chance that a child of theirs will be a taster albino if the wife is heterozygous for albinism?

6. There is a case of disputed paternity, involving a woman (W) and her children (i, ii, iii, iv) and two men (Y and Z). The analysis is limited to the ABO and MN blood group systems. The phenotypes are as follows:

father:

W: A, MN	i: A, MN	_____
Y: B, MN	ii: A, M	_____
Z: AB, N	iii. AB, M	_____
	iv. O, N	_____

Assuming that only Y or Z could be the father of these children, assign the children to their appropriate father. In the ABO blood group system, A and B are codominant, and both are dominant over the recessive O allele. In the MN blood group system, M and N are codominant. You can solve this problem either with Punnett squares for both possible parental crosses (W with Y; W with Z) or without a Punnett square, working with a process of elimination of possibilities.

7. You are typing your blood. What is your blood type if:

a. There is no agglutination?

b. There is agglutination with anti-A but not anti-B?

c. There is agglutination with both anti-A and anti-B?

Which blood type is known as a universal donor? _____

Why?

e. Which blood type is known as a universal receiver? _____

Why?

8. A female who is a PTC taster and a tongue-roller mates with a male who is also a PTC taster but is not a tongue-roller. Use the letters T,t (for PTC tasting) and R,r (tongue-rolling). The ability to taste is dominant, and the ability to tongue-roll is dominant.

a. What do we know of their genotypes? Female _____ Male _____
   (Fill in only the alleles you know at this point, without looking ahead.)

b. They have three kids with the following phenotypes:
   Kid 1: PTC taster and tongue-roller
   Kid 2: PTC taster and non-tongue roller
   Kid 3: PTC non-taster and tongue-roller

c. With the knowledge of the next generation's phenotypes, now what do we know of the genotypes of the parents?

   Female _____ Male _____

9. In a case of disputed paternity, a woman has a daughter with type A, Rh^+ blood. The woman's blood type is A, Rh^-. What blood types could a possible father have?

10. How is it possible that a set of parents with brown eyes produces a child with blue eyes?

Sex-Linked Traits

Sex-linked traits can be coded for by genes on either the X or the Y chromosome. Traits coded for by genes on the X chromosome are X-linked, and those on the Y chromosome are Y-linked. Most traits that are sex-linked are X-linked because X is a much larger chromosome, possessing many more genes than the Y chromosome. Genes on the Y chromosome relate to male sexual development. Most genes on the X chromosome have nothing to do with female sexual development but are vital for individuals of both sexes.

One example of an X-linked trait is red/green color-blindness. On the X chromosome is a gene coding for **opsin** proteins (proteins in cone cells of the retina that enable us to perceive color); these opsins bind to visual pigments in the red-sensitive cones, green-sensitive cones, or blue-sensitive cones, making the visual pigment/opsin complex sensitive to light of a particular wavelength. If the opsin protein (a product of a gene, via protein synthesis) is absent or defective, the color vision is affected.

The vast majority (93%) of people who are colorblind are males, because this trait is transmitted by a recessive gene on the X chromosome. When denoting the genotype for a sex-linked trait, *always include the sex chromosomes*, X and Y, as shown below. This is important because the pattern of transmission of a sex-linked trait differs for males versus females. Below, C denotes the normal, dominant allele, and c the recessive, faulty allele. The genotypes for males and for females are as follows:

Genotypes for Males	Phenotypes
X^CY	Male with normal color vision
X^cY	Colorblind male

Genotypes for Females	Phenotypes
X^CX^C	Female with normal color vision (non-carrier)
X^CX^c	**Carrier** for colorblindness (but normal color vision)
X^cX^c	Colorblind female

Note that females can be homozygous dominant, heterozygous, or homozygous recessive. Because males have only one X chromosome, and thus one allele for each trait coded for by this chromosome, they cannot be referred to as any of these! They are **hemizygous.** Recessive alleles on the X chromosome are always expressed in males, because there is no dominant allele to "compensate."

The steps for predicting outcomes for a sex-linked trait are demonstrated by this example. A man with normal color vision and a woman who is a carrier for colorblindness are about to have a child. What are the possible genotypes for the child?

1. List the genotypes of each parent. Man: X^CY

   Woman: X^CX^c

2. Set up your Punnett square, remembering to include the sex chromosomes with the allele that is on it, as shown below.

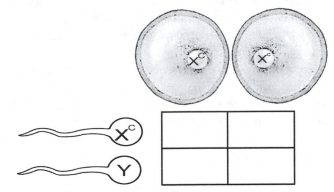

FIGURE 5.8 *Punnett Square for X-linked Trait, Colorblindness*

3. Fill in the Punnett square with the expected types of offspring.

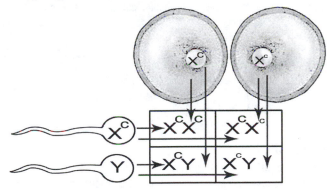

FIGURE 5.11 *Completed Punnett Square for Colorblindness*

4. List the possible genotypes and phenotypes of each, and their associated probabilities of occurrence.

Genotypes	Phenotypes	Probability
X^CX^C	normal female	1/4 (25%)
X^CX^c	carrier female	1/4 (25%)
X^CY	normal male	1/4 (25%)
X^cY	colorblind male	1/4 (25%)

Pedigrees

An important part of the study of inheritance is the search for patterns of transmission of traits from one generation to the next. Does a specific trait follow a definite and predictable pattern of transmission? Knowledge of the mode of inheritance has important implications for biomedical research, genetics studies, and genetic counseling.

We can visualize patterns of inheritance by constructing a **pedigree**, which is a diagram that delineates the genetic relationships of family members over two or more generations. **Segregation analysis** is used to determine which of several modes of inheritance is responsible for producing specific patterns in a familial line. This involves proposing a genetic hypothesis (a possible mode of transmission), testing it, and continuing the process until a hypothesis is proposed that accounts for the observed patterns of inheritance with a high degree of accuracy and cannot be rejected.

The five modes of inheritance (which follow a Mendelian pattern) discussed here are: autosomal recessive, autosomal dominant, sex-linked recessive, sex-linked dominant, and Y-linked. Each has a set of characteristics than can be used to identify it from a pedigree, listed in the accompanying box.

The way to "test" a hypothesis is to provisionally assume a particular mode of inheritance, and try out associated genotypes to see which fits for parents and offspring. Below are examples of abbreviated pedigrees for autosomal and sex-linked traits, with sample genotypes and explanations. Keep in mind that to determine a pattern of inheritance, one normally would observe several generations of a family or extended family rather than only a set of parents and their offspring. Read over the boxed information, then try these out. The actual mode of inheritance for each is listed at the end of this section.

Characteristics of Modes of Mendelian Inheritance

Autosomal Recessive
- Most affected individuals are children of unaffected parents
- All children of two affected parents (homozygous recessive) are affected
- Expressed in males and females to (approximately) same degree
- May skip generations

Autosomal Dominant
- Each affected individual has at least one affected parent
- Number of affected males and females is roughly equal
- Two affected individuals may have unaffected child (because affected individuals can be heterozygotes)

Sex-linked

X-linked Dominant
- Affected males produce all affected daughters and no affected sons
- A heterozygous-affected female will transmit the trait to half her children, with males and females equally affected.
- Twice as many females affected, on average, as males.

X-linked Recessive
- Hemizygous males and homozygous females are affected
- Males express the trait when present (because hemizygous)
- More common in males than in females
- Affected males get mutant allele from mother
- Males transmit allele to all daughters (via X chromosome), but not to sons (pass only Y to sons)
- May skip generations

Y-linked
- Appears only in males
- Affected males pass trait to sons but not to daughters
- Every Y-linked trait should be expressed

Key to Symbols

□ male   ■ affected male
○ female ● affected female
mating □—○
sibship

Aa Aa

a.

aa

Rr Rr

b.

rr

XY^{TDF} XX

c.

XY^{TDF}

$X^H X^h$ $X^h Y$

d.

$X^h Y$

$X^C X^C$ $X^c Y$

e.

$X^C X^c$

a. *Autosomal recessive:* If two unaffected parents have an affected offspring, the trait must be "hidden" in the parents' genotypes, and thus be recessive. If the trait were dominant, at least one parent would be affected.

b. *Autosomal dominant:* If two affected parents have an unaffected offspring, the trait must be dominant. Two affected parents with a recessive disorder would have all affected children.

c. *Y-linked:* Father-to-son transmission rules out X-linked inheritance. All sons of affected fathers are affected; no females are affected.

d. *X-linked dominant:* Affected woman with unaffected son rules out X-linked recessive, since both of her chromosomes would have recessive alleles—so son would be affected, but he is not.

e. *X-linked recessive:* Unaffected daughter from affected father can't be X-linked dominant, because father has only one type of X (with affected allele) to give a daughter, so she would also be affected.

Genetics Recap

By this point, you have gone through the major genetics processes. Try to keep the big picture in mind, from the DNA comprising the chromosomes in all of our cells, to the expression of our physical characteristics via protein synthesis, and their probability of occurrence from generation to generation. Remember also how we got our particular set of genes in the first place—from the meeting of the nucleus of our mother's egg cell and that of our father's sperm cell. The contents of the nucleus of all of our somatic cells are basically photocopies of that original cell, the zygote.

As for the genetic material we contribute to the next generation, in the process of producing our sperm or egg cells, we shuffle up the DNA sequences we received from our father and mother before passing it on to our children. Individuals together comprise populations, the sum total of our genetic contributions to the next generation results in the gene pool. The difference in the gene frequency between the gene pools of succeeding generations is evolution.

LAB EXERCISE 5.2

NAME _____ SECTION _____ DATE _____

1. Your instructor should provide you with a colorblindness chart from the online Instructor's Manual. If you can see the reddish number against the green background, you have normal color vision. If you cannot distinguish the number, you are (red/green) colorblind.

   a. Do you have normal color vision?

   b. What is your genotype, or your possible genotypes, for the colorblindness trait?

      (Remember, because it's a sex-linked trait, you will include the sex chromosomes in your genotype.)

2. With a lab partner, you will use coin-tossing to simulate the random nature of allele combinations in offspring, and "create" a family for which you will construct a pedigree. Use the boxed information and the sample short pedigrees from earlier in this chapter for directions on the symbols to use. Although a Punnett square gives you all of the *possible* outcomes of various crosses and their probabilities of occurrence, this method will mimic the passing on of alleles for the *particular outcome* determined by your coin tosses.

   Begin with a woman and a man with the following genotypes for the colorblindness trait:

   Woman: $X^C X^c$ Man: $X^C Y$

   a. Start your pedigree by putting the symbols for this couple at the top (center) of a blank piece of paper. Fill in the blanks below as well as recording the genotypes next to the male/female symbols on the pedigree itself. Throughout the pedigree, remember to darken the symbol if an individual is affected by colorblindness.

   b. This couple will produce gametes with what kind of alleles?

      Woman: _____   Man: _____

   c. This couple has three children whose sex and color-vision acuity are determined by your coin tosses.
      • The *first coin toss* will be to determine which chromosome (X or Y) the father contributes. Use heads for the X chromosome and tails for the Y chromosome.
      • The *second coin toss* will be to determine which of the two X chromosomes the offspring receives from the mother. Use heads for an X chromosome with a dominant allele and tails for an X chromosome with a recessive allele.

   Offspring 1

   Chromosome contributed by the father? _____ (determines sex of offspring)

   Chromosome contributed by the mother? _____

   Genotype of offspring? _____

   Offspring 2

   Chromosome contributed by the father? _____ (determines sex of offspring)

   Chromosome contributed by the mother? _____

   Genotype of offspring? _____

Offspring 3

Chromosome contributed by the father? _____ (determines sex of offspring)

Chromosome contributed by the mother? _____

Genotype of offspring? _____

d. Add these three offspring to your pedigree, and write the genotypes next to the symbols for each.

e. "Create" mates for each of these offspring—you will know the sex of the mate, because it will be opposite from the offspring. Flip a coin to determine whether a male mate carries a *C* or a *c* on his X chromosomes, and to determine whether a female carries a *C* or a *c* on each of her X chromosomes. Draw these mates on your pedigree.

f. Produce one offspring for each of these second-generation couples by coin-tossing for sex and to determine which alleles are passed on for the color vision trait. Depending upon the parents' genotypes, you may have to toss either more or fewer coins.

Record the genotypes for your third generation.

Offspring Couple 1   *Offspring Couple 2*   *Offspring Couple 3*

_____   _____   _____

g. Add them to your pedigree.

h. Compare your three generations to those of at least three lab partner pairs, and briefly comment on those comparisons.

SELF-TEST 5.2

NAME _____ SECTION _____ DATE _____

1. Hemophilia is a rare, sex-linked recessive trait. It may help to make a Punnett square to answer some of these questions. Use the letter *H, h* to represent the dominant and recessive allele.

   a. What is the genotype of a male with hemophilia?

   b. What is the genotype of a female who is a carrier?

   c. If a female who is a carrier mates with a normal male, what are the chances that they will have an offspring with hemophilia?

   d. Will this offspring (with hemophilia) be a male or a female?

   e. What are the chances of their having a carrier daughter?

2. What is the probability that a colorblind male and a colorblind female will have an offspring with normal vision?

3. A cross between a colorblind man and a woman who is a carrier will result in what "kinds" of offspring, and in what proportions?

6. The Major Forces of Evolution

"Have you ever wondered...?"

- What processes actually cause evolution to occur?
- What does "survival of the fittest" mean?
- What is the role of competition in evolution?

OBJECTIVES

- Understand each of the four evolutionary forces and how they cause changes in gene frequency between generations (evolution)

- Understand the role of probability in the change in gene frequency between generations in a population

- Understand the "mechanics" of each evolutionary force by reenacting them and following-through the results of their actions on changes in gene frequency in populations

- Learn to "translate" allele and genotype frequencies into a mathematical formula (Hardy-Weinberg formula)

- Learn to use the Hardy-Weinberg formula to determine change in gene frequency in populations and determine allele frequency from genotype frequency, and vice versa

- Understand the influence of population size on gene frequency size, especially with regard to small populations

Evolutionary forces are factors that cause a change in gene frequency in a population over time. Remember that this change in gene frequency *is* evolution. The four forces of evolution are: **natural selection, migration (gene flow), genetic drift,** and **mutation.** The first three cause change in the frequency of various genes in the population by "redistributing" the existing alleles, while the fourth, mutation, is the only one to introduce new variation into the gene pool.

Natural Selection

Two important scientists—Charles Darwin (1809–1882) and Alfred Russell Wallace (1823–1913)—were independently involved in formulating a unified theory of evolution. Both realized that several factors were involved: the struggle for existence, extinction of species, variation, and adaptation. But how did these fit together? Darwin knew about **artificial selection** but knew of no mechanism for selection in nature, or **natural selection.** A key question for each dealt with population growth. If human (and therefore animal) population growth could increase at high rates, why weren't species overrunning the earth?

Both Darwin and Wallace had read an essay by the economist Thomas Robert Malthus (first published in 1798), which stated that "animal population growth was checked [stopped] in the struggle for existence," but humans had to artificially restrain population growth. The earth's resources are limited while potential population growth is unlimited.

Darwin realized that not all individuals could survive, so "favorable variations would tend to be preserved, and unfavorable ones destroyed," and that this would result in change within a species. He realized that *selection acts upon the individual.* Wallace, while suffering from a bout of malaria in Indonesia, also solved his problem of why species don't overrun the earth, and why some species become extinct and others continue to live: "The less well adapted don't survive, and the best-adapted survive." Social scientist Herbert Spencer coined the now-familiar phrase "survival of the fittest" to describe the process, although he used it in relation to human societies rather than in nature.

The steps in natural selection are:

1. Within all populations of a species, more individuals are produced than can survive.

2. A great deal of variation exists within each population and, as a result of this variation, some individuals are better adapted to their environment than others (see Figure 6.1).

3. Members of a population compete for limited resources. (Other factors that limit survival and reproduction include death from disease, predation, and so on.)

4. Those best adapted to their environment, because of their inherited traits, will be more likely to survive to reproductive age—and to reproduce—than those that are less well-adapted. Therefore, the genes coding for the well-adapted traits will be passed onto the next generation in higher numbers than the genes for the less well-adapted traits. *At this point, gene frequency change, and thus evolution, has occurred.*

5. If populations of a species become reproductively isolated from each other, many generations of accumulated genetic change between the populations eventually may result in sufficient differences between their genetic makeup to prevent interbreeding. At this point, speciation, or the production of new species, has occurred.

For natural selection to occur, traits must be:

✋ *Variable:* Variation must be present in the population for natural selection to act upon; individuals must differ from each other in the expression of traits. For example, there may be individual differences in thickness of the enamel covering the teeth, length of limbs, thickness of fur, attractiveness to members of the opposite sex, or susceptibility to disease. Darwin and Wallace knew the importance of variation but did not know from where it arose. The field of genetics has provided us with that information.

✋ *Heritable:* The trait(s) must be inherited through the genes passed by the parents rather than acquired in an individual's lifetime or influenced by the environment.

Natural selection acts on *individuals*, not species. Each individual either reproduces a lot, or only a little, or not at all (see Figure 6.2). The additive effects of this **differential reproductive success** result in a population's change in gene frequency. Individuals with inherited traits that are better adapted to their environment will leave more descendants than others. Perhaps some are better able to crack harder

FIGURE 6.1 *Natural Selection Occurring in a Population, Resulting in More Thick-Furred Individuals*

FIGURE 6.2 *Differential Reproductive Success*

nuts because of their thicker tooth enamel, or more efficient at escaping from predators because of their longer limbs, or better able to deal with extreme temperatures because of their thicker fur, or more successful at attracting more (or better quality) mates. The **fitness** (reproductive success) of any variation will change as the environment changes. A result of natural selection is **adaptation**.

Mutation

A heritable change in the genetic material (DNA) is a mutation (see Figure 6.3), a vital source of new variation in a population. Overall, mutation rates tend to be low, so mutations rarely have a great effect on gene frequency change by themselves. But the action of natural selection together with mutation, particularly in small populations, can change gene frequency more rapidly.

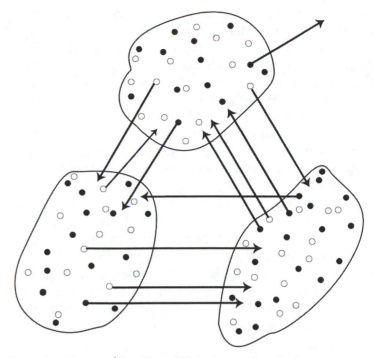

FIGURE 6.4 *Migration/Gene Flow of Alleles Among Gene Pools*

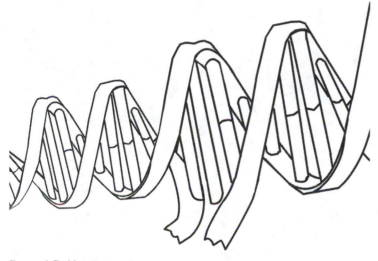

FIGURE 6.3 *Mutation*

As you learned in Chapter 3, mutations can occur at various levels of the genome, from a "mistake" of a single base to entire sets of chromosomes. A mutation can occur during various genetic processes—mitosis, meiosis, DNA replication, or protein synthesis. Mutations are random; they do not occur due to an organism's "need," although they occasionally can provide a benefit in a specific environment. Some specific parts of certain chromosomes are more susceptible to mutation, and environmental **mutagens** such as some chemicals or radiation also can cause mutation.

Migration (Gene Flow)

Migration occurs constantly among populations within a species. When individuals move from one population to another, they obviously take their genes with them! Thus, an individual who has type AB blood takes his or her *A* allele and *B* allele along, thereby taking away an *A* allele and a *B* allele from the old population and contributing these to the

new population. This change—obviously minor in the case of one individual—changes the gene frequency for ABO bloodtype in the population that was left behind, as well as the population the individual moves into.

If we think of a population as being made up of genes rather than individuals, we are referring to the **gene pool**. A gene pool comprises all the genes in a population. As individuals of each species move among populations, **gene flow** causes gene frequencies to fluctuate, resulting in evolutionary change.

Figure 6.4 depicts three gene pools experiencing losses and gains in various genes as individuals move among them. The shaded and unshaded dots represent different alleles for a given trait.

Random Genetic Drift

The gene frequency of populations fluctuates over time. From one generation to the next, random events cause changes in the gene pool. One generation's gene frequencies may not accurately represent the frequency of its previous generation's genes. Two frequent causes of these fluctuations are the **founder effect** and **population bottleneck**.

Genetic drift is similar to a *sampling error* in that the smaller the sample, the less likely it is that the sample will be representative of the population at large. A common analogy is coin-tossing. If you toss a coin four times, the probability that it will come up heads and tails an equal number of times is relatively low. You're quite likely to toss three heads or all four, rather than the number expected relative to the possibilities—two heads and two tails. If you toss a coin 100 times, you're more likely to come up with a "representative sample" of tosses—approximately 50 heads and 50 tails.

Or, say you have a huge vat of marbles, half red and half blue, well-mixed. You reach in and grab eight marbles (see Figure 6.5). Because of this small sample, you might just as readily draw three blue and five red marbles as four and four, or even seven blue marbles and one red marble. If you scoop 200 marbles out of a pitcher full of marbles, this larger sample is more likely to accurately reflect the color proportion of the entire marble "pool," and to be made up of half red and half blue marbles.

Genes in a gene pool can be envisioned in a way similar to the marble example. A small sub-population that separates itself from the rest of the population to "found" a new population will not represent accurately the frequency of the genes in the population at large, called the parent population. The parental gene frequency will exhibit fewer differences in a larger population than in a smaller population. This is the *founder effect* (see Figure 6.6). Results of such small populations include:

✋ A higher proportion of recessive genes, which can be "lost" more easily in a large population

✋ A greater chance of two recessive alleles coming together in zygote formation

✋ More recessively expressed traits, sometimes including genetic diseases

✋ Loss of genetic diversity overall, because fewer individuals contribute their genes to the gene pool

A similar effect is achieved by a drastic reduction in the number of individuals in a population. This is called a *population bottleneck* (see Figure 6.7). Highly endangered species,

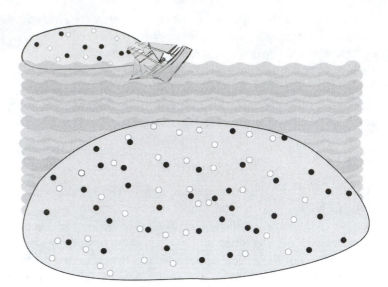

FIGURE 6.6 *Founder Effect: Founding a New Population*

FIGURE 6.7 *Population Bottleneck Resulting from Reduced Population Size*

such as the cheetah, have suffered from such a phenomenon. Their reduced genetic diversity and some recessive traits relating to fertility hinder their chances for future survival as a species.

By summing up the reproductive success of all the individuals in a population resulting from selective processes in nature and adding the influence of mutation, migration/gene flow, and genetic drift, the gene frequency of an entire population will be affected. These are evolutionary changes. Therefore, *the "unit" of evolution is the population.*

FIGURE 6.5 *Genetic Drift Similar to Sampling Error*

LAB EXERCISE 6.1

NAME _____ SECTION _____ DATE _____

In this lab we will be tracking, and actually *causing* the changes in, allele frequency of an imaginary population and documenting the effects of all four evolutionary forces.

We will simulate the action of the four evolutionary forces over a few generations. You will be working in pairs.

Our study animal is a species of a small African mammal similar to a raccoon, as illustrated. These animals are omnivorous and spend most of their time on the ground. Although they sometimes search for food in trees, their climbing abilities are limited so they often must wait for fruit to fall to the ground. Their environment is woodland, consisting of small patches of forest with interspersed savannah; it is more wooded along the Pengbai River that runs through their habitat.

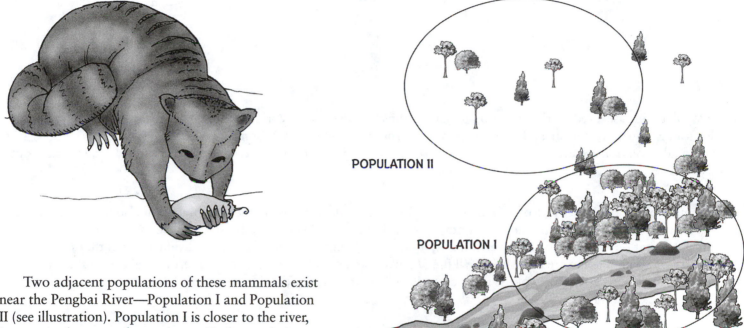

Two adjacent populations of these mammals exist near the Pengbai River—Population I and Population II (see illustration). Population I is closer to the river, in a somewhat more forested area. Each population consists of 50 individuals, so for any given trait there are 100 alleles in the gene pool. We'll use toothpicks to represent alleles and a pair of toothpicks to represent the genotype of an individual. Set up Population I and Population II by placing 100 "alleles" (toothpicks) within the boundaries of a piece of string.

Mutation

Let's cause a mutation. This mutation occurs on chromosome 16, on the short (p) arm. At a specific locus on this portion of the chromosome is a gene that dictates muscle development, and particularly affects a muscle that inserts on the big toe. The DNA sequence for a portion of this gene normally reads: TAC GGG TGA CGC ACT. After the mutation, it reads: T A C G G G *G* G A C G C A C T.

mRNA   __ __ __   __ __ __   __ __ __   __ __ __   __ __ __

tRNA   __ __ __   __ __ __   __ __ __   __ __ __   __ __ __

amino acid   _____   _____   _____   _____   _____

1. Fill in the blanks for the mRNA codons on the strand, and the anticodons on the tRNA.

2. What amino acids will the tRNAs carry to the mRNA strand?

Use the genetic code chart in Chapter 3 (Table 3.1) to see which amino acids will be coded-for during protein synthesis. Fill in the blanks.

3. What amino acid is normally coded-for by the third codon on the mRNA strand (in the *non-mutated* sequence)?

_____

In our hypothetical mammal species, the resulting phenotypic difference from this mutation is increased development in the abductor hallucis muscle, which increases grasping strength for the big toe, and therefore greatly enhances climbing ability. The illustration of chromosome 16 shows the region of the mutated gene causing excessive toe muscle development.

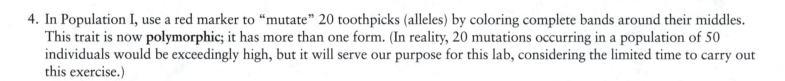

4. In Population I, use a red marker to "mutate" 20 toothpicks (alleles) by coloring complete bands around their middles. This trait is now **polymorphic**; it has more than one form. (In reality, 20 mutations occurring in a population of 50 individuals would be exceedingly high, but it will serve our purpose for this lab, considering the limited time to carry out this exercise.)

5. In Population II, also consisting of 50 individuals (100 alleles in the gene pool), the same mutation also occurs, but at a lower rate. Use a marker to "mutate" 10 toothpicks (alleles) by coloring red bands around them.

  This mutation is inherited recessively; that is, it is expressed in the phenotype of an individual only if the alleles inherited from both parents are recessive. We'll use *H* and *h* to represent the dominant and recessive alleles, respectively, for this trait. The recessive form of the trait results in enhanced muscular development; only homozygous recessive (*hh*) individuals exhibit the trait.

6. Record the allele frequency for your baseline below.

   Population I:

   h allele = 20/100, so 20%

   H allele = 80/100, so 80%

   Population II:

   h allele = _____

   H allele = _____

Natural Selection

In the current woodland environment, there is little recognizable difference in the activities or fitness of individuals on the basis of their genes for the abductor hallucis muscle, and the animals continue to feed on insects, roots, and fallen fruits. Let's focus on Population I to emulate the selection process.

  First, although we know how many *H* and *h* alleles are in the gene pool, we don't know how many individuals are homozygous dominant, heterozygous, or homozygous recessive. Actually, we can use a simple formula, called the **Hardy-Weinberg formula**, to figure that out. Wilhelm Weinberg (1908) and Godfrey H. Hardy (1908) independently stated that in a large, randomly mating population, there is a mathematical relationship between allele frequency and genotype frequency such that the frequencies of particular genotypes can be predicted from allele frequencies.

The **Hardy-Weinberg law** also states that allele and genotype frequencies will remain constant from one generation to the next (in equilibrium) if the following conditions are met:

- random mating,
- no selection or genetic drift, and
- neither migration nor mutation.

This equilibrium has not been observed to be maintained in natural populations, but it is basically a "null hypothesis" and can be used as a model against which we can measure genetic change.

The Hardy-Weinberg formula is:

$$p^2 = 2pq + q^2 = 1$$

where *p* represents the dominant allele and *q* the recessive allele, and

the number 1 represents the entire population (100%).

We will use this formula to estimate the actual *genotypes* from the number of *H* and *h* alleles in the population. In our Population I:

p is 80%, and q is 20%.

Adding these two, we get 100%, or 1.

because p + q = 1, p = .8 and q = .2.

Look at the formula above.

- p^2 represents the number of homozygous dominants
- 2pq represents the number of heterozygotes
- q^2 represents the number of homozygous recessives.

Simply plug our numbers into the above formula. Remember: p = .8 and q = .2.

$p^2 = .8^2 = .64$ (64%)

2pq (this translates to $2 \times p \times q$) = $2 \times .8 \times .2 = .32$ (32%)

$q^2 = .2^2 = .04$ (4%)

We now know how many of each genotype is expected to exist in our population. In reality, the numbers *may* differ somewhat from these *expected numbers* of individuals with the three genotypes, as you'll see.

$$
\begin{array}{lll}
HH & = 64\% & = 32 \\
Hh & = 32\% & = 16 \\
hh & = \underline{4\%} & = \underline{2} \\
   & 100\% & 50 \text{ individuals}
\end{array}
$$

The results indicate that we would expect 64% homozygous dominant, 32% heterozygous, and 4% homozygous recessive individuals. Only the latter, *hh*, would have the enhanced toe muscle development. In our population of 50 individuals, the expected numbers would be 32 *HH*, 16 *Hh*, and 2 *hh*.

1. How do these expected numbers compare to *your population*? Mix up the toothpicks thoroughly, then close your eyes and put all of them into pairs to emulate gametes coming together to form a zygote (an individual). Each pair of alleles represents the genotype of an individual.

    _____ individuals, or _____% *HH*

    _____ individuals, or _____% *Hh*

    _____ individuals, or _____% *hh*

    50   indviduals   100 %

Your random combinations of alleles are probably similar to the expected numbers.

2. Now let's produce another generation to see what happens to our gene pool. Taking our allele pairs as representatives of one of our individual mammals, we will pair individuals into "couples." We'll assume that each individual reproduces with one other individual. Close your eyes, or by using some other random process, pair up your individuals (toothpick/ allele pairs) into couples. (Continue to maintain the integrity of the individuals throughout the exercise, until directed otherwise.) When this pairing process is done, you will have 25 groups of four toothpicks.

3. Fill in the Outcomes Chart #1. First list all 25 of the parental crosses, then fill in probabilities for each kind of genotype. For example:

Pair #1	Cross	Homozygous dominant	Heterozygous	Homozygous recessive
1	HH × Hh	2	2	0

Outcomes Chart #1

Pair #___	Parental cross	Homozygous dominant	Heterozygous	Homozygous recessive
1				
2				
3				
4				
5				
6				
7				
8				
9				
10				
11				
12				
13				
14				
15				
16				
17				
18				
19				
20				
21				
22				
23				
24				
25				
Totals				100%

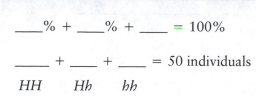

4. How do the genotype frequencies of the parental generation (p. 89) compare with those of their offspring?

5. Compare your results to those of at least one other set of lab partners, and note your comparisons here.

Selective Pressure

We now know how many individuals of the various genotypes are in Population I. Suddenly, a change in climate occurs. It becomes cool and dry, and shortened fruiting seasons soon result. Fallen fruit now is increasingly scarce, and the climatic change affects the entire food web, influencing the availability of foods for our little mammal. Younger trees become less likely to survive because of the lack of moisture, causing some shrinking of forests in areas farther away from the Pengbai River. Along the river, the forests continue to be lush and green.

Individuals who are homozygous recessive (*hh*) for the abductor hallucis trait can move around more efficiently in the trees and thus exploit a wider part of their habitat. They no longer have to wait for fruit to fall to the ground but can get to the increasingly hard-to-obtain fruit by seeking it out where it grows. In doing so, they also have learned about a new source of food: birds' eggs. These individuals fulfill their dietary requirements more easily and have more energy available to seek mates and reproduce successfully.

Previously, the likelihood of reproduction was equal for all individuals. Now we have a **selective pressure** that acts to enhance the fitness for some and lower the fitness for other individuals. Individuals with the **hh** genotype are highly likely to reach reproductive age and reproduce successfully. Those with either *Hh* or *HH* are only half as likely to survive to reach reproductive age and reproduce.

We now will see how selection acts to change gene frequencies in the next generation, and how selection is a nonrandom process, acting on existing variation in the gene pool.

1. Modify your Population I individuals so the number of *HH*, *Hh*, and *hh* offspring match up with the second generation's genotypes (the outcomes ratios from beneath Outcomes Chart #1). For example, if you had 30 *HH* individuals from Outcomes Chart #1, set aside 30 pairs of unmarked toothpicks. Do the same for *Hh* (pairs consisting of one marked and one unmarked toothpick) and *hh* (two marked toothpicks). Your frequencies may not have all been whole numbers; if there are numbers beyond the decimal point, you will have to round up or down slightly. Also, depending upon your numbers in Chart #1, you may have to get (or create) more marked or unmarked toothpicks.

2. Now you are going to apply your selective pressure, with the climatic change selecting for the *hh* individuals. Because *HH* and *Hh* are only half as likely to reach reproductive age, choose half of the *HH* and *Hh* individuals and "select them out" of the gene pool, leaving an even number of individuals (even if you have to leave in an extra pair of toothpicks). Remember—the individuals represented here are not necessarily dying off but simply are not reproducing.

3. For the remaining toothpicks, close your eyes (or use some other random process) and pair them up into "couples."

4. For each couple, produce offspring by closing your eyes (or otherwise randomly choosing) and picking one allele to be passed on from each member of the pair. Obviously, if an individual is homozygous (either *HH* or *hh*), it has only one possible allele to pass on. Use new (marked and unmarked) toothpicks to "create" an offspring for each couple according to the allele combination you have randomly selected from the parents.

5. Place each offspring directly below the parents so you can record the frequencies of their genotypes in Outcomes Chart #2.

Outcomes Chart #2

Homozygous dominant	Heterozygous	Homozygous recessive	Total # Offspring
			N =
			100%

You now have genotype frequencies for Population I from before and after the action of natural selection. Describe this change between the two generations.

The size of Population I appears smaller, because you have removed the nonreproducing individuals (one-half of the *HH* and *Hh*), and the couples have produced only one offspring each thus far. But before the next breeding season . . .

Genetic Drift

Population I is located closer to the Pengbai River and its associated forested area than is Population II. The river is quite low in the dry season, at which time animals cross back and forth over it on the exposed large rocks in a shallow portion. During the wet season, however, our mammal species typically stays within its more familiar range on the side of the river within the boundaries of Population I (or II).

In one year during the dry season, 10 members of Population I are foraging on the other side of the river, when a deluge quickly fills the river and covers the usually-exposed rocks. These terrified little mammals are very wet and, further, are trapped. While they are isolated on the far side of the river, the water level doesn't decrease enough during the dry season for them to return. They go on about their daily lives, which end up being spent on the far side of the river because a geographical barrier has now formed. They will produce offspring, thereby founding a new population, Population III. As mentioned previously, the type of genetic drift that changes gene frequency by formation of a population from a small splinter subgroup is called the founder effect.

1. Close your eyes, choose 10 individuals from Population I (these may be parents or offspring), and set them apart from the others with a string around them. You have just formed Population III.

2. a. What is the allele frequency of this new population?

    H _____ + *h* _____ = 20

    H _____% + *h* _____% = 100%

   b. What is the genotype frequency? Use the Hardy-Weinberg formula: $p^2 + 2pq + q^2 = 1$

      (p = % of *H* alleles; q = % of *h* alleles)

      HH   *Hh*   *hh*

      _____% + _____% + _____% = 100%

3. Compare the allele and genotype frequencies to Population I from the beginning of the lab exercise (p. 89). How different are these proportions?

4. This small population will serve as the *founder* of subsequent generations. The *next generation's* genes will represent the actual evolutionary change that has occurred. What effect will continued selective pressure have on this small population?

5. What might have happened if the climatic change had occurred but the mutation on chromosome 16 had not?

Migration (Gene Flow)

Let's go back briefly to our Population I, to the members that did not become stranded on the opposite side of the river. We'll look at the action of the final evolutionary force by causing the migration of individuals between Populations I and II.

1. From Population I, close your eyes and choose 10 individuals. Likewise, from Population II, randomly select 10 pairs of alleles (toothpicks) to represent 10 individuals. Switch them between populations.

2. What is the allele frequency now for each population? Compare this to before migration occurred.

Population I

H _____ + h _____ = _____ alleles

H _____% + h _____% = 100%

Population II

H _____ + h _____ = _____ alleles

H _____% + h _____% = 100%

You now have reenacted all four evolutionary forces and seen firsthand how gene frequencies fluctuate within populations based upon both random and nonrandom factors.

NAME _____ SECTION _____ DATE _____

1. Using the example of our hypothetical mammal populations, briefly explain how each of the four evolutionary forces causes evolution to occur.

2. Which evolutionary force would seem to change gene frequency the fastest? Why?

3. Which evolutionary forces seem to work together to cause evolution?

4. To which evolutionary force does the saying "survival of the fittest" apply?

5. In which evolutionary force does competition play the biggest role?

6. What evolutionary force is represented by founder effect and population bottleneck? How are these similar to a "sampling error?"

7. In a population of 200, an allele Z has a frequency of 80%. What is the frequency of allele z? Using the Hardy-Weinberg equation, estimate the numbers of homozygous dominant, heterozygous, and homozygous recessive genotypes. (Remember that the formula is: $p^2 + 2pq + q^2 = 1$, where p represents the dominant allele and q the recessive allele. The number 1 represents the entire population, or 100%.)

7. The Bones Within Us

"Have you ever wondered...?"

✋ Is bone alive?

The human skeleton is composed of bones and cartilage, assembled into a rigid framework that has a variety of functions during life and can offer a wealth of information after death. This lab focuses on the structure and function of bone, along with the terminology used to describe the position of various bones in the body.

Bones are actually organs, but they are solid because of the deposition of mineral salts around protein fibers. Although the bones you'll be studying in this lab appear to be dead, bone is a living, dynamic tissue. It changes during life in response to forces placed upon it, as well as to disease and injury. Running through bone are channels of nervous tissue and blood vessels. Bones are part of the phenotype (physical appearance), and therefore are the products of both the genotype (genetic makeup) and the environment. As you'll notice, bones have a great deal of individual variation because of differences in age, sex, geographic origin, activity during life, and diseases or injuries.

Functions of the Skeleton

The skeleton has various functions, which are summarized as follows.

1. *support:* structural support, framework for attachment of soft tissues, holds organs

2. *protection:* protects vital organs (for example, the cranium protects the brain, the rib cage protects the heart and lungs, the vertebral column protects the spinal cord)

3. *movement/leverage:* framework for muscle attachment, allows movement at the joints

4. *mineral and lipid (fat) storage:* stores calcium and phosphate, which can be released as needed to maintain normal concentration of these ions in body fluids (calcium is the most abundant mineral in the body, with one to two kilograms in each individual; energy reserves are stored as lipids in yellow bone marrow)

5. *blood cell formation* (hemopoiesis) and *storage:* blood cells are produced in red bone marrow; in children this occurs in long bones, in adults in the ribs, spleen, and **diploë** (porous portion of flat bones of skull)

What Can We Tell From Bones?

The types of information that can be obtained from bone include age, sex, race, and physical activities that were important in an individual's life. Upon closer analysis, especially with a narrow range of possible identities, unknown skeletons can be identified on the basis of X-rays—for example, comparing teeth to dental records, or skeletal elements with healed fractures to medical records. Also, we often can diagnose disease from bone, even from prehistoric populations. By observing the form of bones and the joint surfaces of human or nonhuman remains, we can make inferences about how they moved around, whether bipedal, quadrupedal, climbing, or leaping.

Classification, Development, and Anatomy of Bone

Bones can be divided into four main categories, or classes (see Figure 7.1).

1. *long bones:* the limb bones as well as finger and toe bones
2. *short bones:* the blocky, often cube-shaped bones of the wrist and ankle, as well as sesamoid bones (these form within a tendon, such as the patella)
3. *flat bones:* those of the cranium, shoulder, pelvis, and rib cage
4. *irregular bones:* the vertebrae, facial bones, and some bones of the wrist and ankle

The skeleton of the fetus serves as a cartilaginous model upon which the adult bony skeleton is based. The skeleton can be separated into two main portions, according to its developmental sequence before birth (Figure 7.2).

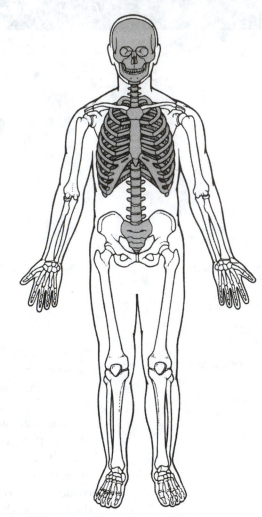

FIGURE 7.2 *Axial (Shaded) and Appendicular (Unshaded) Skeleton*

long bones

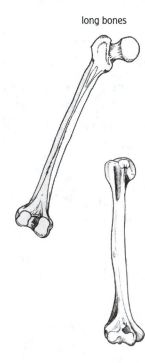

short bones

flat bones

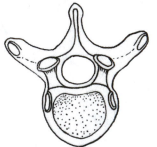

irregular bones

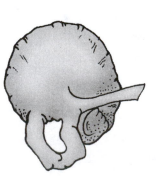

FIGURE 7.1 *Categories of Bone*

The **axial skeleton** develops first, and consists of the midline structures, such as the skull, vertebral column, rib cage, sternum, and hyoid. The **appendicular skeleton,** which develops later, consists of the limb bones and their connections to the axial skeleton (pelvic and pectoral girdles).

A typical long bone, such as the humerus (upper arm bone) consists of the following portions (see Figure 7.3 and *Atlas* pp. 186–187):

1. *diaphysis:* the shaft, or main portion of the bone

2. *epiphyses:* portions at the extremities, or ends of the bone

3. *articular cartilage:* a cartilaginous layer covering the epiphyseal ends

4. *metaphysis:* the region in a mature bone where the diaphysis meets the epiphysis; in growing bone, it is where calcified cartilage is replaced by bone

5. *epiphyseal line:* the remnant of epiphyseal plate, which consisted of hyaline cartilage before being replaced by bone; same area as the metaphysis

6. *periosteum:* the connective tissue covering bone in places where there is no articular cartilage; consists of an outer fibrous layer of connective tissue with blood vessels, lymph vessels, and nerves that pass into bone, and an inner layer that is involved with the production of new bone for growth and repair

7. *medullary (or marrow) cavity:* the space along the inside of the diaphysis that contains yellow marrow (in adults), consisting mostly of fat cells and some scattered blood cells

Throughout the skeleton there are two distinct types of bone based upon differences in the cellular (or histological) makeup. These are **compact bone,** or **dense bone**, usually in the more external portions of bone. It is deposited in a layer over the other bone type, the **spongy bone**, and is thickest in the diaphysis of long bones. Compact bone provides protection and support and resists stress. **Spongy bone,** or **cancellous bone,** usually is found more internally within bone. This is the type of bone that surrounds the marrow cavity and is found within the ends of long bones. Spongy bone contains many large spaces, which are filled with mostly red marrow.

Anatomical Terminology

Osteologists and anatomists often describe bones, or parts of bones, in what is called **anatomical terminology.** They use terms that describe the relationship of the bone to a body in **anatomical position.** Anatomical position for **orthograde** (bipedal) animals such as humans is a standing position with the arms down at the sides and the palms of the hands facing forward with the thumbs out to the sides. Undoubtedly, some of the anatomical terminology outlined below will be familiar to you. Again, when using these terms, we must assume the body to be in anatomical position.

Just like any three-dimensional object, the body can be divided by three basic imaginary planes (see Figure 7.4):

1. *midsagittal*, or *median plane:* divides the body into equal left and right halves (see *Atlas* p. 23; br. ed. p. 23)

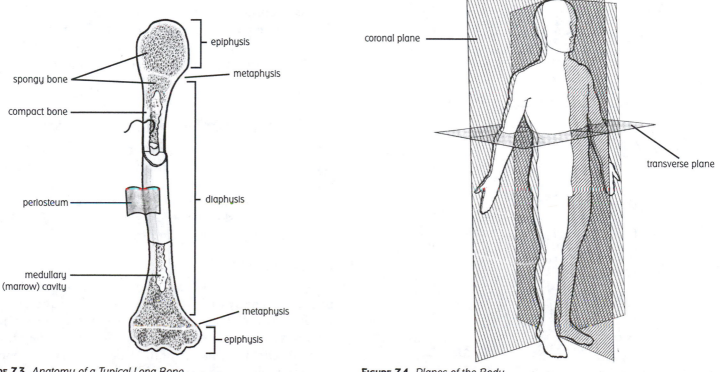

FIGURE 7.3 *Anatomy of a Typical Long Bone*

FIGURE 7.4 *Planes of the Body*

2. *coronal,* or *frontal plane*: divides the body into front and back portions,

3. *transverse,* or *horizontal plane*: divides the body into upper and lower parts.

Many anatomical terms describe the position of structures based on their relationship to these three planes, when the body is in anatomical position (Figure. 7.5). These terms are often used to describe the position of one structure relative to another. The major terms are follows:

medial:	closer to the midline, or the median plane
lateral:	farther from the midline, or the median plane
anterior:	toward the front
posterior:	toward the back
superior:	above
inferior:	below
superficial:	near the body's surface
deep:	away from the body's surface; internal

A specific set of terms refers to how far up or down a limb a particular point lies. These terms are:

proximal:	closer to the attachment of the limb to trunk of body (nearer the hip or shoulder)
distal:	farther from the attachment of the limb to trunk of body (away from the hip or shoulder)

Some examples of how these terms are used are the following.

🖐 The ears are *lateral* to the nose.

🖐 The wrist is *distal* to the elbow.

🖐 The head is *superior* to the feet.

🖐 The thumb is *lateral* to the fourth digit (in anatomical position!).

Keep in mind that some of these terms do not apply as well to **pronograde** (quadrupedal) animals, in which the backbone is parallel to the ground. Terms that help to avoid confusion are:

ventral:	closer to the belly
dorsal:	closer to the back

(These also are used sometimes to refer to structures in humans, similar to anterior/posterior.)

cranial:	closer to the head
caudal:	closer to the tip of the tail

Features of Bone

The human body normally has 206 complete bones, each of which is influenced during life by the soft tissues that surround it. Raised areas or lumps on bone appear where the tendons of muscles attach. The bones may have grooves where blood vessels lie over the surface. Vessels and nerves enter bones by holes called *foramina* (singular: *foramen*). These bumps, grooves, and so on, referred to collectively as **features,** present us with important information. Features on bone can indicate the level of activity to which a limb was subjected during life, and they allow us to distinguish bones that came from the right versus the left side of the body.

In the following discussion, we will cover the bones of the skull. Then we will review a sample of the features found on each bone.

Axial Skeleton Part 1: The Skull

The 22 skull bones are separated from one another by **sutures,** which allow them to grow independently of one another. These sutures are highly visible in the skull of a young individual and become obliterated with advancing age. Some of the skull bones are paired, with a left and a right. The bones in the midline are single.

Bones of the Skull

Using the description of each of the skull bones listed on page 101, identify each bone on a real skull (if available). As you identify each bone, pay attention also to the surrounding bones. With which bones do they articulate (are they adjacent to)? Often, the nature of the articulation of two bones determines their shape at the joint ends, depending upon

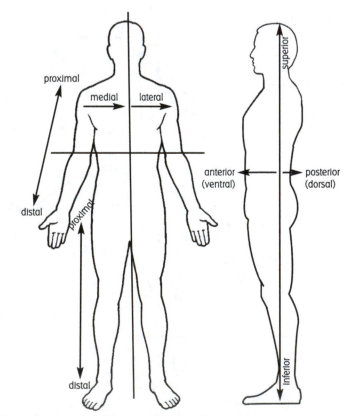

FIGURE 7.5 *Anatomical Position: Directional Terms*

the type of joint that occurs between them. If no skull is available, you may use Photos 7.1 through 7.3 (see also *Atlas* p. 78) instead. This list refers to Photo 7.1

1. *frontal*: The "forehead bone" is a single bone whose lower margins are occupied largely by the *orbits*, or eye sockets.

2. *parietals*: These paired bones articulate with the frontal bone; they make up the "walls" of the skull, meeting at the suture that runs in the midsagittal plane on the top of the head.

3. *temporals*: This pair of bones on sides of head, houses "ear holes" and provides articulation for the mandible (lower jaw).

4. *occipital*: The midline bone at back of skull houses the large hole (foramen magnum) at base of the skull for passage of the spinal cord.

5. *maxilla*: These paired bones make up much of the face between the orbits and the mouth.

6. *zygomatics*: These are the paired "cheekbones."

7. *nasals*: These small, paired bones lie just superior to the nasal opening, between the orbits.

8. *ethmoid*: A single bone entirely within the skull, it can be seen from the frontal view (at the back of the orbit, medial side) or the lateral view (just posterior to lacrimals in orbits) or the superior view with the top of skull removed.

9. *sphenoid*: The large, butterfly-shaped single bone is mostly within skull, but portions are visible laterally

(anterior to the temporals), inferiorly (much of underside of the skull posterior to the maxillae, anterior to the occipital), anteriorly (back of orbits lateral to the ethmoid), and superiorly with the top of the skull removed.

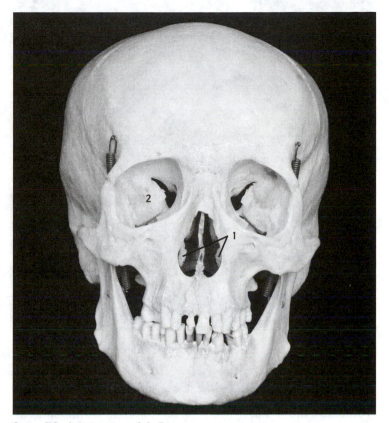

PHOTO 7.2 *Anterior view of skull*

1. inferior nasal conchae   2. sphenoid

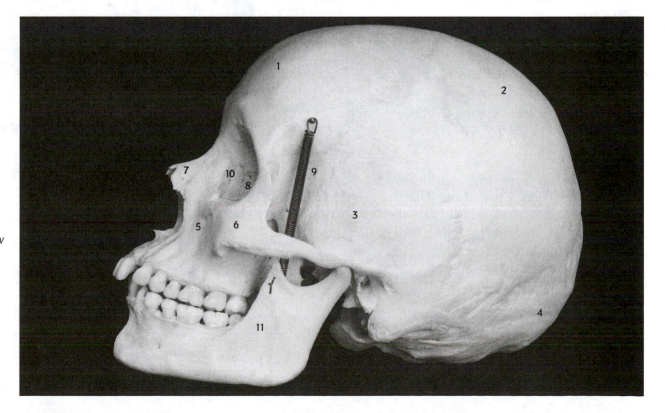

PHOTO 7.1 *Lateral view of skull*

1. frontal
2. parietal
3. temporal
4. occipital
5. maxilla
6. zygomatic
7. nasal
8. ethmoid
9. sphenoid
10. lacrimal
11. mandible

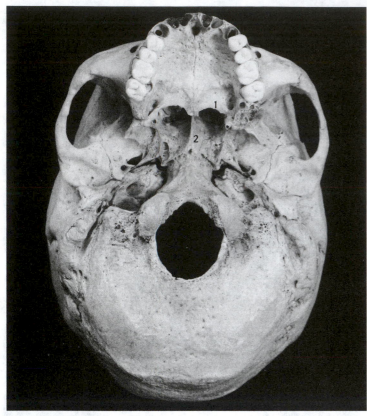

PHOTO 7.3 *Inferior view of skull*
  1. palatine   2. vomer

10. *lacrimals*: Small, delicate, paired bones just inside the rim of the orbits, houses canal for tear ducts (lacrimal ducts)

11. *mandible*: Lower jaw (single bone after about one year of age)

12. *inferior nasal conchae*: small, curved bones; one on each side within nasal opening (Photo 7.2)

13. *palatine*: small, paired bones just posterior to bony palate (of the maxillae) (Photo 7.3)

14. *vomer*: single midline bone visible just posterior to palatine (Photo 7.3)

Skull Sutures

The skull has many sutures, usually named for the two bones they separate (Photos 7.4–7.6 and *Atlas* pp. 83, 85, 88, 89). The primary five sutures, though, have their own names. Identify each of the following major skull sutures on a skull.

1. *sagittal:* separates the two parietal bones; along the midsagittal plane.

2. *coronal:* separates the frontal from the two parietal bones.

3. *squamosal:* separates the parietal from the temporal bone.

4. *lambdoidal:* separating the parietal bones from the occipital bone.

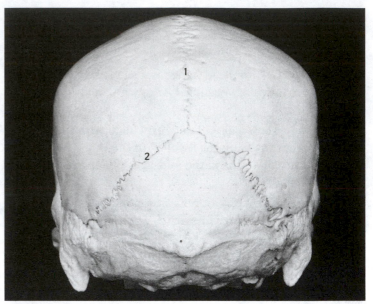

PHOTO 7.4 *Sutures, posterior view*
  1. sagittal suture   2. lambdoidal suture

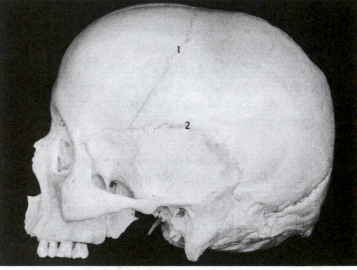

PHOTO 7.5 *Sutures, lateral view*
  1. coronal suture   2. squamosal suture

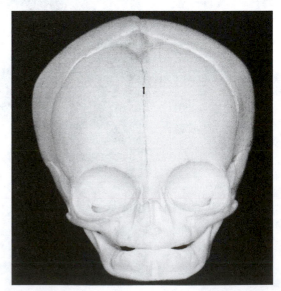

PHOTO 7.6
Sutures: fetal skull, anterior view
  1. metopic suture

5. *metopic:* separates the two halves of the frontal bone until approximately 2 years of age in humans; in most mammals and in some primates it is retained throughout life.

Middle Ear Bones

The mammalian ear is a complex organ, originally derived from ancestral reptilian bones that made up the articulation of the mandible with the cranium! The *ear canal* is the portion (in humans, taking the form of a bony tube) that leads to the tympanic membrane, or eardrum. This is the point of entrance to the *middle ear,* a space that houses the three small ear bones, or *ossicles:* the *malleus, incus,* and *stapes* (see Figure 7.6).

Incoming sound waves vibrate the tympanic membrane, which in turn vibrates the three ossicles. The last of these, the stapes, vibrates against the membrane leading to the *inner ear,* which contains the cochlea and the semicircular canals. It is in the cochlea that nerve receptors reside that transmit impulses via the acoustic nerve, to be perceived by the brain. The middle ear is housed inside of a highly mineralized part of the temporal bone, the *petrous portion* (Gr. *petr:* rock).

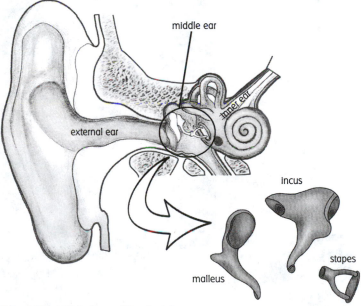

FIGURE 7.6 *Middle Ear and Ear Ossicles*

The Teeth

As mammals, we have a heterodont (G *hetero:* different; *dont:* tooth) dentition, with teeth specialized for different functions. Our four different types of teeth—*incisors, canines, premolars,* and *molars*—allow us to process various foods efficiently. As adults, we typically have 32 teeth (assuming that none have been removed). The deciduous dentition, or set of baby teeth (G *decid:* falling off) is composed of 20 teeth.

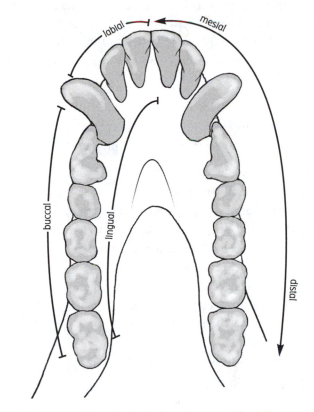

FIGURE 7.7 *Directional Terms for Tooth Row; Functional Tooth Types*

Look at the teeth of a skull, and identify the four types of teeth. The incisors and canines are blade-like and chiseled. The premolars (often called bicuspids; L *bi:* two) have two cusps, and the molars (L *mola:* grind) have four or five.

In one quadrant of the jaw, a human with a full complement of teeth has two incisors, one canine, two premolars, and three molars (see Figure 7.7). This is known as the **dental formula**. Because it is the same for the top and the bottom in humans, the dental formula is $\frac{2}{2}\frac{1}{1}\frac{2}{2}\frac{3}{3}$. Children's teeth are all deciduous until about age 6, when these begin to be replaced by permanent teeth. Thus, they have the dental formula $\frac{2}{2}\frac{1}{1}\frac{0}{0}\frac{2}{2}$. The mouth has its own set of directional terms, as shown in Figure 7.7 and *Atlas* p. 22; br. ed. p. 22.

Features on Skull Bones

Now that you have identified all of the skull bones, you are prepared to learn some of the *features* found on these bones. (Again, features are the bumps, crests, and grooves that result from the influence of soft tissue during development; and each feature has its own name). These features can be used for diagnostic purposes that allow us to distinguish female from male skulls and evaluate sites for muscle attachment (for example, the size of a bump indicates the size of a muscle during life).

Some of the terminology used for features throughout the skeleton is defined below. Many specific features include one of these words as a part of their name. You are not expected to memorize this list.

Terms that describe raised area on bone are:

process: general term for an area that protrudes on bone

Articular surface found at a movable joint:

condyle: large, rounded articular projection or surface
head: dome-shaped articular projection

Areas of muscle attachment:

tubercle: small rounded process
tuberosity: large rounded, rough process
trochanter: large blunt process (only on femur)
ridge: raised, elongated area of bone
torus: thickened ridge
crest: relatively sharp, narrow ridge
linea or *line*:   raised, elongated area that is not as marked as a ridge or a crest
spine: sharp slender projection
epicondyle: prominence above a condyle

Terms that refer to concave areas on bone:

fissure: narrow, crack-like opening
foramen: holes for blood vessels and nerves to pass through (*plural*: foramina)
meatus: short canal
sulcus: furrow-like depression
fossa: dug-out area, depression
notch: indentation

An additional term is:

facet: a smooth, flat surface for articulation; typically where little movement occurs

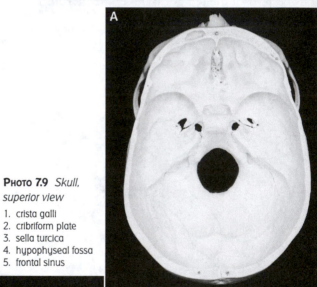

PHOTO 7.8
Skull: inferior view

1. mandibular fossa
2. occipital condyle
3. foramen magnum
4. hard palate (palatine process)

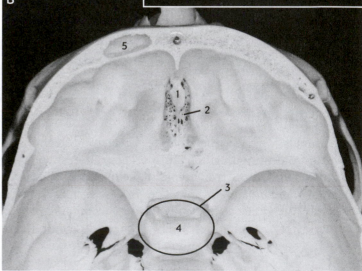

PHOTO 7.9 *Skull, superior view*

1. crista galli
2. cribriform plate
3. sella turcica
4. hypophyseal fossa
5. frontal sinus

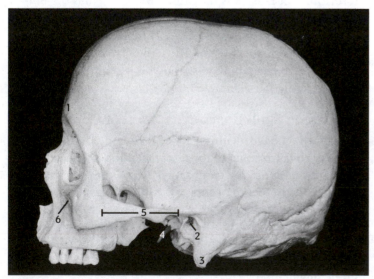

PHOTO 7.7 *Skull: lateral view*

1. supraorbital ridge   3. mastoid process   5. zygomatic arch
2. external auditory meatus   4. styloid process   6. infraorbital foramen

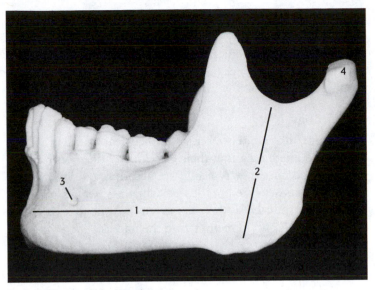

PHOTO 7.10 *Mandible, lateral view*

1. body
2. ramus
3. mental foramen
4. mandibular condyle (condyloid process)

Selected Skull Features Below are some examples of prominent features found on some of the skull bones. Keep in mind that there are a multitude of such features. Your instructor may want to add more features to this list. Refer to a skull and to Photos 7.7–7.10 (and *Atlas* pp. 78, 83, 86, 87) to identify these features.

Skull bones:
   Temporal (Photos 7.7, 7.8):
      external auditory meatus
      mastoid process
      styloid process
      mandibular fossa
      zygomatic process of zygomatic arch (together with
         zygomatic bone)

   Occipital (Photo 7.8):
      occipital condyles
      foramen magnum

   Maxilla (photos 7.7, 7.8):
      infraorbital foramen
      hard palate (palatine process)

   Zygomatic (Photo 7.7):
      zygomatic arch (together with the temporal bone)

   Ethmoid (Photo 7.9):
      crista galli
      cribriform plate (where olfactory bulbs sit)

   Sphenoid (Photo 7.9):
      sella turcica (the "compartment" for the pituitary
         gland; the gland "sits" in a depression called the
         hypophyseal fossa)

Mandible (Photo 7.10):
   mental foramen
   mandibular condyles (condyloid process)
   body
   ramus

Fetal Skull A fetal or an infant skull exhibits some important differences from an adult skull. Take a look at a fetal skull and/or at Photo 7.11 and *Atlas* pp. 95 and 97. Notice the open sutures, allowing room for growth, and the large spaces between some of the bones. These spaces, termed **fontanels**, are the so-called "soft spots" on a baby's skull. Review the **metopic suture** in Photo 7.6. In an infant, the frontal bone and the mandible are composed of two bones. As the metopic suture and the mandibular symphysis *fuse, or ossify*, by 1 or 2 years of age, these bones combine into one.

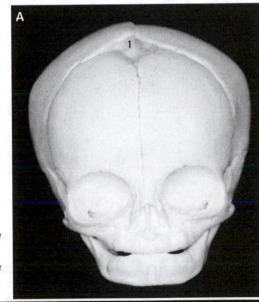

PHOTO 7.11 *Fetal skull*

1. anterior fontanelle
2. sphenoidal fontanelle
3. mastoid fontanelle

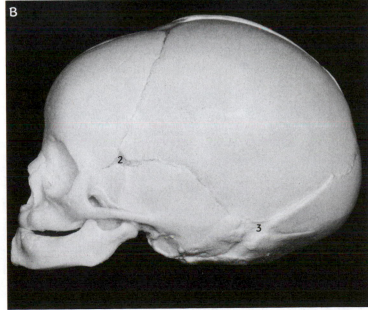

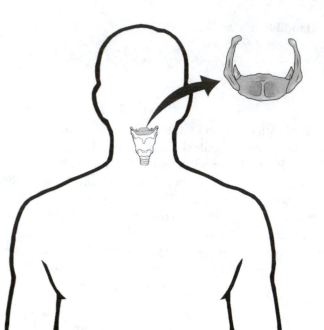

FIGURE 7.8 *Hyoid Bone*

Hyoid Bone

The bony support for your larynx, or voice box, is the hyoid bone. It is connected via muscles and ligaments to the larynx and the temporal bones (see Figure 7.8). It is the only bone in the body without any direct bony articulations.

Etymology

In learning the names of bones and their features, it is helpful to know something about their Greek or Latin roots (etymology), because they typically are descriptive terms. Some of these roots are listed in the text when new bones or features are introduced. Others are given in Appendix B. The roots can be useful in memorizing the names.

LAB EXERCISE 7.1

NAME _____ SECTION _____ DATE _____

1. Label the parts of a typical long bone.

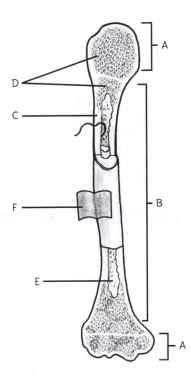

2. Label the planes of the body on the diagram at right.

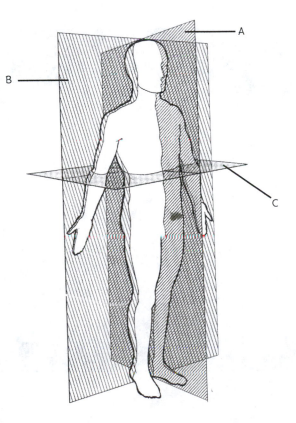

3. Your knee is _____ relative to your navel.

4. Your navel is _____ relative to your right side.

5. Your nose is _____ relative to your ears.

6. Your ankle is _____ relative to your hip.

7. Provide labels for all of the bones learned so far.

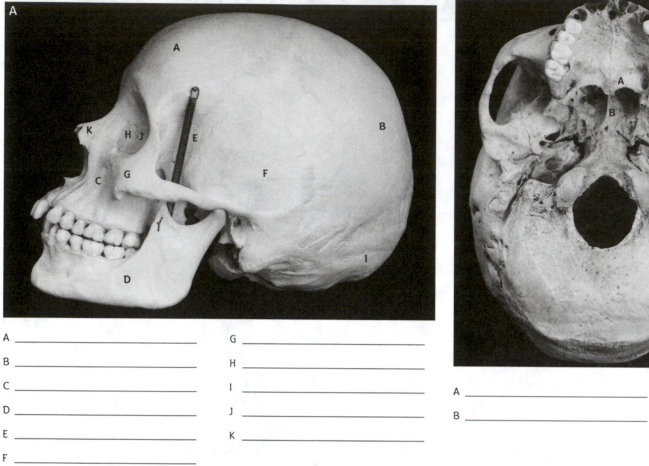

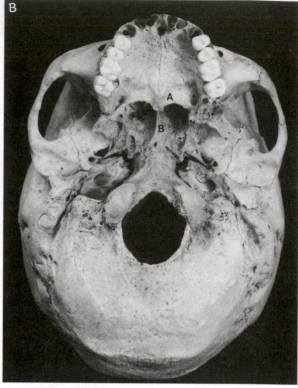

A _____

B _____

C _____

D _____

E _____

F _____

G _____

H _____

I _____

J _____

K _____

A _____

B _____

8. Label the four main sutures on the adult skull and the one learned for the fetal skull.

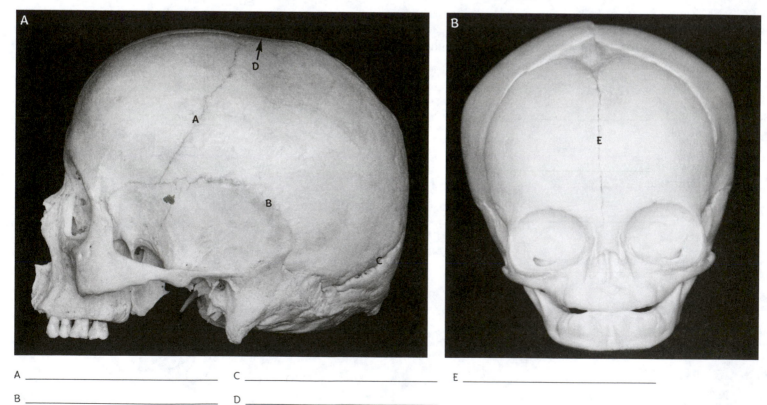

A _____

B _____

C _____

D _____

E _____

9. Which is which? Label each of the middle ear ossicles.

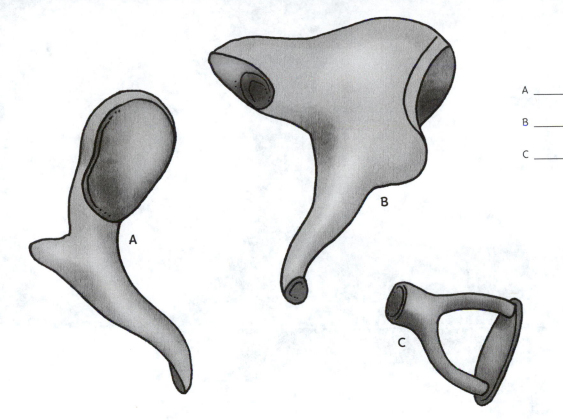

A _____

B _____

C _____

10. How many teeth, and of which type, do you have in your mouth? Which have been pulled, or otherwise lost?

11. Your canine is _____ relative to your first molar. (Use the directional terms for the tooth row.)

12. Provide labels for all of the features learned so far.

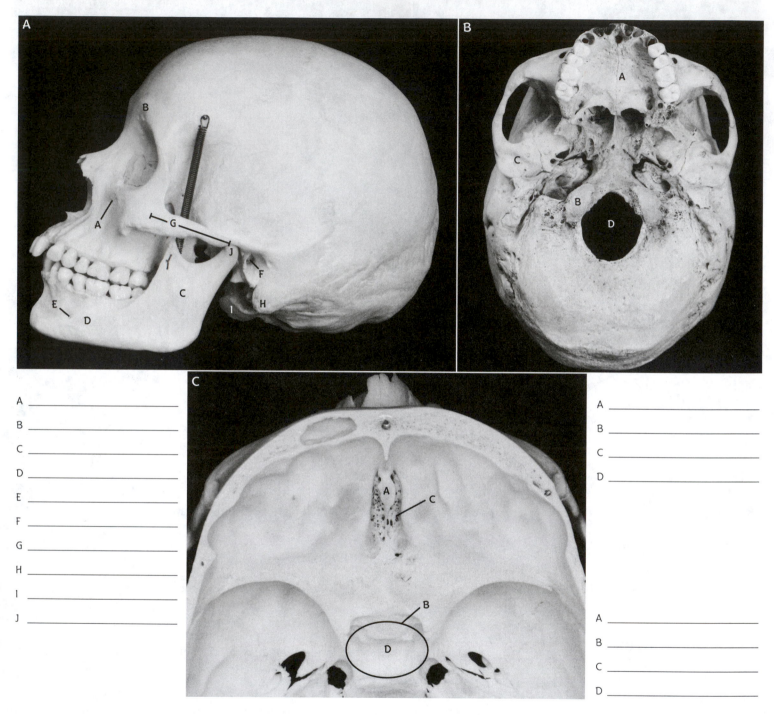

A _____

B _____

C _____

D _____

E _____

F _____

G _____

H _____

I _____

J _____

A _____

B _____

C _____

D _____

A _____

B _____

C _____

D _____

13. Take a look at the frontal bone. With which other bones does it articulate?

14. The bump on your skull just posterior to your ear is the _____.

15. Which bone is visible from anterior, lateral, and inferior views, and articulates anteriorly with the temporal bone?

SELF-TEST 7.1

NAME _____ SECTION _____ DATE _____

1. What are the five main functions of the skeleton? Briefly explain each.

2. What are some kinds of information that can be obtained from a skeleton?

3. What is an example of a long bone?

4. What are the two "portions" of the skeleton?

    Which appears first developmentally?

5. What are the two types of bone?

6. What set of terms is used specifically to refer to a position up or down the limbs?

7. What plane divides the body into left and right halves? Into front and back portions?

8. The name for the structures separating skull bones is _____.

9. In directional terms, where is:

   a. your thumb relative to your palm?

   b. a dog's tail relative to its lumbar vertebrae?

   c. your shin relative to your calf?

   d. a horse's belly relative to its back?

   e. your pinkie relative to your elbow?

10. The ear ossicles are found in the _____. Name these three bones.

11. What is the dental formula for humans (adults)?

12. If a mammal's entire top row of teeth consists of four incisors, two canines, two premolars, and four molars, and its lower tooth row consist of four incisors, two canines, two premolars, and two molars, what is its dental formula? (Remember: Dental formulae refer to one *quadrant* of a jaw!)

13. Where is the ethmoid bone relative to the lacrimal bone?

14. The name for a hole through bone is _____.

15. The real name for the "soft spots" on an infant's skull is _____.

16. The only bone in the body that does not articulate with any other bone is the _____.

Axial Skeleton Part II: Vertebral Column

The vertebral column is made up of five main regions, each of which has vertebrae with distinguishing characteristics based upon their function and their position in the column. Look at Figure 7.9 and *Atlas* p. 158. As you follow the vertebrae inferiorly, you'll see how they become larger and larger as they provide support for more and more body weight. Also notice the various regions of the spine and the characteristic curves, which together serve to bring the weight-bearing axis directly under the body.

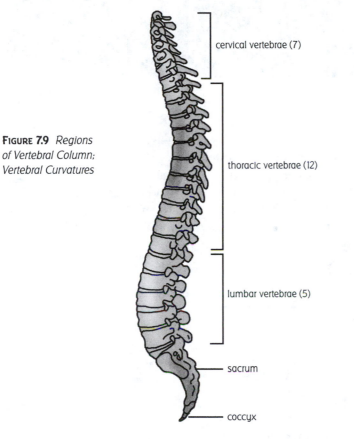

FIGURE 7.9 *Regions of Vertebral Column; Vertebral Curvatures*

cervical vertebrae (7)

thoracic vertebrae (12)

lumbar vertebrae (5)

sacrum

coccyx

All four types of vertebrae share several features. Photo 7.12 uses a thoracic vertebra as an example. The features found on most vertebrae include:

- ☙ *body*
- ☙ *arch*
- ☙ *vertebral foramen*
- ☙ *spinous process*
- ☙ *transverse processes*
- ☙ *superior and inferior articulating surfaces.*

You should be able to identify each of these listed features on a vertebra (preferably a thoracic or lumbar), using Photo 7.12 as a guide.

Next we will learn the characteristics of individual types of vertebrae.

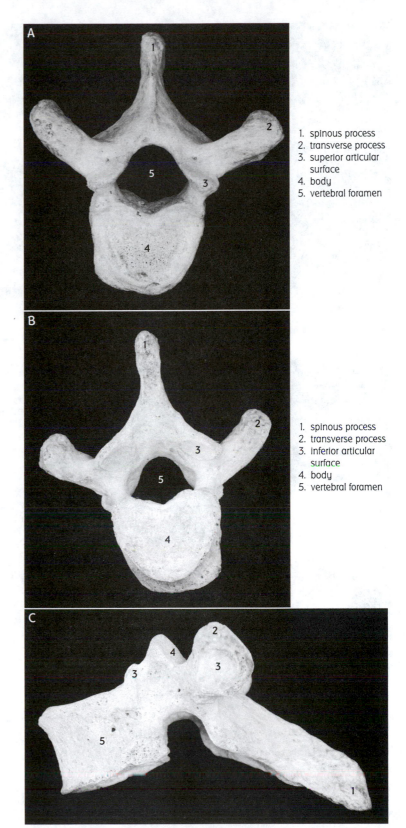

A

1. spinous process
2. transverse process
3. superior articular surface
4. body
5. vertebral foramen

B

1. spinous process
2. transverse process
3. inferior articular surface
4. body
5. vertebral foramen

C

1. spinous process   3. rib facets (only on thoracic)   5. body
2. transverse process   4. superior articular surface

PHOTO 7.12 *Features of a typical vertebra (shown is a thoracic): (A) superior view, (B) inferior view, (C) lateral view*

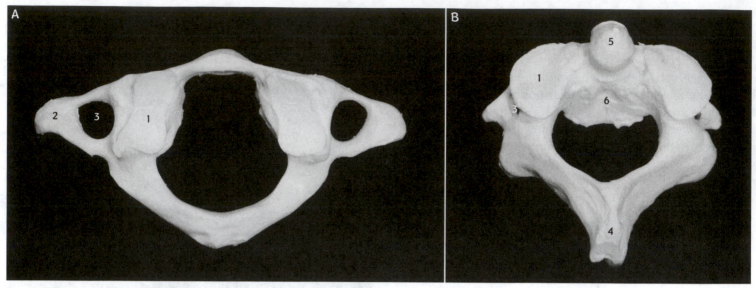

| 1. superior articular surface | 2. transverse process | 3. transverse foramen | 4. spinous process | 5. dens | 6. body |

PHOTO 7.13 *Features of an atlas (A) and an axis (B), superior view*

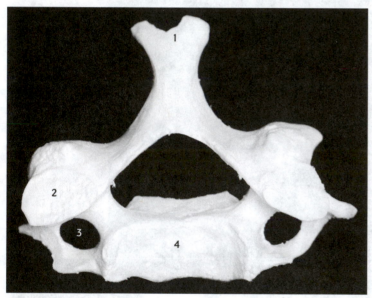

PHOTO 7.14 *Cervical vertebrae C3–C7, superior view*

| 1. spinous process | 3. transverse foramen |
| 2. superior articular surface | 4. body |

Cervical Vertebrae

The neck vertebrae are called *cervical vertebrae* (L *cervi:* neck). The homologous condition of the number of cervical vertebrae—seven—is common to all mammals and presumably is inherited from the mammalian common ancestor.

The two most superior vertebrae have some distinguishing features because of their unique role relative to the other vertebrae. The *atlas (CI)* supports the skull and has large articular facets for a wide range of movement (Photo 7.13A). The *axis (C2)*, just inferior to the atlas, has a superior projection, the *dens,* which serves as an axis for the atlas to move about (Photo 7.13B). The other cervical vertebrae (C3 through C7) are more similar to one another (see Photo 7.14).

All seven cervical vertebrae have transverse foramina for passage of the transverse artery, vein, and nerve. Once in the thorax, this nerve/blood supply bundle takes a different route, running anterior to, rather than within, the vertebral column. Features of the cervical vertebrae are as follows (see also *Atlas* pp. 159, 160).

atlas (C1):
- no body
- large superior articulating facets
- barely discernable spinous process

axis (C2):
- dens (odontoid process)
- larger body than atlas

C3–C7:
- larger body than atlas or axis
- more prominent spinous process
- spinous process often bifid (forked)

Thoracic Vertebrae

The *thoracic vertebrae* all articulate with ribs; hence, there are 12 of them. (Refer again to Photo 7.12, and *Atlas* pp. 161, 162). Features are:

🖐 long, skinny, spinous process (except for the most inferior thoracic vertebrae)

🖐 transverse process thick compared to those of lumbar vertebrae

🖐 superior and inferior articular surfaces oriented laterally (side to side)

🖐 rib facets on body of vertebra and on transverse process

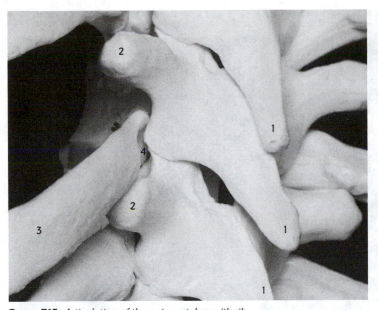

PHOTO 7.15 *Articulation of thoracic vertebra with rib*

1. spinous process   2. transverse process   3. rib   4. articular facet on rib

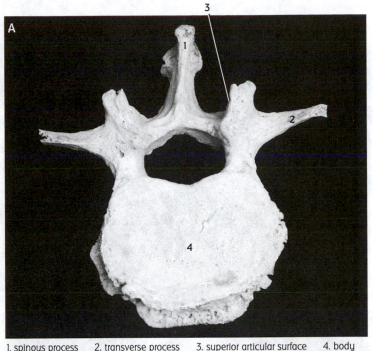

1. spinous process   2. transverse process   3. superior articular surface   4. body

Looking at an articulated skeleton (or, in its absence, Photo 7.15), observe the articulations of the ribs with the thoracic vertebrae. Most of the ribs articulate with the thoracic vertebrae in two places, on the flattened **facets** located laterally on the body and on the transverse processes.

Lumbar Vertebrae

The five *lumbar vertebrae* bear the most weight and thus are the largest vertebrae (*see* Photo 7.16 and *Atlas* pp. 163, 164). Spinous process short and squared-off.

✋ superior and inferior articular surfaces oriented antero-posteriorly (front to back)

✋ no rib facets

The adjacent 12th thoracic vertebra and first lumbar vertebra are similar in size and overall shape. Photo 7.17 highlights the differences so you can learn to distinguish them from each other (see also *Atlas* p. 162, Figure 5.13).

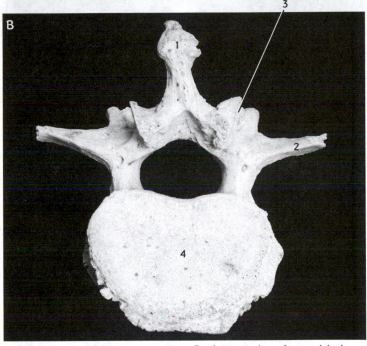

1. spinous process   2. transverse process   3. inferior articular surface   4. body

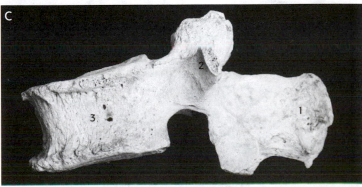

1. spinous process   2. transverse process   3. body

PHOTO 7.16 *Lumbar vertebrae, (A) superior view, (B) inferior view, (C) lateral view*

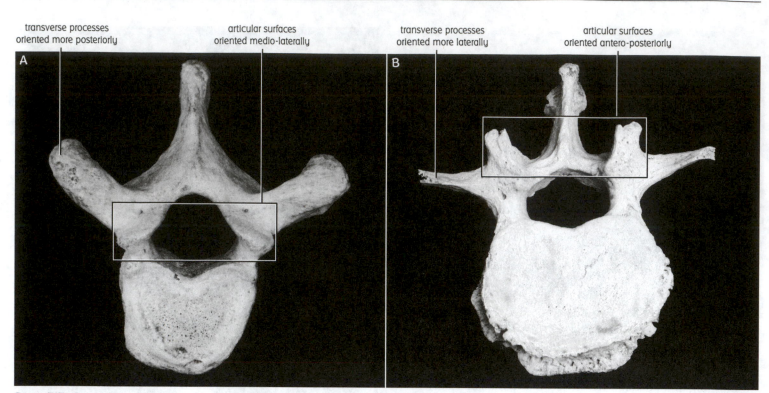

A — transverse processes oriented more posteriorly — articular surfaces oriented medio-laterally

B — transverse processes oriented more laterally — articular surfaces oriented antero-posteriorly

PHOTO 7.17 *Comparison of thoracic and lumbar vertebrae, superior view*

Sacrum

The *sacrum* is made up of vertebrae that fuse near adulthood (see Figure 7.10 and *Atlas* p.165). Together, the sacrum and the two pelvic (innominate) bones form the pelvis, which has these features:

☟ made up of five fused vertebrae

☟ forms theof sacroiliac joint (articulation of pelvic bones and sacrum)

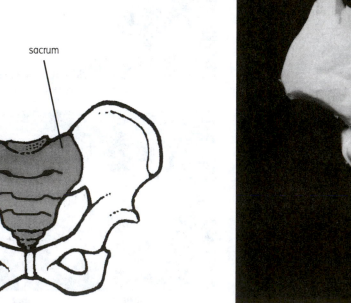

sacrum

FIGURE 7.10 *Pelvis with Sacrum Highlighted*

Coccyx

The *coccyx* is the small remnant of the caudal vertebrae that make up the tail in most vertebrates—hence the nickname "*tailbone.*" It is made up of about four fused vertebrae (see Photo 7.18 and *Atlas* p. 165).

☟ sometimes fused to the sacrum

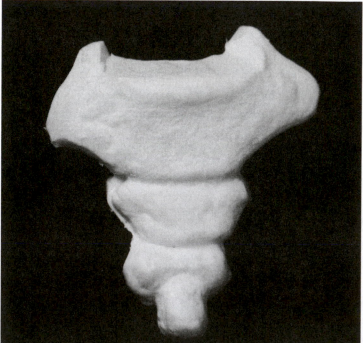

PHOTO 7.18 *Coccyx*

Axial Skeleton Part III: Thorax

The bony thorax provides protection for the heart and lungs. It consists of

✋ the *sternum* (breastbone),

✋ the *ribs*,

✋ the *costal cartilage*.

Referring to Photo 7.19, the uppermost seven ribs (the "true" ribs) articulate with the thoracic vertebrae posteriorly, then come around anteriorly to articulate with the sternum. In the 8th through the 10th ribs (called "false" ribs), there is no direct connection. Here, a cartilaginous structure, the costal cartilage (L *cost*: rib), stretches between the anterior margin of the ribs and the sternum. In the photo, particularly note the 11th and 12th ribs. These, the smallest and most inferior ribs, articulate posteriorly with the 11th and 12th thoracic vertebrae. Because they have no anterior connection, they are called "floating" ribs. There are no differences between the sexes in numbers of ribs—both males and females have 12!

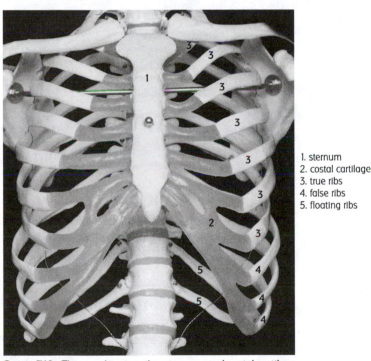

1. sternum
2. costal cartilage
3. true ribs
4. false ribs
5. floating ribs

PHOTO 7.19 *Thorax, showing ribs, sternum, and costal cartilage*

Sternum

The three main parts of the sternum are (see Photo 7.20 and *Atlas* p. 166)

✋ *manubrium*

✋ *body*

✋ *xiphoid process*.

Obvious features include the *clavicular notches* and the *jugular notch* (both on the manubrium, but not shown here), and the *costal notches* for the attachment of the ribs (or the costal cartilage) on the body of the sternum.

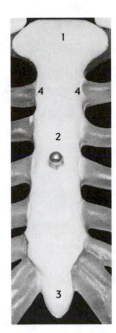

PHOTO 7.20
Features of the sternum

1. manubrium
2. body
3. xiphoid process
4. costal notches

Ribs

Most ribs have the following features (see Photo 7.21 and *Atlas* pp. 166, 167):

✋ *head*: articulates with the rib facet on the transverse process of a thoracic vertebra

✋ *tubercle*: a process near the head for articulation with the rib facet on the body of a thoracic vertebra

✋ sharpened inferior border, useful for siding the ribs

To distinguish the left from the right ribs, find the sharpened lower (inferior) border of the rib, then orient it so the head of the rib is on the posterior aspect.

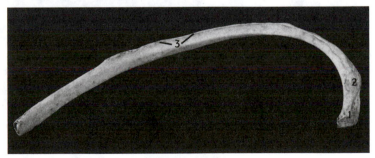

PHOTO 7.21 *Features of a typical "true" rib, inferior view*

1. head   2. tubercle   3. inferior border

LAB EXERCISE 7.2

NAME _____ SECTION _____ DATE _____

1. In your lab, find and identify the following vertebrae, then note, below, the features you used for your identifications. If no skeletal material is available, use Photos A–E (not all vertebrae are represented by photos here):

atlas:

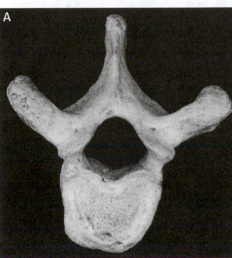

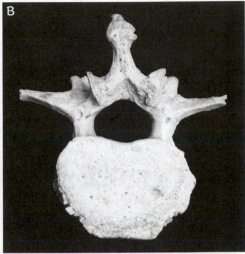

axis:

representative of C3–C7:

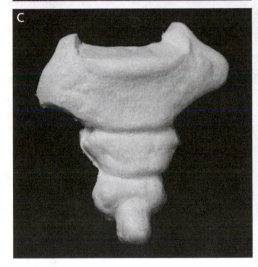

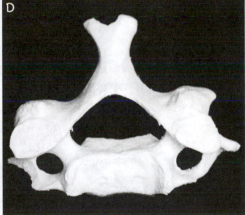

thoracic vertebra:

lumbar vertebra:

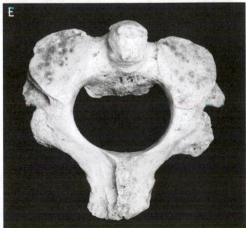

sacrum:

coccyx:

2. Observe a sternum (or a photo). Identify and list the three main portions. Identify the costal notches.

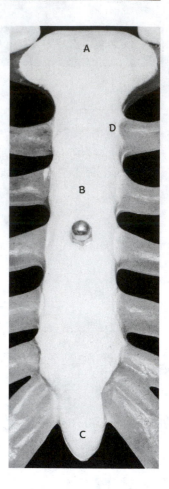

3. In your lab collection, side three ribs (the top ones are more difficult, so you may want to choose other, more "typical" ribs). How did you go about determining which side of the body they were from?

4. Look at a rib and a thoracic vertebra. Identify the head and the tubercle of a rib. Point out the corresponding points of articulation on a thoracic vertebra, and fit them (at least approximately) together.

SELF-TEST 7.2

NAME _____ SECTION _____ DATE _____

1. What are the components of the axial skeleton?

2. What are the five kinds of vertebrae?

3. Name a feature that differentiates all seven cervical vertebrae from the other vertebrae.

4. For the cervical, thoracic, and lumbar vertebrae, name two features that are used to distinguish them from one another.

   cervical:

   lumbar:

5. Why are their curves in the human vertebral column?

6. What are the three parts of the thorax?

7. What are the differences between a true rib, a false rib, and a floating rib?

8. Point to the approximate location of the xiphoid process on yourself. (Don't push too hard!).

Appendicular Skeleton

The human body is unique among primates in many ways, including our form of locomotion. We exhibit features in the *postcranial* skeleton (the skeleton from the neck down) that reflect our ancestry as well as those that evolved as a result of our upright posture and striding gait. We evolved from arboreal hominoids with a highly mobile upper limb, which we still possess. Our lower limb obviously is adapted for bipedalism, for which we use only two limbs to support all of our body weight. Therefore, we have a robust and relatively long lower limb.

We will explore the relationship between body form and function further in Chapter 9. For the remainder of this chapter, we will learn the bones and relevant features and, further, how form influences factors such as muscle function, range of motion, and weight-bearing capabilities.

You will work your way through the appendicular skeleton (the appendages and their bony attachments to the axial skeleton), identifying the bones and their features using the figures in this chapter and any laboratory material available to you. In learning the features, pay close attention to their location on the bone (using anatomical terminology). Knowledge of the position of features on paired bones will allow you to successfully distinguish whether a specific bone is from the right or the left side of the body. To "side" a bone, hold it close to your body as if it were your own bone.

Muscle Attachments

Muscles insert onto bone via tendons; most muscles cross one joint, *originating* on one bone and *inserting* on another. When a muscle contracts, it shortens and reduces the angle between the two bones. A muscle **origin** is the site from which a muscle arises. A muscle pulls toward its origin, which usually is fixed and more proximal. A muscle **insertion** is the site where a muscle grabs hold of the second bone. This site is usually on the mobile bone and is more distal.

By contracting, muscles are responsible for performing various actions. The location of the origin and insertion (how near to or far from a joint) and the size of the muscle determine the magnitude of its strength and its speed. Many *muscle actions* are paired and opposites; one set of muscles produces a certain action at a joint, and another produces the opposite action. Many of the following muscle actions will be familiar to you already.

flexion:	acts to bend or reduce the angle between two bones
extension:	acts to increase the angle between two bones
abduction:	movement of a body part away from the longitudinal axis of the body (or, in the hand, from a specified digit)
adduction:	movement of a body part toward the longitudinal body axis (or toward a specified digit)

rotation:	the act of a bone turning around its axis; for example, rotation of the radius around the ulna produces the specific actions:
pronation:	palm of the hand turning toward the posterior aspect
supination:	palm of the hand turning toward the anterior aspect
inversion:	turns the sole of the foot inward
eversion:	turns the sole of the foot outward
protraction:	a bone is drawn forward
retraction:	a bone is drawn backward
circumduction:	a circular movement at a joint, produced by numerous individual muscle actions (for example, making a cone shape with the arm, a movement produced at the shoulder joint)

Pectoral (Shoulder) Girdle

Typically, a "girdle" is a stable feature that encircles (more like the pelvic girdle). Earlier vertebrate ancestors had a more stable, encircling pectoral girdle, whereas ours is adapted to mobility. The pectoral girdle consists of two bones:

✋ *clavicle*

✋ *scapula*.

Both of these names probably are familiar to you, but they are known more commonly as the collarbone and the shoulder blade, respectively. The articulation between these two bones is only superficial and occurs at the lateral end of the clavicle (see Photo 7.22 and *Atlas* p. 168).

Feel along your clavicle out toward the lateral end. When you get to a bump, you've probably found the articulation between the lateral (acromial) end of the clavicle and the *acromion* process of the scapula.

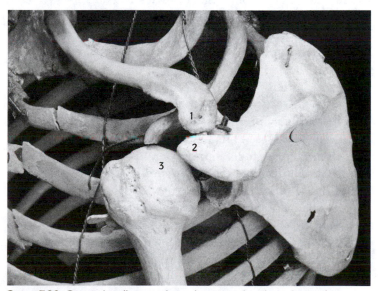

PHOTO 7.22 *Pectoral girdle; articulation between clavicle and scapula*
1. acromial end of clavicle   2. acromion process of scapula   3. head of humerus

Clavicle

The clavicle acts as a "strut" to keep the upper limb away from the body, providing greater leverage for muscle actions taking place at the shoulder joint. It is "S"-shaped, which resists fracture more efficiently than would a straight bone. Even so, clavicles sometimes do fracture as a result of falls of great force to the hands, if the arms remains straight. The *inferior surface* tends to be more *rugose*, or rough, than the *superior surface*, because more muscle insertions occur on the underside of the clavicle (see Photo 7.23 and *Atlas* p. 170). The *sternal end* is "fatter" and rounder than is the *acromial end*. (Remember that the sternal end is positioned medially in the body and the acromial end is lateral.)

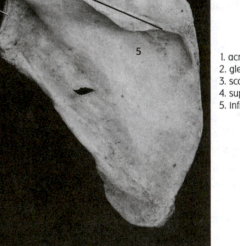

1. acromion process
2. coracoid process
3. subscapular fossa

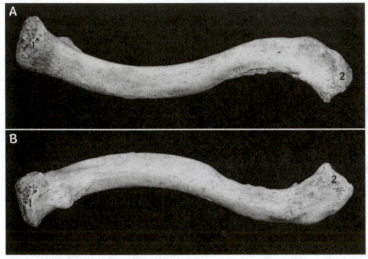

PHOTO 7.23 *Features of the clavicle (left side): (A) superior view and (B) inferior view*

1. sternal end   2. acromial end

Scapula

The scapula slides around on your back as you shrug your shoulders or move your shoulder forward or backward. It has muscular attachments to the vertebral column and to the humerus. The anterior, or ventral, side of the scapula has a somewhat "scooped out" appearance; thus, this depression is the *subscapular fossa* (see Photo 7.24 and *Atlas* p. 168. The posterior, or dorsal, aspect has more features.

The *scapular spine* is one of the attachment sites for an important muscle that lifts the arm, the deltoid. The scapular spine divides the scapula into upper and lower sections, the *supraspinous fossa* and the *infraspinous fossa*. The articulation of the head of the humerus with the scapula occurs at the pear-shaped depression, the *glenoid fossa*. Two other important features are the *acromion process,* to which you were introduced as the articulation with the lateral end of the clavicle, and the beak-like *coracoid process* (G *cora*: crow, raven).

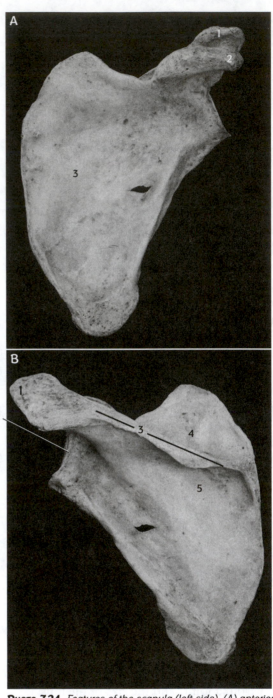

1. acromion process
2. glenoid fossa
3. scapular spine
4. supraspinous fossa
5. infraspinous fossa

PHOTO 7.24 *Features of the scapula (left side): (A) anterior view and (B) posterior view*

Study a clavicle and scapula to identify the features labeled in Photos 7.23 and 7.24, and *Atlas* p. 168–170.

Upper Limb

The upper limb articulates with the body axis at the *shoulder joint,* which is the connection between the scapula and the humerus. This type of articulation is referred to as a *ball-and-socket joint* and allows for a wide range of motion, particularly because there are few bony constraints surrounding the joint.

Humerus

The upper arm has a single bone, the *humerus*. Locate the listed features at the proximal and distal ends of the humerus on Photo 7.25 (and *Atlas* p. 171) and on an actual bone. The main features located at the proximal humerus are:

head: articulates with glenoid fossa of scapula

greater tubercle: point of origin for rotator cuff muscles; anteriorly located

lesser tubercle: smaller process, antero-medially located

bicipital groove   (intertubercular sulcus): tendon for a portion of the biceps muscle runs through this groove; anterior

About halfway down the *shaft* of the humerus lies the *deltoid tuberosity*: place of insertion for deltoid muscle

At the distal humerus, the main features are:

olecranon fossa: depression for articulation with the olecranon process of the proximal ulna; on posterior side

trochlea: spool-shaped feature that articulates with ulna

capitulum: rounded feature for articulation with depression at head of radius

lateral epicondyle: protrusion superior to capitulum; on lateral side

medial epicondyle: protrusion superior to trochlea; on medial side

For siding purposes, remember that the humeral head faces medially (toward the glenoid of the scapula) and the olecranon fossa is posterior.

Radius

The *radius* and the *ulna* together make up the bones of the forearm. You can palpate (feel) them in your own arm, particularly distally near your wrist. Both bones articulate with the humerus at their proximal end. The radius is located on the lateral side of the ulna. Remember to picture the body in *anatomical position*, with palms facing forward and thumbs out to the sides. When you *pronate* your hand at the wrist, you cause the distal end of the radius to cross over the ulna.

At the proximal end of the radius, the primary features (Photo 7.26 and *Atlas* p. 174) are the

head: shaped like a horse's hoof, the very end is depressed for articulation with the rounded capitulum of the humerus

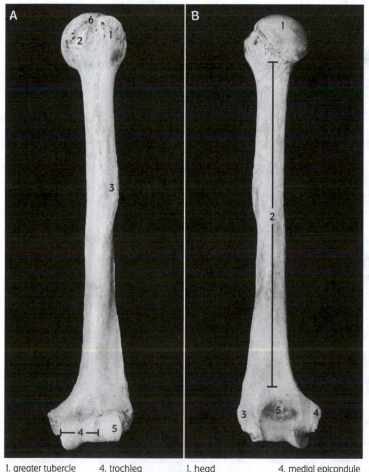

1. greater tubercle   4. trochlea   1. head   4. medial epicondyle
2. lesser tubercle   5. capitulum   2. shaft   5. olecranon fossa
3. deltoid tuberosity 6. bicipital groove 3. lateral epicondyle

PHOTO 7.25 *Features of the humerus (left side): (A) anterior view and (B) posterior view*

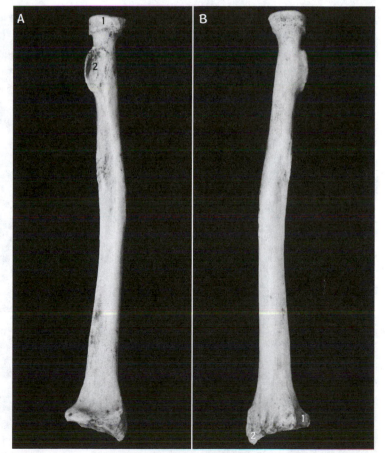

1. head   2. radial tuberosity   1. ulnar notch   2. styloid process

PHOTO 7.26 *Features of the radius (left side): (A) anterior view and (B) posterior view*

radial tuberosity: bump near radial head; muscle attachment site

ulnar notch: semilunar-shaped depression found on the medial aspect for articulation with the ulna

The main feature at the distal end is the

styloid process: distal extended tip of radius

Ulna

At the proximal end are the two primary features (Photo 7.27 and *Atlas* p. 176):

olecranon process: uppermost posterior portion of the ulna; in humans and apes, it is not prominent, but in quadrupeds it is large and prevents full extension of the arm at the elbow

radial notch: a depression for articulation of the rounded portion of the radial head

At the distal end of the ulna is the

styloid process: sharper than the like-named feature on the radius, it is a pointy extension

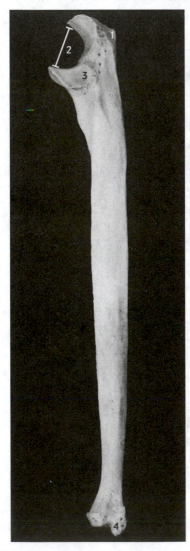

PHOTO 7.27
Features of the ulna (left side)

1. olecranon process
2. trochlear notch
3. radial notch
4. styloid process

Carpal Bones

The bones of the wrist are referred to as *carpal bones* (G *carp:* wrist). The anatomical term for the wrist is the *carpus*. Humans have eight carpal bones; apes have nine. The bones of the wrist can be roughly divided into a proximal row and a distal row (Photo 7.28 and *Atlas* p. 178). The proximal row, from the medial to the lateral side, consists of the *pisiform, triquetrum (triquetral), lunate,* and *scaphoid (navicular).* The distal row contains the *hamate, capitate, trapezoid,* and *trapezium.*

Hand Bones

The row of bones immediately distal to the carpals consists of the *metacarpals* (see Photo 7.28 and *Atlas* p. 179). These can be easily palpated between your palm and the back of your hand. The bones making up your fingers and thumb are *phalanges* (singular: *phalanx*). The first row, articulating with the metacarpals, consists of the *proximal phalanges.* You can see these as the first section of each finger and of your thumb. The next row consists of the *middle phalanges* and is found only in your fingers. Note that your thumb consists of only two sections (and thus two bones). Your finger and thumb tips are on your *distal phalanges.* The fingers are numbered one through five, with Digit I referring to the thumb, and Digit V the pinkie.

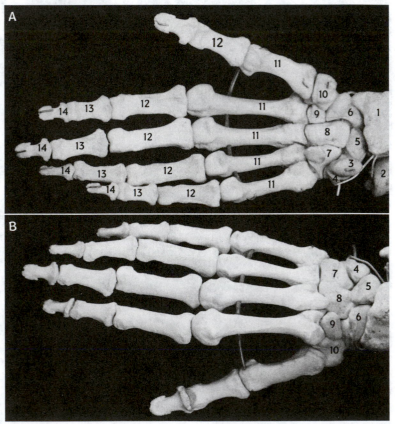

PHOTO 7.28 *Hand and carpal bones (right side): (A) palmar view and (B) dorsal view*

1. distal radius	5. lunate	9. trapezoid	13. middle
2. distal ulna	6. scaphoid	10. trapezium	phalanges
3. pisiform	7. hamate	11. metacarpals	14. distal phalanges
4. triquetrum	8. capitate	12. proximal phalanges	

LAB EXERCISE 7.3

NAME _____ SECTION _____ DATE _____

1. Side a clavicle.

2. Side a scapula.

3. Find a clavicle and a scapula from the same side, then articulate them properly, using an articulated skeleton or Photo 7.22 as a guide.

4. Find a humerus, or use the photo of the humerus (at right).

   a. Side the humerus.

   b. List the features you used to orient the bone and determine the side.

   c. Locate and list two features at the anterior end of the humerus, and two at the distal end.

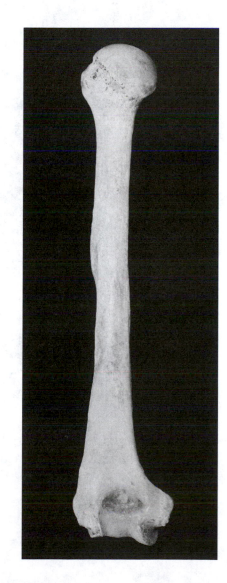

5. Find a radius and an ulna from the same side, then articulate them properly, using an articulated skeleton or the photo as a guide.

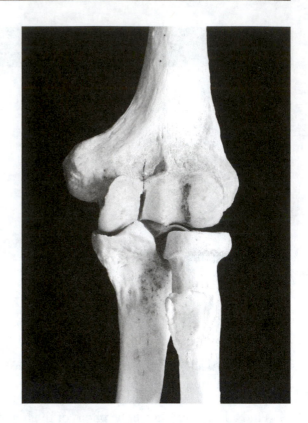

6. Two relatively easily identifiable carpal bones are the pisiform (G *pis*: pea; this is a hint!) and the hamate. The pisiform is the medial-most bone, and the hamate has an appropriately named feature called a *hook* on the anterior (palmar) side. Identify these bones on either a disarticulated or an articulated hand (or use the photo below).

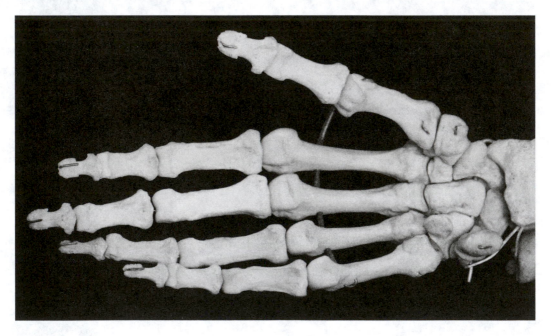

7. Observe the very tip of the distal phalanx of the thumb. You will notice a slightly rounded, expanded, roughened area. What do you think this feature relates to, and why might it be much smaller in our close relatives, the apes?

SELF-TEST 7.3

NAME _____ SECTION _____ DATE _____

1. What is the difference between the appendicular skeleton and the postcranial skeleton?

2. Briefly explain the basic way by which muscles function.

3. What is the difference between the pectoral girdle and the shoulder joint?

4. What are the points of articulation between the humerus and the scapula?

5. What are the features that serve as the articulating points between the humerus and the ulna?

Between the humerus and the radius?

Between the radius and the ulna?

6. What is the anatomical name for the wrist bones?

7. The first row of bones immediately distal to the wrist bones consists of _____.

8. The name of the bone underneath the fingertip of your index finger is the _____ _____

of digit _____.

Pelvic Girdle

Numerous features apparent in the bones of the pelvic girdle relate to bipedalism and differ from the form of these bones in the apes. Again, the pelvic girdle is composed of the two pelvic (*innominate*) bones and the sacrum (*Atlas* p. 181)

Innominate Bones The two innominate bones are each made up of three bones that fuse during the early teen years—the *ilium*, the *ischium*, and the *pubis* (*Atlas* p. 182). The pelvis is extremely useful for distinguishing the sex of skeletons. The numerous differences between male and female human pelves relate primarily to the widening of the female pelvis to allow for more efficient childbirth. As you orient the pelvis, note that the ischium is wider than the pubis. The two innominate bones articulate with each other at the pubis, where a pad of fibrocartilage makes up the *pubic symphysis*.

The pelvic features labeled in Photo 7.29 (see also *Atlas* p. 182) will be used later to side the bones, to determine sex, and to make comparisons with nonhuman primates and with fossil specimens. These include the:

iliac crest:	ridge of bone along the superior margin of the ilium
iliac fossa:	internal portion of the ilium, a large scooped-out area
anterior inferior iliac spine:	large process on anterior aspect of ilium; origin for *rectus femoris* muscle, a key muscle for propulsion in bipedal locomotion
greater sciatic notch:	large notch on posterior aspect of ilium; helpful in making determination of sex
acetabulum:	large fossa for articulation with femoral head; hip socket
obturator foramen:	large foramen on anterior aspect of pelvis
ischial tuberosity:	roughened areas on the inferior-most portion of the ischium; the area we sit on
pubic symphysis:	the joining of the pubic regions of two innominates

1. Put your hands on your hips. You're putting your hands on the iliac crest (with a few layers of tissue between your hands and the actual pelvis, of course).

2. Sit down hard on a hard surface (but don't break your coccyx!). Those are your ischial tuberosities you can feel in contact with the substrate.

3. Pick up an innominate bone. Hold it in front of your own hips, and orient it the way it would be placed if it were in your body. Remember—the pubis is anterior and

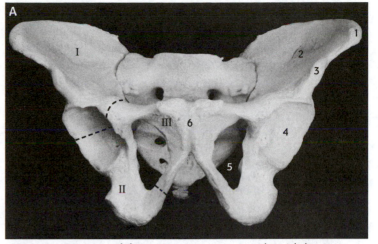

I Ilium	1. Iliac crest	4. acetabulum
II Ischium	2. Iliac fossa	5. obturator foramen
III pubis	3. anterior inferior iliac spine	6. pubic symphysis

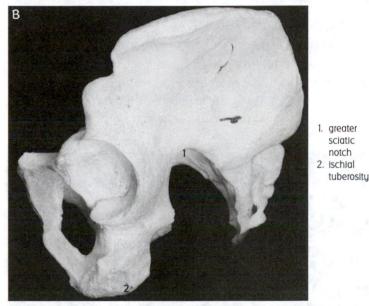

1. greater sciatic notch
2. ischial tuberosity

PHOTO 7.29 *Features of the innominate: (A) anterior, and (B) and lateral*

must point (orient) medially if it is to meet up with the pubis from the other innominate bone.

4. Side the bone, using what you know about the position of the pubis and the ischium, and/or using an articulated skeleton or referring to Photo 7.29 of the innominate.

Lower Limb

The lower limb articulates with the body axis at the *hip joint*, which is the connection between the pelvis and the femur. Like the articulation between the scapula and humerus, this is a ball-and-socket joint, although the range of motion is less because of more bony constraints. The acetabulum of the pelvis is much more stable and protective than is the glenoid fossa of the scapula. This is necessary because the hip, unlike the shoulder, is a weight-bearing joint. Numerous changes in the lower limb occurred during the evolution of our quadrupedal ancestors to efficient bipeds.

Femur

The femur is relatively large and robust and is oriented inward from hip to knee. This brings the weight-bearing load more in line with our center of gravity. The features highlighted in the photo are important either for siding the bone or making comparisons of the adaptations of our extant and extinct relatives (Photo 7.30 and *Atlas* pp. 186–187).

At the proximal end, the key features are the

head: large and robust in humans, it is set off from the shaft of the femur by a *neck*; faces medially for articulation with acetabulum of pelvic bones

greater trochanter: large superior projection; attachment point for hip muscles

lesser trochanter: smaller process on posterior aspect

On the posterior aspect, running down much of the femoral shaft, is the

linea aspera (L *lin*: line; *asper*: rough):   insertion of the adductor muscles, which bring the leg around to the center with each step, an important aspect of human bipedalism

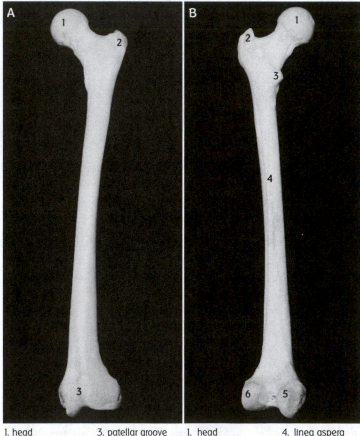

1. head
2. greater tuberosity
3. patellar groove

1. head
2. greater tuberosity
3. lesser tuberosity
4. linea aspera
5. medial condyle
6. lateral condyle

PHOTO 7.30 *Features of the femur (left side): (A) anterior view and (B) posterior view*

The primary features at the distal end are the

medial condyle: rounded articulation area for the medial condyle of the tibia

lateral condyle: rounded articulation area for the lateral condyle of the tibia

patellar groove: depression, the sides of which are formed by the medial and lateral condyles; the patella rests in this groove

Patella

The patella is a *sesamoid* (G *sesam*: sesame) bone. Sesamoid bones form within the tendons of some joints, acting rather like a pulley to move a muscle away from a joint to provide enhanced leverage for the muscle's action. The patella is the largest sesamoid in the body; most of the others are so small (and because they do not articulate directly with other bones) that they are rarely found with a skeleton.

Besides being able to tell anterior from posterior (the posterior side is smooth from articulation with the femur), the important distinctions to make are between these two features:

apex: pointed end; distal-most part of the patella

base: gently rounded end; proximal portion of the patella

The facet for the lateral condyle of the femur is larger than for the medial side, and the entire lateral side of the patella is somewhat larger and heavier (Photo 7.31 and *Atlas* p. 191). This makes siding the patella very simple.

To side a patella:

1. Identify the apex and the posterior (dorsal) surface of the patella.

2. Point the apex away from you, and put the patella down on its posterior surface, balancing it momentarily on the ridge between the facets for the medial and lateral femoral condyles.

3. Let go. The patella will tip toward the lateral side. Thus, if it falls to the right, it is a right patella.

Tibia

The tibia articulates distally with the femur. Together, the tibia and the fibula comprise the lower leg bones (Photo 7.32 and *Atlas* p. 189). The tibia is commonly referred to as the shin bone.

medial condyle: articulates proximally with the medial condyle of the femur

lateral condyle: articulates proximally with the lateral condyle of the femur

anterior tibial tuberosity: roughened area on anterior aspect; insertion of *rectus femoris* muscle; can be palpated as a bump just distal to the patella

PHOTO 7.31 *Patella (left side; note the arthritic growth): (A) anterior view and (B) posterior view*

1. base   2. apex

medial malleolus: distally located process on tibia; useful for siding the bone; located on medial side

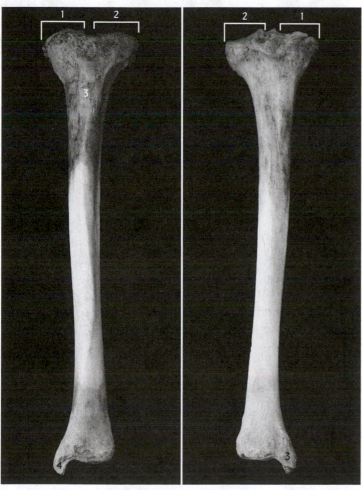

1. medial condyle   4. medial malleolus
2. lateral condyle
3. anterior tibial tuberosity

1. medial condyle   3. medial malleolus
2. lateral condyle

PHOTO 7.32 *Features of the tibia (left side): (A) anterior view and (B) posterior view*

Fibula

The fibula is a long, skinny bone that articulates laterally with the tibia (Photo 7.33 and *Atlas* p. 191). The proximal and distal ends initially can be difficult to distinguish from one another.

head: proximally located feature, which is "blockier" and more compressed than the distal-end

lateral malleolus: distal end of tibia; longer and more drawn-out than the head, almost arowhead-shaped

PHOTO 7.33 *Features of the fibula (left side)*

1. head   2. lateral malleolus

The medial malleolus of the tibia and the lateral malleolus of the fibula together enclose the most proximal of the ankle bones, the *talus.* Both of these processes can be felt as bumps on the medial and lateral sides of the ankle.

Tarsal Bones

The bones of the ankle are referred to as *tarsal bones* (G *tars:* ankle). The anatomical term for the ankle is the *tarsus.* Humans have seven tarsal bones. The two largest bones are also the most proximally located: the *calcaneus* (heel bone) and the *talus* (astragalus). The talus articulates distally with the *navicular,* and the rest of the tarsal bones—*cuboid, lateral cuneiform, intermediate cuneiform, and medial cuneiform—*

form a row that articulates with the foot bones (*see* Photo 7.34 and *Atlas* p. 192).

Foot Bones

The row of bones immediately distal to the tarsals consists of the *metatarsals* (Photo 7.34 and *Atlas* p. 192). These can be easily palpated between the sole and the back of your foot. As in the fingers, the bones making up the toes are the

phalanges (singular: *phalanx*). The first row, articulating with the metatarsals, consists of the *proximal phalanges*. The next row contains *middle phalanges* (except in the big toe, which, like the thumb, has only two bones). The tips of the toes are the *distal phalanges*. As in the hand, the toes are numbered one through five, with Digit I referring to the big toe and Digit V, the little toe.

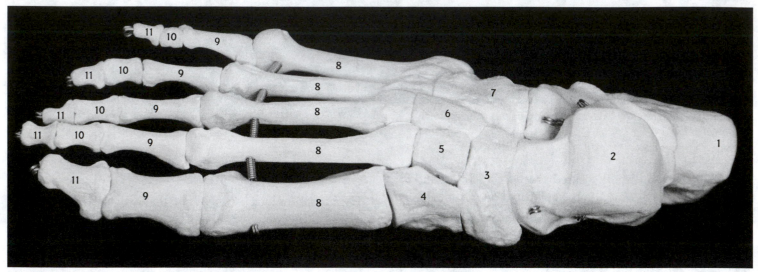

PHOTO 7.34 *Tarsal and foot bones (right side), dorsal view*

1. calcaneus
2. talus
3. navicular
4. medial cuneiform
5. intermediate cuneiform
6. lateral cuneiform
7. cuboid
8. metatarsals
9. proximal phalanges
10. middle phalanges
11. distal phalanges

LAB EXERCISE 7.4

NAME _____ SECTION _____ DATE _____

1. Identify the following features on an innominate bone (or use the photo for identification):

   anterior inferior iliac spine: sciatic notch: pubis: ischium: obturator foramen:

   Side the bone (for a specimen in your lab).

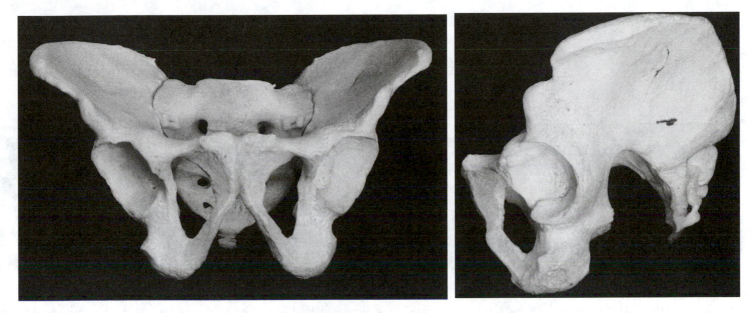

2. Side a femur. What features did you use to determine the side? (Use the photo for reference.)

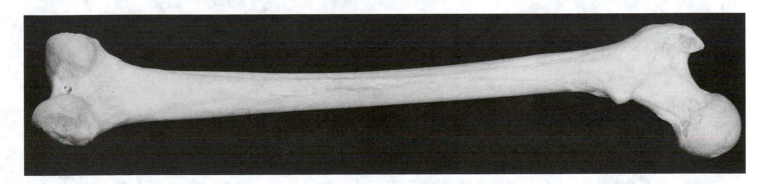

3. Identify the *linea aspera* on a femur (or on the photo). What directional term best describes the location of this feature on the femur?

4. Find a tibia that comes from the same side as the femur, and articulate the two bones. What features did you use to determine the side of the tibia?

5. For a fibula, determine which is the proximal and which is the distal end. What are the names of the features at each end?

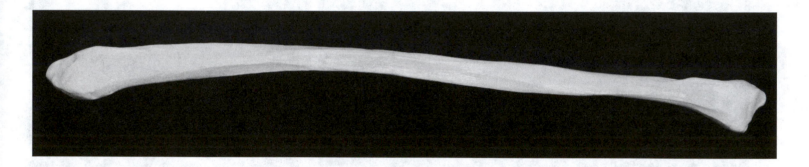

6. Identify the calcaneus and the talus on an articulated foot, disarticulated bones, or on the photo. Also identify the proximal phalanx of Digit V.

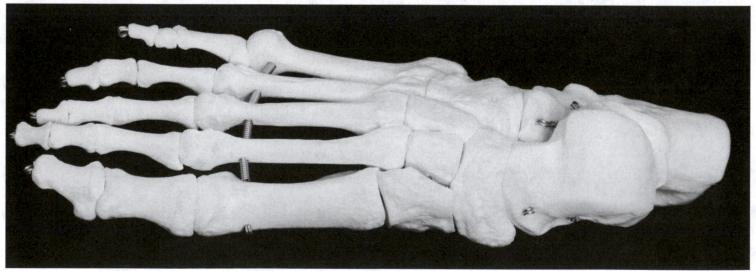

SELF-TEST 7.4

NAME _____ SECTION _____ DATE _____

1. How can you tell the difference between a humerus and a femur?

2. What bones make up the pelvic girdle?

3. Which three fused bones makes up each innominate bone?

4. What is the name for the heel bone?

5. Which is the lateral of the two lower leg bones?

6. What is the anatomical name for the ankle bones?

7. The first row of bones distal to the ankle bones are the _____.

8. What is the name for the points of articulation between the femur and the innominate?

9. The talus is enclosed by the _____ _____ of the tibia and the _____

_____ of the fibula.

8. Forensic Anthropology

"Have you ever wondered...?"

How can you tell a male skeleton from a female skeleton?

NOTE: You will need a calculator for this lab.

OBJECTIVES

- Become aware of the range of information that can be obtained from a skeleton
- Understand the sources of biological variation of the skeleton
- Learn to use anthropometric tools
- Learn anthropometric techniques and gain experience in data collection
- Learn examples of qualitative and quantitative skeletal traits to estimate/determine age, sex, ancestry, and stature

Forensic anthropologists work with law enforcement officials to help identify skeletal remains. Remember from Chapter 7 that a great deal of information can be obtained from bone. Biological variation among humans results from age differences, sex, ancestry, nutrition and disease, and type and extent of activity during life. Knowledge of how these factors affect a skeleton provides the forensic anthropologist with information necessary to piece together the puzzle and gain either an accurate description of a person's characteristics when alive, or to provide a positive identification of a skeleton. Forensic anthropologists frequently collaborate with medical professionals in comparing bones with diagnostic tests such as X-rays, or with dental records.

Measuring Human Biological Variation

To measure the variations in human biology, two tools are anthropometry and osteometry. **Anthropometry** refers to the measurement of humans, often of living individuals. **Osteometry** is a subcategory of anthropometry that deals strictly with the measurement of the skeleton. In today's lab we'll use both skeletal material and your fellow students as your experimental subjects. Osteometric techniques, together with qualitative assessment of skeletal material, provide the basis for conducting forensic anthropology analyses.

Standard methods of measuring the human body are in place for both living and skeletal specimens. The first step is to identify a few of the many sites on the skull that serve as **landmarks** (Photo 8.1) for measurement and allow us to take the same measurement consistently on a number of individuals.

Examples of landmarks for the skull are:

glabella: the most prominent point on the midline of the supraorbital ridge

opisthocranion: not a fixed point, but the point on the occipital bone that occurs the greatest distance from glabella (in the mid-sagittal plane)

nasion: the most superior point of articulation of the two nasal bones, where both articulate with the frontal bone

nasospinale: the midline point of the inferior margin of the nasal aperture (opening)

alare: most lateral point of each side of the nasal aperture

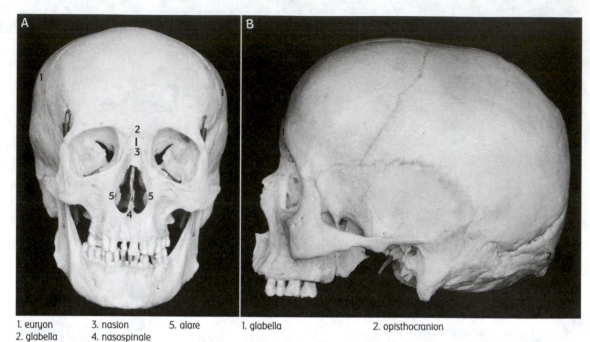

PHOTO 8.1 *Landmarks of the skull: (A) anterior, (B) and lateral views*

| 1. euryon | 3. nasion | 5. alare | 1. glabella | 2. opisthocranion |
| 2. glabella | 4. nasospinale | | | |

☙ *euryon:* most lateral point on each side of the skull (on parietals)

A more complete listing of landmarks can be found in the *Atlas*, pp. 206–210.

Anthropometric Techniques

The main tools for collecting data on skeletal material (particularly on skulls) are *spreading calipers* (see Figures 8.1 and 8.2) and *sliding calipers* (see Figures 8.3 and 8.4). Your instructor will review the proper use of the calipers. Take each measurement two times to ensure accuracy. Record all measurements using the metric system (in cm), which is the international system for scientific measurements.

Head Shape

A common set of measurements used for anthropometry is related to shape of the head. Head shape is one of the many features considered in determining an individual's ancestry. The two measurements and the formula presented below can be applied to skulls as well as the heads of living humans. For **cranial** measurements, use the spreading calipers.

☙ *cranial breadth:* This is the maximum transverse diameter of the skull (the maximum width). Take the measurement by moving the points of the spreading caliper along the parietal bones until the maximum diameter is found, at *euryon* (Figure 8.1) on both sides of the skull.

☙ *cranial length:* This measurement quantifies the anterior–posterior maximum length of the skull, measured from *glabella* to *opisthocranion*. Fix one end of the spreading caliper on glabella and hold it with one hand. With the other hand move the other end of the caliper around until you find the maximum reading (Figure 8.2).

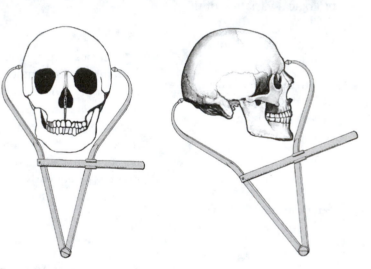

FIGURE 8.1 *Measuring Cranial Breadth*   **FIGURE 8.2** *Measuring Cranial Length*

With the measurements you have obtained, you now can draw some useful information about the overall appearance of these skulls. To gauge how round-headed versus how long-headed an individual is, you would use the cranial, or **cephalic,** index:

$$\text{Cranial index} = \frac{\text{Cranial breadth} \times 100}{\text{Cranial length}}$$

The following categories have been created for results of the cranial index (*e.g.,* Bass, 1995):

	Index
Narrow or long-headed (*dolichocephalic*)	up to 74.9
Average (*mesocephalic*)	75.0–79.9
Round-headed (*brachycephalic*)	80.0–84.9
Very round-headed (*hyperbrachycephalic*)	more than 85.0

Nasal Region

Also commonly measured is the **nasal** region, which can be useful for determining ancestry, especially when taken together with several qualitative features. The following measurements relate to the overall width of the nose. For the nasal measurements, use the sliding calipers (carefully—they're sharp!).

✋ *nasal breadth:* Measure the widest portion of the nasal aperture; between the two *alare* landmarks (Figure 8.3).

✋ *nasal height:* Measure from *nasion* to *nasospinale*; remember—you are not measuring only the nasal opening but actually from the inferior margin of the nasal opening to the superior margin of the nasal bones (see Figure 8.4).

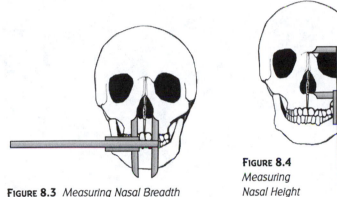

FIGURE 8.4
*Measuring
Nasal Height*

FIGURE 8.3 *Measuring Nasal Breadth*

You then will apply the *nasal index* to your results.

$$\text{Nasal index} = \frac{\text{Nasal breadth} \times 100}{\text{Nasal height}}$$

	Index
Wide-nosed (*platyrrhiny*)	53 and up
Medium-nosed (*mesorrhiny*)	48–52.9
Narrow-nosed (*leptorrhiny*)	up to 47.9

(e.g., Bass, 1995)

LAB EXERCISE 8.1

NAME _____ SECTION _____ DATE _____

Using your fellow students as laboratory subjects, conduct the following measurements to determine their head shape, referring to Figures 8.1 and 8.2. Use the spreading calipers (and take care to not poke out anyone's eye!) to measure, then calculate, the cranial index.

	Individual #1	Individual #2
Cranial breadth		
Cranial length		
Cranial index		

Next you will collect some osteometric data, taking these same measurements on three skulls.

	Skull 1	Skull 2	Skull 3
Cranial breadth			
Cranial length			
Cranial index			

Practice using the sliding calipers for some nasal measurements, filling out the chart below. Referring to Figures 8.3 and 8.4 again, use the sharper, pointed part of the calipers. Be gentle in taking these measurements, especially for nasal breadth, as the nasal region is fragile. Calculate the nasal index for each skull.

	Skull 1	Skull 2	Skull 3
Nasal breadth			
Nasal length			
Nasal index			

S E L F - T E S T   8 . 1

NAME _____ SECTION _____ DATE _____

1. Which measurements can be taken with sliding calipers?

2. Which measurements can be taken with spreading calipers?

3. What does the cranial index tell you?

Male or Female?

To determine the sex of an individual, evidence is taken from the skull and the pelvis.

Evidence from the Skull

You undoubtedly have noticed that humans possess characteristics that vary according to the sex of an individual. **Sexual dimorphism** refers to differences in shape or size between the sexes of a species. Living human males and females exhibit obvious differences, and skeletal correlates exist for some of these soft anatomical differences. These features relate mainly to differences in muscle development and to the widened birth canal in females.

Rugose (rough) areas—raised processes, or areas, on bone—often appear where the tendons of muscles attach. In general, male skeletons have more rugose areas than female skeletons at muscle attachment sites, because of their greater muscle mass (*e.g.,* France, 1986). Females usually are smaller and have shorter, more slender bones. The most distinctive differences occur on the skull and in the pelvis (Giles and Elliot, 1963; Phenice, 1969).

In today's lab you will determine the sex of some individuals by examining several features of the cranial and post-cranial skeleton. Table 8.1 lists several of the many features that differ on the skulls of males and females. Most of these are observable in the photo (Photo 8.2).

Keep in mind that because skeletons vary greatly, most skulls have at least a few characteristics that appear to belong to the opposite sex. Therefore, a suite of several features must be taken together to determine sex reliably.

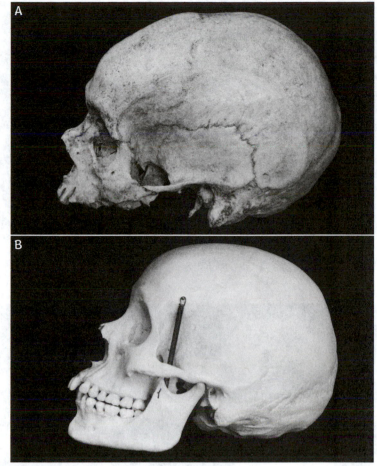

PHOTO 8.2 *(A) Male skull and (B) female skull*

Evidence from the Pelvis

Numerous features exist on the postcranium, particularly on the pelvis, that can indicate an individual's sex. Some of the features of the innominate bone illustrated in Figure 8.5 are listed in Table 8.2. As with the skull, there is overlap between the sexes and a pelvis may exhibit a mix of "male" and "female" features (see Photos 8.3 and 8.4).

TABLE 8.1: Selected Traits for Determining Sex from Skull		
Skull Features	**Form in Male**	**Form in Female**
Overall skull size	larger, more robust	smaller, more gracile
Shape of forehead	sloping	more vertical, rounded
Supraorbital ridge	more prominent, thicker	less prominent, smaller
Mastoid process	larger	smaller
Orbital shape	squared, low, broad	rounded, set higher
Nuchal area and occipital protuberance	more pronounced	less pronounced
Chin shape	more squared, broader	more rounded, narrower

TABLE 8.2: Selected Traits for Determining Sex from Pelvis		
Features of Innominate	**Form in Male**	**Form in Female**
Sub-pubic arch size	narrower, more V-shaped	wider, more rounded
Pubic symphysis (height versus width)	longer, narrower	shorter, wider
Ventral arc	absent	present
Pelvic inlet	narrower, heart-shaped	broader, more oval
Greater sciatic notch	narrower, deeper	wider, shallower
Preauricular sulcus	usually absent	usually present

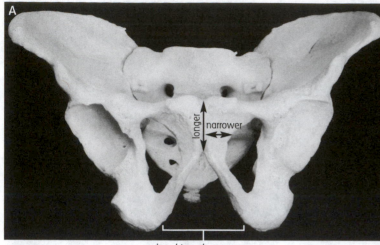

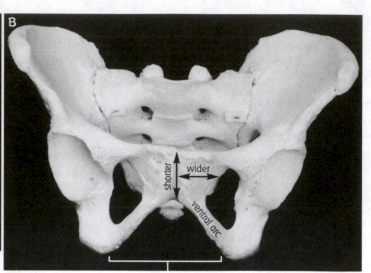

Photo 8.3 *(A) Male pelvis and (B) female pelvis*

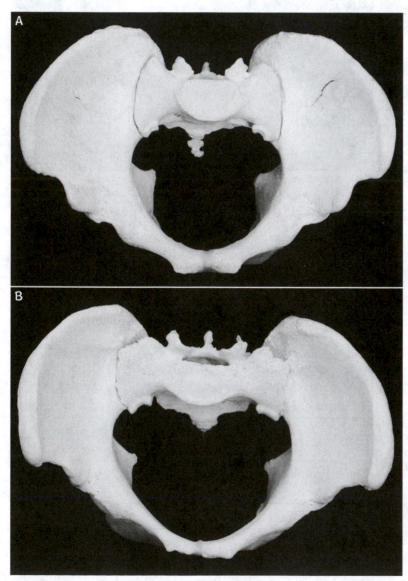

Photo 8.4 *Pelvic inlet of (A) male and (B) female*

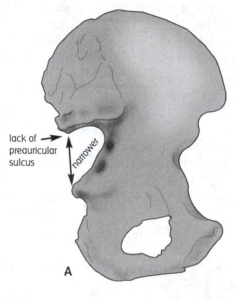

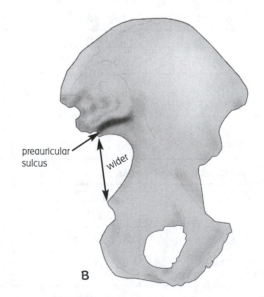

Figure 8.5 *Sciatic Notch Form and Preauricular Sulcus in (A) Male and (B) Female*

LAB EXERCISE 8.2

NAME _____ SECTION _____ DATE _____

1. "Sex" three skulls by filling out the chart below. For each feature, enter an "M" or an "F," indicating whether each feature appears to be more masculine or more feminine, or a "U" to designate "uncertain." For each feature, compare all of the skulls before deciding on a sex. (In the absence of comparative skulls in your lab, use the photos here).

Feature	Skull 1	Skull 2	Skull 3
Overall skull size			
Forehead shape			
Supraorbital ridge size			
Mastoid process			
Nuchal area, occipital protuberance			
Chin shape			
Total number of Ms			
Total number of Fs			
Sex designation			

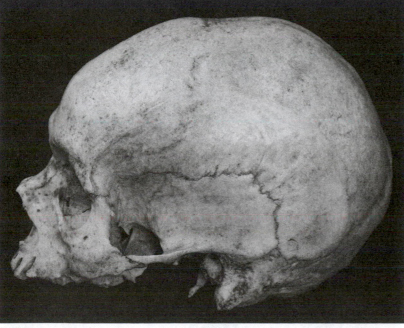

Skull 1

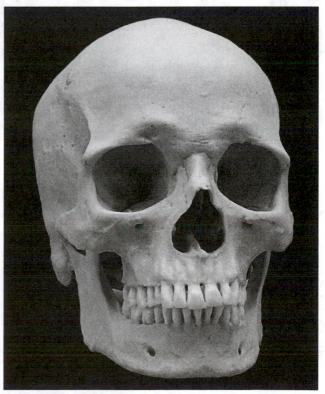

Skull 2

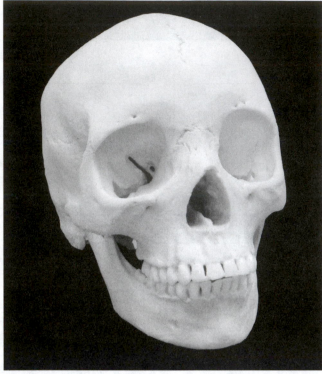

Skull 3

2. Sex three pelves (either entire pelves or casts of parts of the pelvis). Fill in the chart, again using the letters M, F, or U. (In the absence of comparative pelves in your lab, use the photos here. Some of the features listed below may not be observable from the photos.)

Feature (Use M or F)	Pelvis 1	Pelvis 2	Pelvis 3
Sub-pubic arch			
Pubic symphysis			
Ventral arc			
Greater sciatic notch			
Pelvic inlet (for entire pelvis)			
Total number of Ms			
Total number of Fs			
Sex designation			

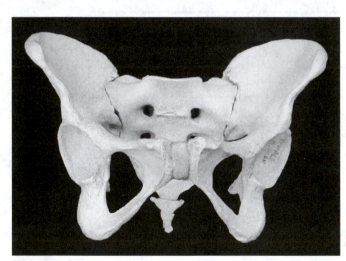

Pelvis 1

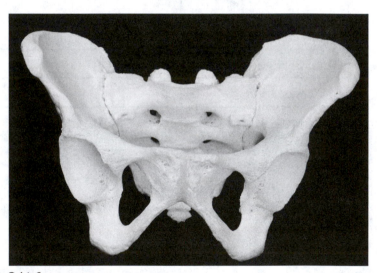

Pelvis 2

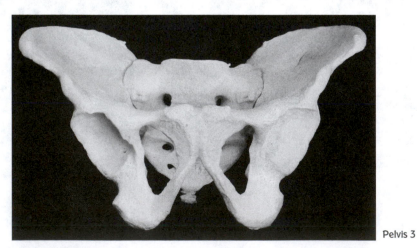

Pelvis 3

SELF-TEST 8.2

NAME _____ SECTION _____ DATE _____

1. a. What are three ways to tell male from female skulls?

   b. What are these differences related to?

2. What are three ways to tell male from female pelves?

   a.

   b.

   c.

   Why do these differences exist?

3. What is the term for differences between males and females within a species that do not relate to reproductive organs?

How Old Were They?

Numerous methods can be used to estimate the age of an individual at death. These methods depend upon knowledge of the **formative changes** that occur as we grow, and the **degenerative changes** that occur as we senesce (grow old). Methods for ageing skeletal material include observations of the dentition, skull suture closure, and growth areas of the long bones. We will look at a few examples.

Formative Changes

Developmental features can be a useful means to determine age until growth stops, because the developmental sequence is predetermined and known. Because individuals vary in their rate of development, the results are presented in terms of a *range* of ages.

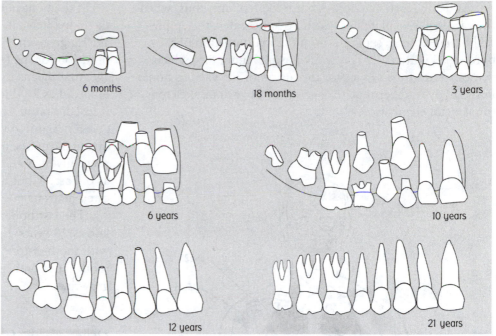

FIGURE 8.6 *Dental Eruption Chart*   Source: Brothwell, D. R. 1981. *Digging Up Bones*, 3d ed. New York: Cornell University Press, p. 64; Ubelaker, D. H. 1978. *Human Sekeletal Remains: Excavation, Analysis, Interpretation*. Chicago: Aldine; Whitehead, P. F., W. K. Sacco, and S. B. Hochgraf. 2005. *A Photographic Atlas for Physical Anthropology*. Englewood, CO: Morton, p. 73.

Age Determination Using the Teeth Several methods involving the dentition are useful. We will deal only with the third method listed here.

1. Examination of *growth ridges of tooth enamel,* which grows at a regular, measurable rate; growth lines form a new ridge each week and can be detected with scanning electron microscopy.

2. Patterns of *tooth root growth patterns* are instructive as well. Even after the full eruption of a tooth, the root grows for as long as 20 years. The tips of the roots remain sharp until about 25 years of age, then they become blunt as cementum is deposited around them. They can be observed by X-ray while in the alveoli (tooth sockets).

3. *Dental eruption* pattern is the most commonly used method. The sequence of appearance of deciduous (baby) and permanent dentition provides a useful tool for determining age (*e.g.,* Ubelaker, 1978). It is most useful through about age 15. Again, in adults, the dental formula is 2 1 2 3 for the upper and lower teeth. The dental formula for deciduous teeth is 2 1 0 2, after which the dentition will consist of a mix of permanent and deciduous teeth for a number of years.

In this lab you will look at some skulls to determine their age using an illustration of the eruption times of various teeth provided in Figure 8.6.

Epiphyseal Closure After birth, bone growth occurs in cartilaginous "plates," in which cartilage cells divide by mitosis for growth. Bone cells then enter via the bloodstream and are "injected" into the cartilage. Later, minerals are deposited

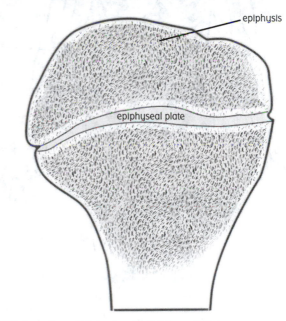

FIGURE 8.7 *Long-Bone Epiphysis with Epiphyseal Plate*

and the bone **ossifies.** Cartilaginous growth plates are evident while bone tissue is being deposited (see Figure 8.7). In the long bones these cartilaginous plates are located between the epiphyses and diaphysis. When the cartilage is replaced by bone, bone growth ends.

Different bones ossify, or "fuse," at different times, generally between the early teens and the mid-20s. Because males and females mature at different rates, a different scale is used for each sex (they are difficult to tell apart before puberty). On average, females mature 1 to 2 years before males (for example, 14–17 if male, 13–16 if female).

At death, cartilage decays but bone remains; thus, when the cartilaginous plate decays and disintegrates, the epiphyseal bone ends can separate from the main portion of the bone (see Figure 8.7). You will be using Figure 8.8, which demonstrates time ranges for the fusion of the various bones in the body to determine the age range of various skeletons (or skeletal elements).

If the bone end (the epiphysis) is fused to the diaphysis, the individual can't be younger than the minimum age of the age range given. For example, if the age range for occurrence of fusion for the femoral head is between 14 and 20 years of age, that means that the head can be fused as young as 14, or as old as 20 (but no older). If you find a femur whose head is fused, that individual is at least 14 years old (you cannot give a maximum value). If the epiphysis is not fused, the individual can't be any older than the maximum age of the age range given. So if the femoral head has not fused, it may be as old as 20, but not older. Use of another epiphyseal end often helps narrow the age range.

The last bone to fuse is the clavicle, which can occur as late as 28 years. Epiphyseal growth often is used together with tooth eruption information, but much of the significant tooth eruption begins much earlier than most epiphyseal growth.

Degenerative Changes

Upon reaching adulthood, wear and disease become increasingly common and observable. Observable changes include the following.

1. Bone microstructure changes such that the bony rings (plates) around the circumference of long bones are replaced by more osteons, which end up closer to the periphery of the bone. This can be studied by taking a thin section of long bone to observe under a microscope.

2. The ratio of two types of aspartic acid (an amino acid) in teeth changes, with one type increasing steadily during life and the other converting (racemizing) to yet another type. Measuring their ratio can yield an estimate of age.

3. The teeth wear down so the cusps become dull, and the enamel wears away to expose the dentin beneath.

4. Bone density decreases with increasing age. Common sites of bone loss (reabsorption) are the clavicle and the femur. The surface porosity of the sternal rib ends, resulting in a "jagged" appearance. This series of transformations can be used as an aging technique.

In this lab we will observe two types of degenerative change: cranial suture closure, and the appearance of the pubic symphyseal surface. Another important way to determine age in adults is attrition, or wear, of the teeth.

Cranial Sutures   As the cranium grows, the spaces making up the sutures close, and eventually they may even become obliterated. Although individuals vary greatly in the timing of suture closure, the method is at least useful to distinguish younger from older adults (Photo 8.5).

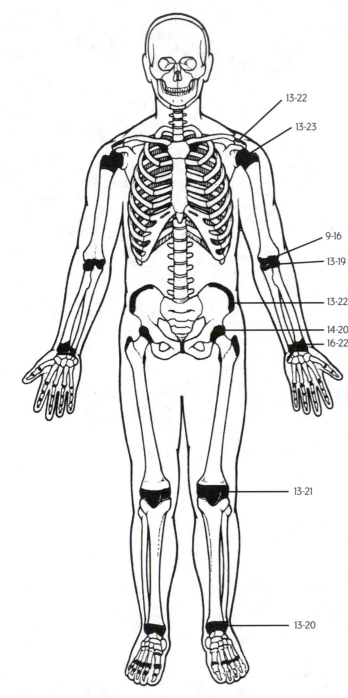

FIGURE 8.8 *Timing of Epiphyseal Union Throughout the Skeleton*

Source: McKern, T. W., and T. D. Stewart. 1957. *Skeletal age changes in young American males. U.S. Army Quartermaster Research and Development Command, Technical Report EP-45*; Buikstra, J. E., and Ubelaker, D. H. 1994. *Standards for Data Collection from Human Skeletal Remains.* Fayetteville: Arkansas Archeological Survey, p. 43; Whitehead, P. F., W. K. Sacco, and S. B. Hochgraf. 2005. *A Photographic Atlas for Physical Anthropology.* Englewood, CO: Morton, p. 157..

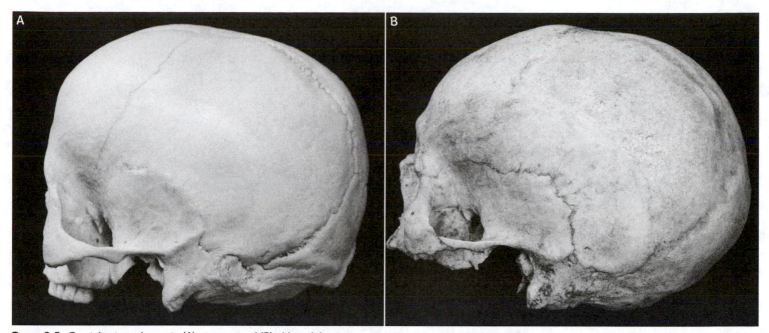

PHOTO 8.5 *Cranial suture closure in (A) younger and (B) older adults*

Pubic Symphysis Surface

The symphyseal "face" of the pubis changes with age, as the distinctive ridges wear down to less evenly placed bumps (Todd, 1920; Todd, 1921; Katz and Suchey, 1986). In females, bony projections form at the birth of each child in response to stresses on that area during childbirth. Figure 8.9 demonstrates a male pubic symphysis and the changes occurring from young adult to older adult.

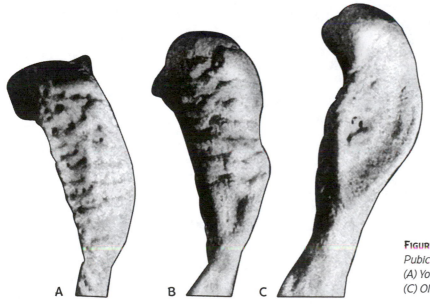

FIGURE 8.9 *Appearance of Male Pubic Symphysis Surface at (A) Younger, (B) Middle, and (C) Older Age*

LAB EXERCISE 8.3

NAME _____ SECTION _____ DATE _____

1. Use the dental eruption chart (Figure 8.6) to gauge the age of these two individuals or skulls in your lab. How old do you think these are?

Dentition A _____   Dentition B _____

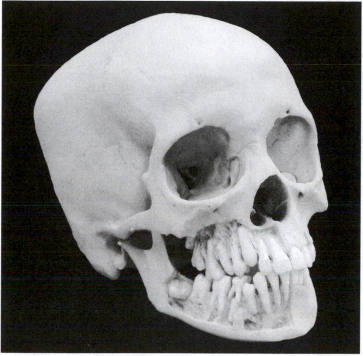

Dentition A

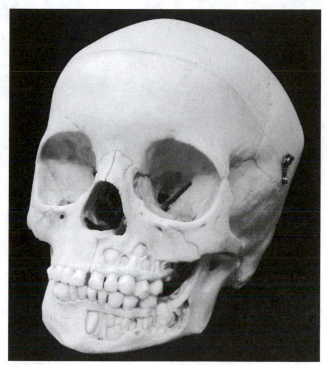

Dentition B

2. To determine the age range for specimens A, B, and C, refer to lab specimens or the illustrations below. Refer to Figure 8.8 for epiphyseal fusion times.

Individual	Epiphyseal End	Age Range
A	Crest of ilium	
B	Humerus	
C	Femur	

What if A and C are from the same individual?

Would that narrow the age range?

If so, how?

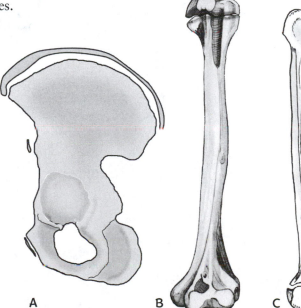

A   B   C

3. Compare the sutures on skulls A and B in the photos or in two skulls from your lab. Look at points 1, 2, and 3 on each, and using the chart below, score them from 0 to 3 according to the closure categories (from Buikstra and Ubelaker, 1994). Normally, one would use 17 such points to gauge suture closure, rather than only a few.

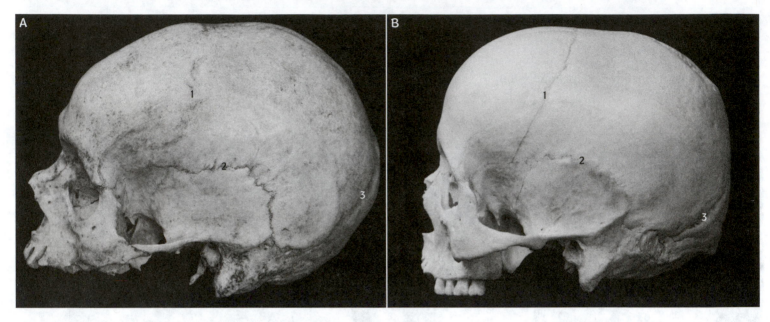

Skull Suture Area	Skull A	Skull B
1		
2		
3		
Average		

Open = 0
Minimal closure = 1
Significant closure = 2
Complete obliteration = 3

Which skull is from an older individual?

4. Look at the illustration (or your lab specimens) to compare the surface of the pubic symphysis of A and B. Which is older? What's the difference between them?

A

B

SELF-TEST 8.3

NAME _____ SECTION _____ DATE _____

1. What are the two main categories of age-related changes the skeleton experiences?

   a.

   b.

2. What are two specific techniques we can use to tell age within each of the categories referred to above? Explain each of them briefly.

   a.

   b.

3. In the following, each of numbers 1–4 represents an individual with bones in various stages of fusion. Using Figure 8.8 on epiphyseal union of bone ends, figure out the age range for each of the bones, then combine the information to estimate the individual's age. A sample is done for you below. Phrase your answer in terms such as "at least ___ years," or "not older than ___ years," or "between ___ and ___ years."

example:	head of humerus fused to diaphysis	at least 13 years
	head of femur unfused to diaphysis	not older than 20 years
	age of individual	between 13 and 20 years

   a. iliac crest unfused to body of ilium   _____

      head of humerus fused to diaphysis   _____

      age of individual   _____

   b. iliac crest fused to body of ilium   _____

      sternal end of clavicle unfused to shaft   _____

      age of individual   _____

c. ischial tuberosity fused to ischium   _____

distal end of tibia unfused to diaphysis   _____

age of individual   _____

Determining Ancestry

Although forensic anthropologists must determine ancestry—also referred to as **race**—as accurately as possible, this is difficult to do. Populations vary widely, with much overlap among various groups. Still, some extent of past reproductive isolation in groups has resulted in features that are found with much greater frequency in some skeletons than in others.

Terminology to describe these categories of people from various geographical regions varies. The three most widely used general categories in the United States are African, Asian, and European ancestry. The European category includes East Indians, and Asian and Native American skulls have many similarities because of their shared ancestry. Australian aboriginal peoples possess a number of distinctive skull features, but such skulls are rarely found in the U.S. Some studies have focused on mainly quantitative, or **osteometric,** traits (*e.g.,* Ayres et al., 1990), while others deal with qualitative, or **anthroposcopic,** traits (e.g., Hrdlička, 1920; Hinkes, 1990; Rhine, 1990). Both types of traits used together provide the greatest accuracy.

Quantitative (Osteometric) Features

Two examples of qualitative traits are cranial shape and nasal shape, which you learned earlier in this lab.

Cranial Index (Ubelaker, 1999; Byers, 2005)

up to 74.9 = narrow or long-headed (dolicocephalic)	more often African Origin
75.0–79.9 = average (mesocephalic)	more often European Origin
80.0–84.9 = round-headed (brachycephalic)	more often Asian Origin
over 85.0 = very round-headed (hyperbrachycephalic)	

Nasal Index (Bass, 1995; Ubelaker, 1999; Byers, 2005)

53 and up = wide-nosed (platyrhiny)	more often African Origin
48–52.9 = medium-nosed (mesorhiny)	more often Asian Origin
up to 47.9 = narrow-nosed (leptorhiny)	more often European Origin

Qualitative Features (Anthroposcopic Traits)

Table 8.3 lists just a small sample of the many traits that are considered when attempting to determine ancestry. Most of these can be observed in Photos 8.6–8.8, as indicated.

TABLE 8.3: Selected Traits for Determining Ancestry

	African Origin	European Origin	Asian Origin
Nasal root (superior nasal margin)	low, gently rounded	high, narrow, peaked	low, peaked
Lower border of nasal aperture	"guttered"	sharp sill, forms ridge	flatter, often indistinct
Orbital shape	rounded	tear-drop, sloping	squared
Malar tubercle	absent	usually absent	usually pronounced, "droopy"
Dental arcade shape	broad anteriorly; rectangular	narrow anteriorly; parabolic	broad posteriorly, rounded
Lingual side of incisors	flat	flat	shovel-shaped

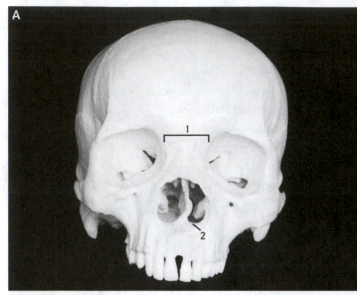

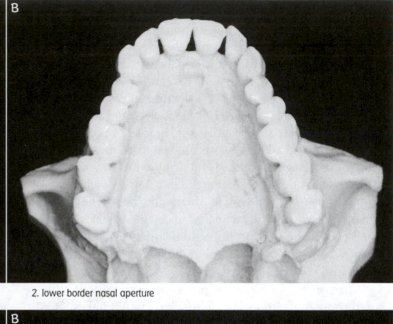

PHOTO 8.6 (A) African skull (B) and dental arcade   1. nasal root   2. lower border nasal aperture

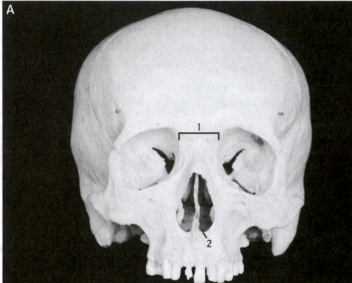

PHOTO 8.7 *(A) European skull and (B) dental arcade*   1. nasal root   2. lower border nasal aperture

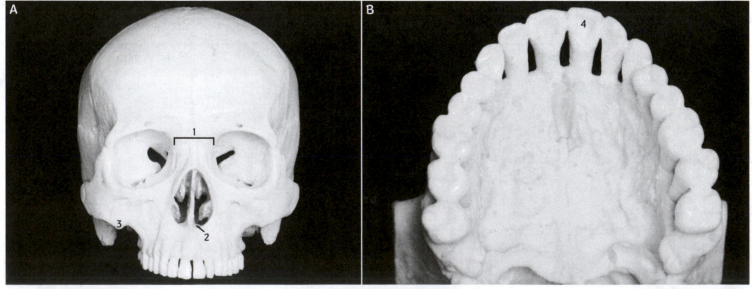

PHOTO 8.8 *(A) Asian skull and (B) dental arcade*   1. nasal root   2. lower border nasal aperture   3. malar tubercle   4. shovel-shaped incisors

How Tall Were They?

We can reconstruct height, or stature, by measuring the length of various long bones. Most accurate is the femur, especially used in combination with other long bones. An anthropometric tool called an *osteometric board* is used to take measurements on various bones (Figure 8.10). The bone measurements are plugged into a formula to give an estimate of total height, accompanied by some margin of error (Trotter, 1970). Because body proportions can differ depending upon sex and ancestry, different formulae are used for different populations (Krogman and Iscan, 1986). Each population, however, experiences more variation within than it does when compared to others.

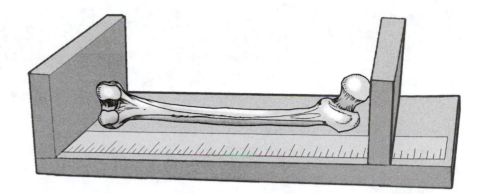

FIGURE 8.10 *Osteometric Board with Femur Being Measured*

LAB EXERCISE 8.4

NAME _____ SECTION _____ DATE _____

1. Measure two skulls from your lab to determine the cranial index (your instructor may have you use measurements taken earlier in this lab or provide you with measurements as a time-saving technique).

$$\text{Cranial index} = \frac{\text{Cranial breadth}}{\text{Cranial length}} \times 100$$

	Skull 1	Skull 2
Cranial breadth		
Cranial length		
Cranial index		

2. Use the sliding calipers to estimate the relative width of the nose on two skulls (don't perform these measurements on a classmate!) by measuring nasal height and nasal breadth. *Please remember to be careful; the bone is extremely delicate in this area.*

$$\text{Nasal index} = \frac{\text{Nasal breadth}}{\text{Nasal height}} \times 100$$

	Skull 1	Skull 2
Nasal breadth		
Nasal height		
Nasal index		

3. Observe the features, and compare them to the three skulls shown in the photos (or your lab collection skulls). Enter an *Af* if you think the form of a feature is more likely to be African, *As* for Asian, and *Eu* for European.

	Skull 1	Skull 2	Skull 3
Nasal root (superior nasal margin			
Lower border of nasal aperture			
Nasal aperture width			
Orbital shape			
Malar tubercle			
Dental arcade shape			
Lingual side of incisors			

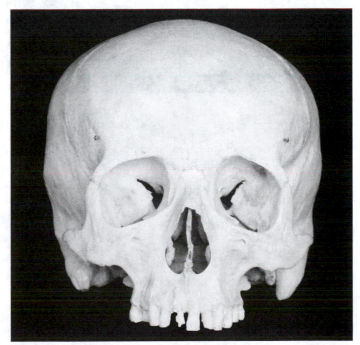

Skull 1

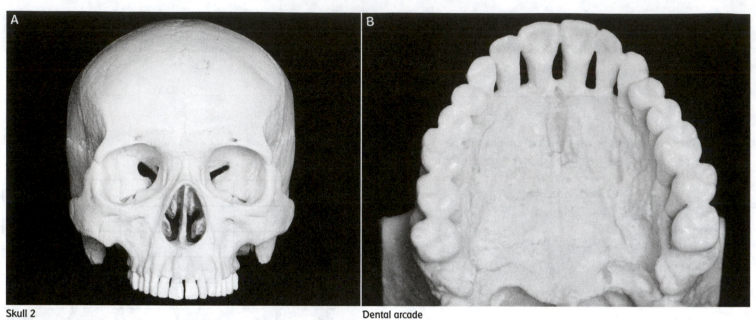

Skull 2   Dental arcade

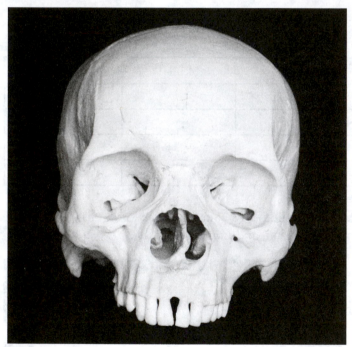

4. If you looked at the same skulls in your lab collection for questions 1 through 3, were your answers consistent for the quantitative together with the qualitative data? Keep in mind that your sample size is small, so inconsistencies between results of the various means of assessing ancestry are likely.

Skull 3

5. In the absence of an osteometric board, you can improvise with a tape measure taped to a table. Measure the maximum length of a femur (in cm), and use the following formula (this one happens to be for Asian males) to reconstruct stature.

femur length: _____

     formula (Trotter, 1970):

     femur (2.15) + 72.57   [femur length × 2.15 + 72.57]

     stature _____ (cm)

     _____ (inches: 2.54 cm = 1 inch)

SELF-TEST 8.4

NAME _____ SECTION _____ DATE _____

1. What are two qualitative and two quantitative methods to determine ancestry?

2. Why is ancestry determination so difficult?

3. If you find a decayed skeleton with only one complete long bone remaining intact and you want to reconstruct the stature of this individual, what steps would you take?

Incidentally, you find your skeleton in Thailand, the bone is a femur, and it measures 52.8 cm long. The diameter of the femoral head falls into the male range.

9. Comparative Osteology and Functional Complexes

"Have you ever wondered...?"

✋ How do scientists know how an individual of an extinct species moved around or what it ate?

OBJECTIVES

- Understand the importance of the comparative perspective
- Understand how form–function relationships work
- Become familiar with form–function relationships in terms of specific dental complexes and locomotor complexes
- Learn to interpret main functional types of teeth for each dietary type
- Recognize various forms of the postcranial skeleton to be able to interpret locomotor behavior

We can look to the past to inform us about present evolutionary relationships and, conversely, study the present to make inferences about the past. We'll look at some **functional complexes** in terms of what can be learned from them. A functional complex will reflect a **form–function** relationship. For example, a **prehensile** tail has certain bony and muscular features (its form) and is directly associated with the grasping abilities (the function) that its form allows. By observing a specific **form** of a feature, together with the manner in which it is used, we can make inferences about its functional significance and possibly about the selective pressures that led to its evolution.

Evidence from the Teeth

The first vertebrates had no teeth, nor jaws to house them. These were the **Agnathans** (G *a*: without; *gnath*: jaws). It is thought that the first vertebrate teeth evolved from fish scales. We've come a long way since then! Because we're mammals, we share with other mammals the feature of differentiated, or **heterodont**, teeth. Mammals have incisors, canines, premolars, and molars (see Figure 9.1B). By contrast, the jaws of reptiles and other nonmammalian vertebrates (illustrated by the crocodile in Figure 9.1A), are populated by one basic form of tooth.

The form of teeth reflects their function in the diet of a species over time. The diet influences the evolution of tooth form and even jaw form. Teeth are by far the most commonly found body part in the fossil record! The teeth are covered with enamel, a hard, highly mineralized substance that often allows them to escape rapid decay. Further, teeth are small enough to escape the effects

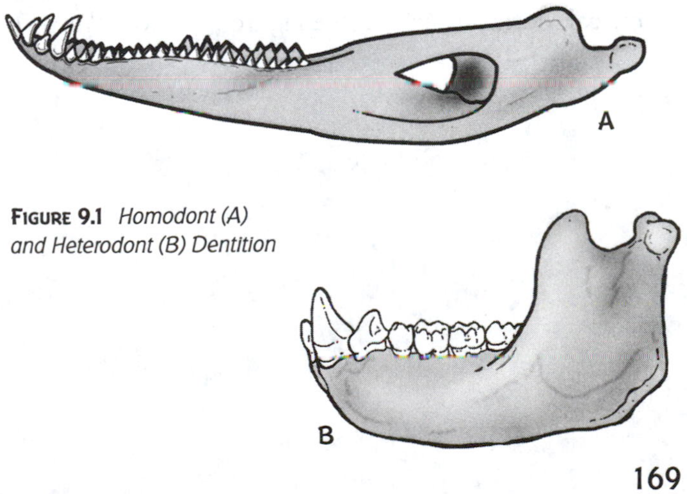

FIGURE 9.1 *Homodont (A) and Heterodont (B) Dentition*

of scavenging, by simply falling to the ground and soon becoming embedded in the sediment and left there as a permanent record of an organism's existence.

The teeth hide many "stories"—if you know how to read them. By studying only a few teeth of an individual, we might be able to learn something about their:

✋ *Age*

- Tooth eruption (poking through the gums)
- Attrition (tooth wear)

✋ *Sex*: The size of teeth and jaws (especially canine tooth size) can differ in males and females.

✋ *Health*: Dental caries and abscesses reflect dental health and general nutrition.

✋ *Mating systems*: The evolution of canine dimorphism may be influenced partly by the type of mating system.

✋ *Behavioral patterns*: The use of specific body parts causes characteristic wear patterns.

✋ *Evolutionary relationships*: Comparative anatomy can indicate an organism's place in the biological classification system.

✋ *Diet*: Tooth morphology is an indication of the diet of extinct species.

In this lab and subsequent ones, we will focus on the last two items on this list. Learning about teeth can establish the *evolutionary relationships* of modern forms based on similarities to extinct ones; and by identifying form/function relationships in modern species, we can make inferences about *diets* of extinct species. We'll review a bit of dental anatomy.

✋ What are the four *types of teeth*, from the front to the back of the tooth row?

✋ Review the anatomical directions for teeth. Draw a *dental arcade*, label anatomical directions: mesial, distal, lingual, buccal, occlusal surface (see Figure 7.7 and *Atlas* p. 22).

✋ Review the *dental formula* concept. Our dental formula, which we share with Old World monkeys and apes (as members of the Infraorder Catarrhini) is $\frac{2}{2}$ $\frac{1}{1}$ $\frac{2}{2}$ $\frac{3}{3}$.

✋ Review *dental terminology*, using humans as an example. I1 and I2 are the central and lateral incisor, and C1 is the canine. P3 and P4 are the third and fourth premolars (P1 and P2 were lost over evolutionary time). M1, M2, and M3 are the first through third molars.

- top versus bottom: I^1, I^2 – I_1, I_2
- left versus right: LM_1 (left lower first molar)
- deciduous versus permanent: d, then lower case tooth (dm: deciduous molar)
- Rdi^2 (right deciduous second/lateral incisor)

On the molars, a great deal of attention is directed to the form of the **occlusal surface** (where the upper and lower teeth oppose each other). All bumps, grooves, valleys, and other defining features have names. The primary features on the molars are the bumps, or cusps (*Atlas* p. 35, Figure 3.9). Mammalian molar teeth evolved from a series of triangles, which pointed toward the tongue in the uppers and away from the tongue in the lowers (Fleagle, 1999).

The evolution of cusp size, form, and position on the tooth can be tracked through time. Primates are *generalized* in that we retain that same basic pattern of distinctive cusps, unlike cows or deer, whose molars have undergone considerable change in adapting to a grazing or browsing diet, and whose cusps are no longer distinguishable from one another.

Tooth Function

Teeth are considered accessory organs to the digestive system, because they assist in beginning the digestive process. Functions of the **anterior dentition** (incisors and canines) differ from those of the **posterior dentition** (premolars and molars). The anterior dentition is responsible for **ingestion**, the taking in of food. The posterior dentition has the task of physically processing food, called **mechanical digestion**. In this part of the process, digestive enzymes separate the food into small pieces for easier breakdown. The form of the posterior dentition (also called cheek teeth) more directly reflects dietary adaptations than does the anterior dentition.

For many mammalian species, the anterior dentition has social functions in addition to dietary ones. In some primates, the incisor form has evolved for a grooming function, and large canines presumably were selected because of the advantage they provide in threat displays and fighting, also apparent in some nonprimates such as the walrus.

The posterior dentition breaks down food mechanically in one of four main ways, depending upon cusp form, as illustrated in the photos:

1. *Puncture-crushing/piercing*: Small, sharp, pointy cusps break up hard insect exoskeletons (Photo 9.1).

2. *Shearing:* High cusps and the crests that link them cut through leafy vegetation (Photo 9.2).

3. *Crushing, grinding:* Low, rounded cusps occlude with low basins to masticate a variety of foods; sometimes useful for hard or slippery foods such as nuts and fruits (Photo 9.3).

4. *Tearing:* Large, pointy cusps with long, sharp edges cut foods into smaller bits without excessive preparation before swallowing; used particularly for meat-eating (Photo 9.4).

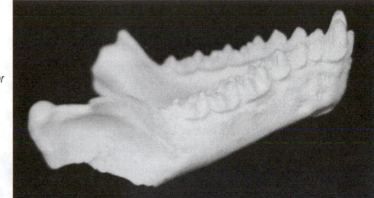

PHOTO 9.1 *Dentition for puncture-crushing/piercing*

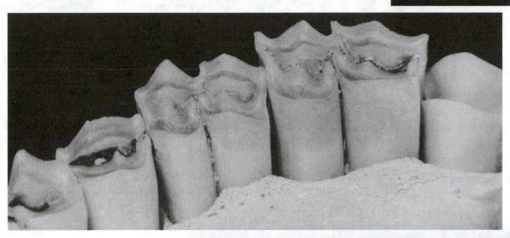

PHOTO 9.2 *Dentition for shearing*

PHOTO 9.3 *Dentition for crushing and grinding*

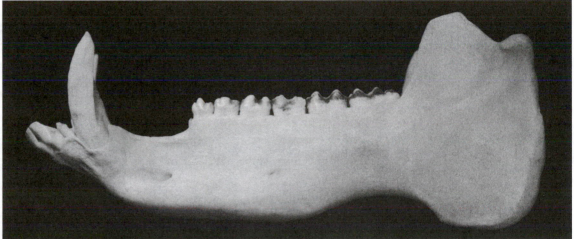

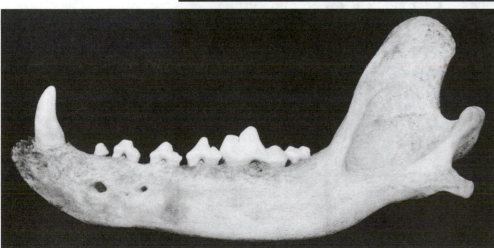

PHOTO 9.4 *Dentition for tearing*

Tooth Form

Molars can be classified in various ways, and the number of terms that refer to types and parts of the teeth is overwhelming. We will mention only several of the main forms. One of the first subcategories to consider is whether the molar teeth of a species are *high-crowned* or *low-crowned*.

High-Crowned Teeth   If a tooth sticks up far above the gumline, it is high-crowned, or *hypsodont* (G *hypso*: high; *dont*: tooth). These teeth are present in herbivores such as deer, cows, and horses. In some species (particularly rodents), teeth continue to grow as they are worn down by abrasive foods, and enamel ridges makes grinding more efficient.

Two types of hypsodont molars are *lophodont* (G *loph*: crest) and *selenodont* (G *selen*: moon) (Photo 9.5). Lophodont teeth have elongated ridges (lophs) that connect the cusps. Selenodont teeth (such as that in deer and cows) have cusps that have been elongated in an anterior–posterior direction to increase cutting surfaces. Old World monkeys possess *bilophodont* (two-crested) molars, in which two crests connect the pairs of cusps in a medio-lateral direction (Photo 9.6).

Low-Crowned Teeth   If a molar tooth is relatively low-crowned, it is described as *brachydont* (G *brachy*: short). One important type of brachydont tooth is that exhibited by many species of mammal that eat a variety of foods (hard, soft, and everything in between). They may have square-ish shaped molars (quadrate), with low, rounded cusps. These teeth, termed *bunodont* (G *bun*: hill, mound), are found in humans (and many other primates), bears, and pigs (Photo 9.7).

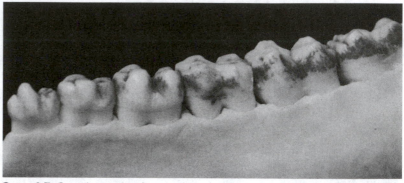

Photo 9.7   *Bunodont molars (peccary)*

Some members of the Order Carnivora (not bears, but dogs and cats) have a last upper premolar and first lower molar that is large and blade-like. These are the *carnassial* (L *carn*: flesh) teeth, used for slicing and chopping (Photo 9.8).

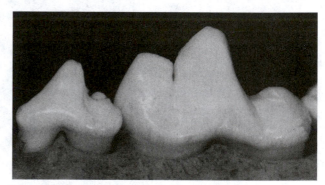

Photo 9.8   *Carnassial teeth (dog).*

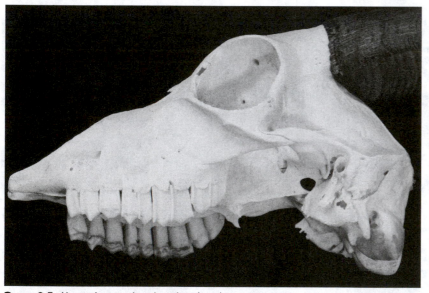

Photo 9.5   *Hypsodont teeth: selenodont (goat)*

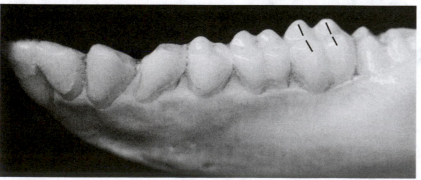

Photo 9.6   *Bilophodont molars (vervet monkey)*

Skull Form

Keep in mind that the bony development of the skull depends on the size and shape of chewing muscles and the magnitude and direction of force generated in the skull while chewing.

- ✋ If you touch the side of your head in the region of your temple and clench and unclench your teeth, you'll feel the action of the temporalis muscle.

- ✋ The next time you have the opportunity to pet a large dog, feel the crown of its head (the top, toward the back). You may feel a bony bump. That is a sagittal crest, the site of attachment for the temporalis muscle.

LAB EXERCISE 9.1

NAME _____ SECTION _____ DATE _____

1. Review the main four molar tooth functions and the tooth types. Then take a look at the dentitions of various mammalian species in your lab, or from a combination of your specimens and these photos. For each, list the type of mechanical breakdown (puncture–crushing, shearing, etc.) presumably undertaken by the molars, as well as its assumed diet. Use the chart on the following page.

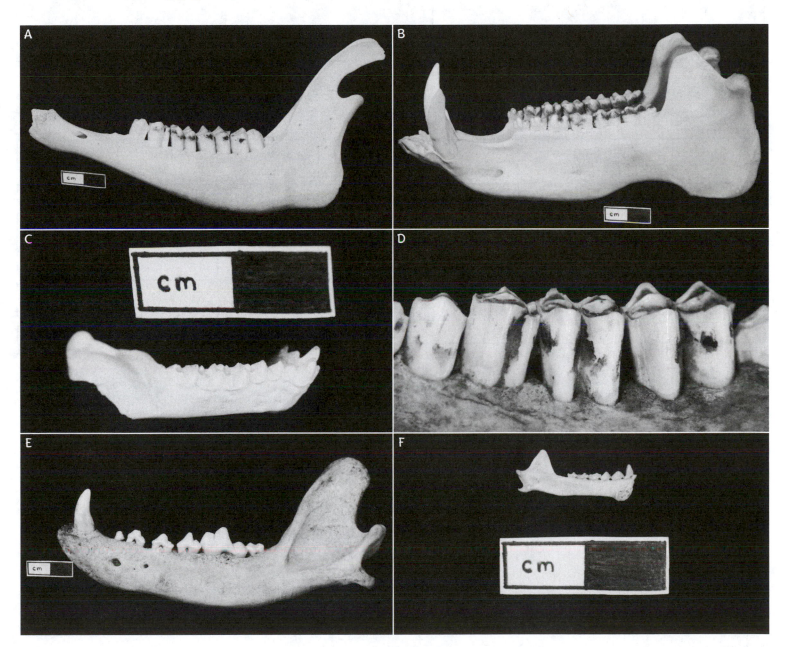

Specimen	Mechanical function	Presumed diet	Species (optional)
A			
B			
C			
D			
E			
F			

2. Experiment to see which foods require processing with which teeth. Try each food type, and fill out the table regarding tooth use and form.

	Sunflower seeds	Carrots	Beef jerky	Spinach or lettuce	Whole apple	*Sunflower seed in shell
Use of anterior dentition? (yes/no)						
Use of posterior dentition? (yes/no)						
Best kind of posterior teeth to break down food						

*This approximates the dentition needed to effectively break down the exoskeleton of a large insect, such as a cockroach or a beetle.

Evidence from the Skeleton

Functional complexes occur throughout the body wherever form/function relationships have developed over time. For example, by looking at the bony human shoulder joint (e.g., the humeral head, how it articulates with the glenoid fossa of the scapula), we can see the potential range of motion. By applying laws of biomechanics, we know that the size and location of muscle attachment sites on bone indicate the size and orientation of muscles, and we can extrapolate the degree of speed or strength generated at that point.

We study postcranial remains for much the same reason as we study dental remains. Once we are familiar with form–function relationships in modern species, we can make inferences about fossils, including our extinct relatives. Just as teeth and diet are directly related, so are postcranial morphology (form) and **positional behavior— posture** and **locomotion**. Within each individual's body, the range of motion at every joint is limited by the morphology of the bone ends contributing to the joint, and the surrounding ligaments and muscle attachments. Because individual variation is found within species, some individuals will have a morphology that is better suited than others to perform a specific motion. The most efficient forms for certain movements are selected by natural selection over time.

Thus, positional behavior is influenced by morphology, as well as by body size and use of substrates. Different forms of features will be selected for in **arboreal** species than in **terrestrial** species, because the challenges of arboreality and terrestriality are different.

The vast majority of primates are quadrupeds —using all four limbs in locomotion. Although many primates are arboreal, some species are terrestrially adapted—spending most of their time on the ground. Two main differences between arboreal and terrestrial quadrupedal primates are in *joint form* and *body segment ratios*.

The joints in arboreal species are mobile, with fewer bony restrictions and more rounded joint surfaces than terrestrial species. Terrestrially adapted species are likely to have more stable joints, and their range of motion is limited by the surrounding bony restrictions. For example, parts of a terrestrial baboon's femur are more similar to a deer's femur than that of a spider monkey! This is an example of convergent evolution, in which a similar form evolves as a result of similar environmental pressures to fulfill a similar function.

In arboreal species, the **center of gravity** tends to be lower, closer to the **base of support.** Arboreal species typically have shorter limbs relative to their trunk, which lowers their body (and center of gravity) and brings it closer to the substrate (see Figure 9.2). Because terrestrial animals do not

have to worry about falling far, these species tend to have longer limbs relative to their trunk, which enhances speed.

The forelimbs and hindlimbs of quadrupeds are approximately equal in length. This is more true for terrestrial quadrupeds than arboreal ones, whose legs (hindlimbs) often are longer, enabling them to leap farther. The relative length of forelimbs and hindlimbs reflects their use. Primates with longer arms have a *forelimb-dominated* mode of locomotion, and longer legs indicate *hindlimb-dominated* locomotion (see Figure 9.3).

In this part of the lab, you will compare various bones to determine functional differences between species. You will be paying particular attention to the articular surface area of a joint. Examples of features to look for on some selected bones are:

🖐 *Femur*: A rounded, globular femoral head with a low-set greater trochanter indicates more mobility and thus arboreality; a less rounded femoral head whose articular (smooth) surface area extends onto the femoral neck, and a greater trochanter that extends considerably higher than the head, act to limit mobility and be more indicative of a terrestrial locomotor mode (Figure 9.4).

🖐 *Humerus*: Similar to the femur, a rounded, globular humeral head, with smaller, lower-set tuberosities, is associated with the greater mobility required for arboreal

FIGURE 9.2 *(A) Arboreal and (B) Terrestrial Primates*

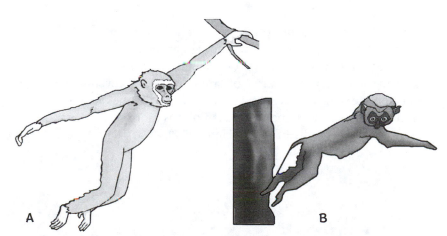

FIGURE 9.3 *Forelimb-dominated (A) and Hindlimb-dominated (B) Locomotion*

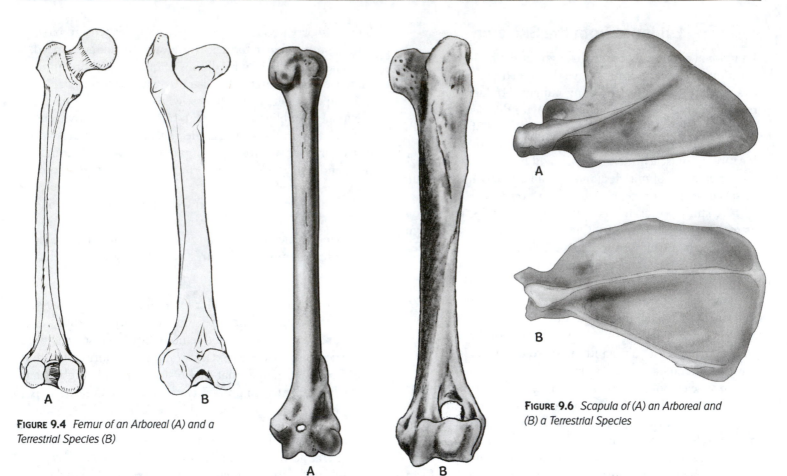

Figure 9.4 *Femur of an Arboreal (A) and a Terrestrial Species (B)*

Figure 9.5 *Humerus of (A) an Arboreal and (B) a Terrestrial Species*

Figure 9.6 *Scapula of (A) an Arboreal and (B) a Terrestrial Species*

Figure 9.7 *Ulna of (A) an Arboreal and (B) a Terrestrial Species*

species; a humeral head that is less rounded and more ovoid, with large, bulky tuberosities, is more likely to be terrestrially adapted (Figure 9.5).

✋ *Scapula:* A broader scapula (like that of a human) and a more dorsal placement is typically associated with a more mobile shoulder joint; a long, narrow scapula that is placed laterally on the thorax functionally lengthens the forelimb for a greater stride length, and indicates terrestriality (Figure 9.6).

✋ *Ulna:* The size of the olecranon process influences the degree of extension an arm can undergo at the elbow. A low olecranon process allows for full elbow extension and, thus, greater mobility. A large olecranon process prevents full elbow extension because it will not fit inside the olecranon fossa of the humerus; such a joint is more stable and more terrestrially adapted (Figure 9.7).

LAB EXERCISE 9.2

NAME _____ SECTION _____ DATE _____

In this exercise you will identify four types of bone (homologous bones) from a few different species and make inferences about the locomotion of each depending upon the morphology of the bone ends. Use the photos in Appendix C in addition to bones from your lab collection. Your instructor may provide some human bones for comparison, and assistance in identifying which bone is of what type.

1. Using ourselves as an example, we first will learn about some general features of locomotion. For this brief "exercise," stand up.

    a. Where is your base of support?

    b. How can you make the base of support wider?

    c. How is your base of support different from that of a gorilla?

    d. Based on our limb-length ratios, our locomotion is _____- dominated.

2. From Appendix C, group the same types of bones together by cutting out the photos and physically putting them together. If available, use your real bone specimens. Which bones did you group together?

    Specimen   Bone

    ___ ___ ___   _____

    ___ ___ ___   _____

    ___ ___ ___   _____

    ___ ___ ___   _____

3. Now you will make some inferences about function for some of these bones. By examining the joint surface and surrounding area, you will determine how mobile or stable a joint is and possibly make inferences about movements that could have taken place at that joint.

Specimen	Emphasis on mobility or stability?	Likely to be terrestrially or arboreally adapted?	Comments
A			
B	N/A		
C			
D			
E			
F	N/A		
I			
L			

S E L F - T E S T 9 . 1

NAME _____ SECTION _____ DATE _____

1. What type of molars do you have, according to the functional categories discussed in this lab?

2. What is your dental formula?

3. How do anterior and posterior dentition differ functionally?

4. What are the four main functional types of posterior dentitions in mammals?

5. Why should we study form–function relationships in living species?

6. Which has a larger base of support, a penguin or a mouse?

7. What is a functional complex?

8. What are the two categories of positional behavior?

   a.

   b.

9. What are some primary differences in articular surface area between arboreally and terrestrially adapted mammal species?

10. What are some primary differences in limb segment ratios between arboreally and terrestrially adapted primates?

10. Biological Classification and the Living Primates

"Have you ever wondered...?"

✋ What is the difference between a monkey and an ape?

OBJECTIVES

- Become familiar with the basis for biological classification
- Understand the concept of homology and its use in classifying living organisms
- Know the characteristics of the primate order
- Distinguish characteristics of the major groups and subgroups of primates
- Learn to identify primate groups based on skeletal features

All living things are related. Some groups share a more recent common ancestry than others, and the farther back in time the common ancestor for two groups goes, the fewer features the descendants will share with each other. Fleas are in the Kingdom Animalia, along with bears—and humans. Animals comprise a diverse group. This will become clear as you think about some characteristics humans share with fleas and some characteristics we share with bears.

Establishing Evolutionary Relationships

Our shared ancestry with the flea can be traced far back in time, before humans, bears, or even mammals or vertebrates existed. Our shared ancestor is found early in the Paleozoic Era, which began about 600 million years ago. Many types of invertebrates existed at that time, but this was long before the first vertebrate appeared.

Over time, vertebrates evolved and diversified into various groups. One of the groups evolved into a creature with live-bearing young, fur, relatively large brain, teeth specialized for different functions, and a constant internal body temperature. These mammals originated within the Mesozoic Era, more than 200 million years ago. Mammals diversified, giving rise to the groups that included the taxonomic Order Carnivora, of which bears are a member, and the Order Primates, the order in which humans are a member.

Thus, the more distant shared ancestry of the human and the flea resulted in few shared features, but the more recent common ancestry of the bear and the human resulted in more shared features, which also are shared with many other mammalian species. The features that groups share as a result of common ancestry are called **homologous features**, or **homologies**. Figure 10.1 illustrates some of the species within the Kingdom Animalia, with a homologous feature (the humerus) illustrated.

The group called the vertebrates contains a bony internal skeleton. It forms the **Subphylum Vertebrata**. Because similar characteristics are used to group (classify) organisms, we have to know how the characteristics that form the basis for our classifications arose in the first place. Similarities between groups of organisms can arise in two primary ways, analogies and homologies.

Analogies

The fish and the dolphin in Figure 10.1 are superficially similar in body form, reflecting adaptations to similar conditions rather than descent from a common ancestor possessing

FIGURE 10.1 *Various Members of the Kingdom Animalia*

marsupial), and aquatic adaptations of seals and sea lions, each of which evolved separately from land-adapted mammals.

Homologies

Alternatively, the features of the two groups may be similar because their common ancestor had the feature and both descendant groups inherited it. As mentioned above, a feature deriving from a common ancestor is termed a **homology**. For example, dogs and bears both have a humerus because they share a common ancestor (some early carnivore) that had a humerus. Cats and crocodiles both have femurs because they share a common ancestor (some early reptile of the Mesozoic Era) that had a femur. The lack of a tail in humans and in apes is another feature in the common ancestry of these groups. *Homologous features are useful for classification, because they reflect evolutionary relationships.*

that body form. This is an example of an **analogy**, in which a feature evolves independently in different groups as a result of similar evolutionary pressures resulting in similar adaptations. Dolphins evolved from land mammals but converged upon a fish body form as a result of their gradually adapting to an aquatic environment. **Convergent evolution** caused analogous features to appear in fish and dolphins, which share a distant ancestry.

The bird's wing and the bat's wing provide another good example of an analogous character that arose independently in the two groups. Other examples of analogies are the body form of a rabbit and that of a bandicoot (an Australian

Primitive Features Versus Derived Features

Two other concepts important in understanding evolutionary relationships are **primitive features** and **derived features**. A vertebral column is a primitive feature for vertebrates; the common ancestor of vertebrates had a vertebral column. Within the vertebrate group are the mammals, those features shared by and unique to mammals among the vertebrates are termed derived features. Derived features are distinct and changed from those of the common ancestor. For example, only primates have opposable thumbs, so this is a derived feature shared only by other primates, not with all mammals.

LAB EXERCISE 10.1

NAME _____ SECTION _____ DATE _____

Of the array of varied creatures within the Kingdom Animalia, some fly, some crawl, some leap, and some swim. This exercise asks you to place a number of them into taxonomic groups and decide which groups are related most closely to which other groups.

1. Start with a small sample to work with first, consisting of: fish, horse, frog, dolphin, butterfly, pigeon, dog, and bat. You could dissect them to see the underlying structures, or refer to Figure 10.1 for the illustrations of various animals in the Kingdom Animalia, with part of the forelimb visible for comparison.

2. What separation would you make first? Which has an ancestry that is the most distant from the others?

   _____. Once that creature is separated from the others, all seven of the other species stand together in a group. What is an important feature common to all seven?

3. Of those seven remaining animals, now figure out which ones are mammals. Which of the following characteristics would help you decide, and why?

   fur   vertebral column

   limbs   mammary glands

   opposable thumbs   homeothermy (warm-blooded)

4. Is the bird and bat humerus an example of analogy or homology? (Check with your instructor on this one!)

Biological Classification

Classifications are information-retrieval systems that order objects into groups on the basis of similarities. These hierarchical systems consist of sets with subsets, each lower set sharing an increasing number of characteristics. Biological classification specifically orders living organisms into groups and subgroups based on their evolutionary relationships.

John Ray (British), **Casper Bauhin** (Swiss), and **Carl Linnaeus** (Swedish) each devised a biological classification system independently. Although Ray and Bauhin lived and worked in an earlier time than Linnaeus did, the latter's work alone is what is remembered. The system of **binomial nomenclature** uses two names, the **genus** and the **species**. For example, in *Australopithecus africanus*, *Australopithecus* is the genus and *africanus*, the most basic unit, is the species.

The **binomen** is a combination of names for genus and species that is unique and universal. Latin, which is no longer the primary language of any country, enables scientists worldwide to communicate without favoring one language over another. Although common names differ among countries, scientific names are the same everywhere. For example, dog is *perro* in Argentina and Mexico, *chien* in Quebec and France, but *Canis familiaris* is the term used by scientists all over the world.

The biological classification hierarchy for the orangutan looks like this:

Kingdom	Animalia
Phylum	Chordata
Subphylum	Vertebrata
Class	Mammalia (mammals—not birds, reptiles)
Order	Primates (prosimians, monkeys, apes)
Family	Pongidae (ape family)
Genus	*Pongo*
Species	*Pongo pygmaeus*

Alternative Classification Schemes

The science of naming organisms is called **taxonomy**. A **taxon** (*pl:* **taxa**) is a taxonomic group. At higher levels of classification, members of a taxon share fewer characteristics and a common ancestor farther back in time. At lower levels, members of a taxon share increasing numbers of characteristics and a more recent common ancestor. Groups of species are classified on the basis of their evolutionary relationships. Alternative ways of classifying organisms are based on two facets of such relationships:

1. Recency of divergence—how recently two groups shared a common ancestor

2. To what extent the groups diverged—how much change has occurred in each group in the time since they shared a common ancestor

Figure 10.2 presents illustrations of three apes and a human. Through biochemical and fossil evidence, we know that orangutans diverged from the evolutionary line leading to African apes (chimpanzees and gorillas) and humans more than 15 million years ago. Therefore, African apes and humans share a more recent common ancestor with one another and are more closely related to each other than any of the three are to the orangutan. Humans, however, have diverged much more since the time of the common ancestor. We differ more from the common ancestor in appearance and (presumably!) in behavior than any of the other great apes.

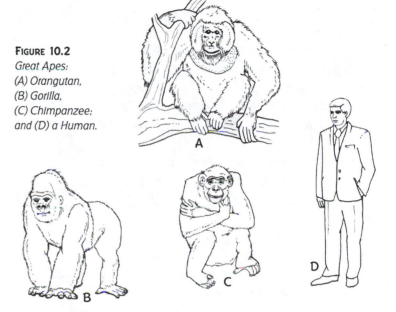

FIGURE 10.2
Great Apes:
(A) Orangutan,
(B) Gorilla,
(C) Chimpanzee;
and (D) a Human.

The more traditional classification, based upon the school of thought called **evolutionary taxonomy,** would place humans apart from all of the great apes because we have diverged more than the other apes since our split from the common ancestor. The newer (now more common) school of thought is **cladistics,** which emphasizes the actual timeframe of evolutionary divergence.

The Order Primates

The primates constitute an order of mammals. Examples of other orders within the Class Mammalia are

✋ Rodentia (rodents)

✋ Chiroptera (bats)

✋ Artiodactyla and Perissodactyla (the two hoofed mammal orders).

It is thought that the Order **Primates** originated from insectivore-like (shrew/hedgehog order) stock approximately

65 million years ago. The evolution of primates is discussed further in Chapter 12.

Homologous skeletal features can be used to classify the primates in terms of their place in the Class Mammalia, and their subgroupings within the primate order. Although we now can also use a number of genetics techniques for classification, in this lab we will cover skeletal features that are useful for grouping the primates. The following is a list of primate characteristics, or evolutionary trends of the order. Figure 10.3 illustrates some of these features that serve to distinguish *most* primates from *most* other mammalian orders. Although some other groups possess some of these features, primates have all or most of these as a *suite* of characteristics.

*1. Unique ear region
 — petrosal bulla (*Atlas*, p. 9, Figure 1.15)

*2. Retention of unspecialized limb skeleton
 — retention of five fingers and five toes and retention of clavicle; this is unlike hoofed mammals, for example, which have lost most of their digits and have no clavicle

*3. Nails (rather than claws) on digits; tactile pads

*4. Grasping hind feet with opposable first toes; grasping hands; some with opposable thumb

*5. Increased emphasis on vision:
 — forward-facing eyes allowing for better depth perception
 — expanded occipital and temporal lobes (visual centers)
 — color vision (in most primates)

*6. Complete ring of bone around orbit: postorbital bar

*7. Enlarged brain relative to body size; complex, more elaborate neocortex

---

* Features that are especially important because they also can be observed in the fossil record.

*8. Decreased emphasis on olfaction:
 — shortened snout
 — small olfactory bulbs

*9. Decrease in number of teeth; primitive cusp pattern preserved

10. Longer fetal nourishment, intrauterine development, prolonged stages of lifespan

11. Longer period of infant dependency and parental care

12. Most are gregarious (live in social groups) with well-developed communication systems

Distribution, Habitat, Diet

Extant (living) primates are distributed throughout much of the tropics and subtropics, although their numbers are drastically declining, mostly a result of habitat encroachment. They occur in tropical Africa, India, and Southeast Asia, as well as South and Central America (and a few even in North America, in Mexico)—see Figure 10.4. The primate inhabitants of Madagascar, besides the relatively recent addition of humans, are a diverse group that includes all lemur-like forms.

Primates inhabit a variety of habitats, from wet rainforest to quite dry savanna. As an order, primates are highly adaptable and sometimes coexist successfully with humans. Most primates eat a basically vegetarian diet, but they may specialize in certain classes of foods. These dietary types are:

✋ *folivory* (leaf-eating)
✋ *frugivory* (fruit-eating)
✋ *gramnivory* (seed-eating)
✋ *gummivory* (gum-eating)

Some are primarily *insectivorous*. Many are *omnivorous* and eat a variety of plant and animal matter. As you saw in Chapter 9, dietary adaptations are reflected in the dentition.

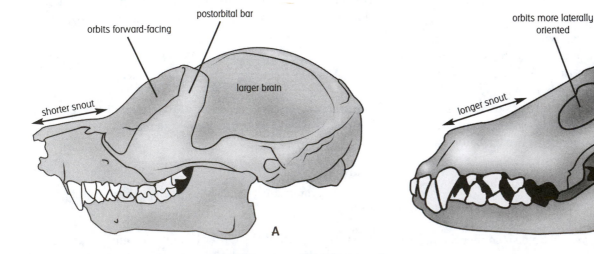

FIGURE 10.3 *Some Comparative Features of (A) Primate and (B) Nonprimate*

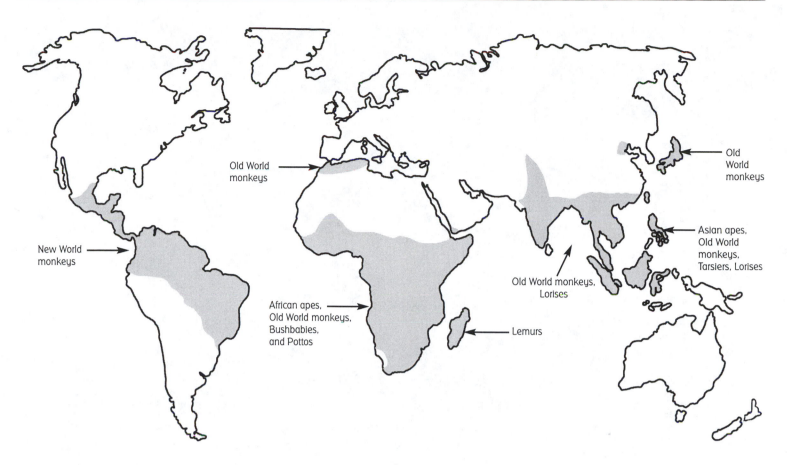

FIGURE 10.4 *Primate Distribution*

LAB EXERCISE 10.2

NAME _____ SECTION _____ DATE _____

In examining a number of mammal skeletons—for example, bear, lion, opossum, wolf, raccoon, pig, and elephant, in addition to several primate species—what characteristics would you use to decide whether a skeleton is a primate or not?

1. Circle the characteristics you would use.

fur   opposable thumbs

forward-facing eyes   relatively small olfactory bulbs

relatively large brain   mammary glands

2. For the characteristics you did not circle, why didn't you think they would be useful to differentiate primates from nonprimates?

3. Fill out the chart below, using the photos on the next page or skulls in your lab collection.

	Dog	Monkey
Postorbital bar?		
Cranium size relative to body size (or face)		
Emphasis on vision versus olfaction		
Type of teeth		
*Opposable first toes or thumbs?		
*Nails or claws?		
*Not observable from the photo		

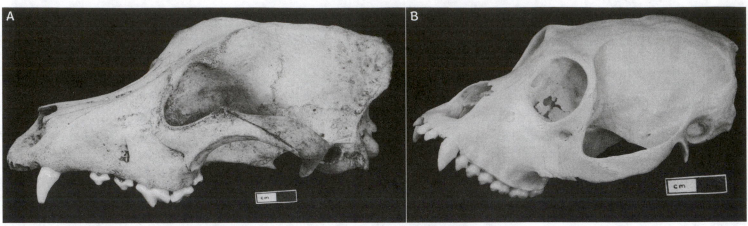

Dog skull   Monkey skull

4. Look at the photos below or your lab specimens and *note the form* of the listed features in the chart below. You later will use your answers to place the specimens into suborders (Strepsirhini and Haplorhini).

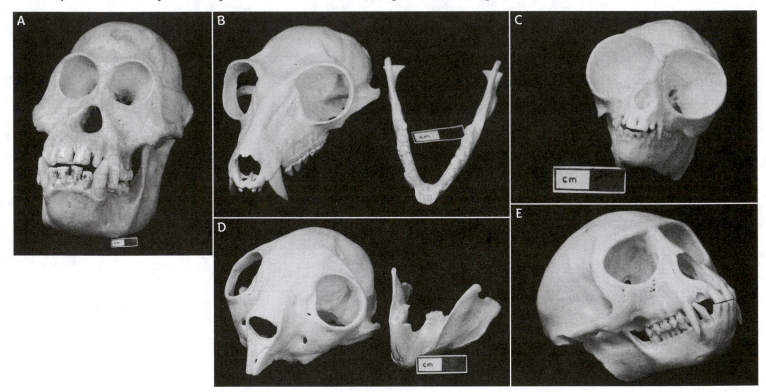

Specimen	Fused mandibular symphysis? (Is the mandible one bone or two)	Cranium size relative to face	Fully enclosed orbit?	Toothcomb? (Lower incisors jut forward)
A				
B				
C				
D				
E				

Primate Classification

The primates can be divided into two suborders, the **Strepsirhini** and the **Haplorhini,** named for the form of their nose. Strepsirhini refers to the "turned nose" (comma-shaped nostrils), as contrasted with Haplorhini, the "simple nose." Each of these two suborders is made up of richly varied primates that can be subclassified into various infraorders, superfamilies, families, and so forth.

✋ Strepsirhines exhibit a number of primitive characteristics that are shared by most mammals, but they are united by two important **derived features** (unique to the group): a toothcomb and a grooming claw. The best-known example of a strepsirhine is a lemur.

✋ The haplorhines are more obviously "human-like" and include monkeys of both the New World (the Americas) and the Old World (Africa and Asia), the apes (chimpanzees, gorillas, orangutans and gibbons), and humans.

Figure 10.5 shows selected examples of these suborders.

Suborders The traditional classification of the primates split the primates into two suborders— **Prosimii** (G *pro* – before; L *simia* – ape) and **Anthropoidea** (G *anthrop* – man; *oid* - like)—instead of Strepsirhini and Haplorhini. The primate members of the two groups in both the traditional and the newer classification are virtually the same, with the exception of the tarsier (discussed next).

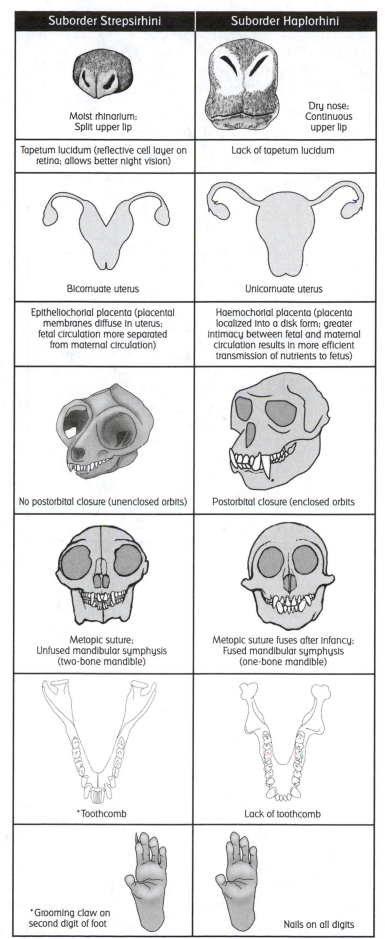

FIGURE **10.5** *Selected Characteristics of the Primate Suborders*

derived features for strepsirhines

Infraorder Levels Strepsirhines and haplorhines each include infraorders and lower-level taxa, but we will focus on the haplorhines only, as they are more closely related to us. Figure 10.6 is a partial classification of the primate order. The Haplorhini has three infraorders:

1. **Tarsiiformes** (tarsiers)
2. **Platyrrhini** (G *plat*: broad; *rhin*: nose)
3. **Catarrhini** (G *cat*: downward; *rhin*: nose)

Tarsiers (see Photo 10.1) are distinct from the other haplorhines and were traditionally classified with the strepsirhines in the old suborder Prosimii. The platyrrhines (New World monkeys) and catarrhines (Old World monkeys, apes, and humans) are more similar to each other. Important differences are found those of the ear region shown in Photo 10.2 (note the bony ear tube, the ectotympanic tube, on the catarrhine), and the nose, in Figure 10.7.

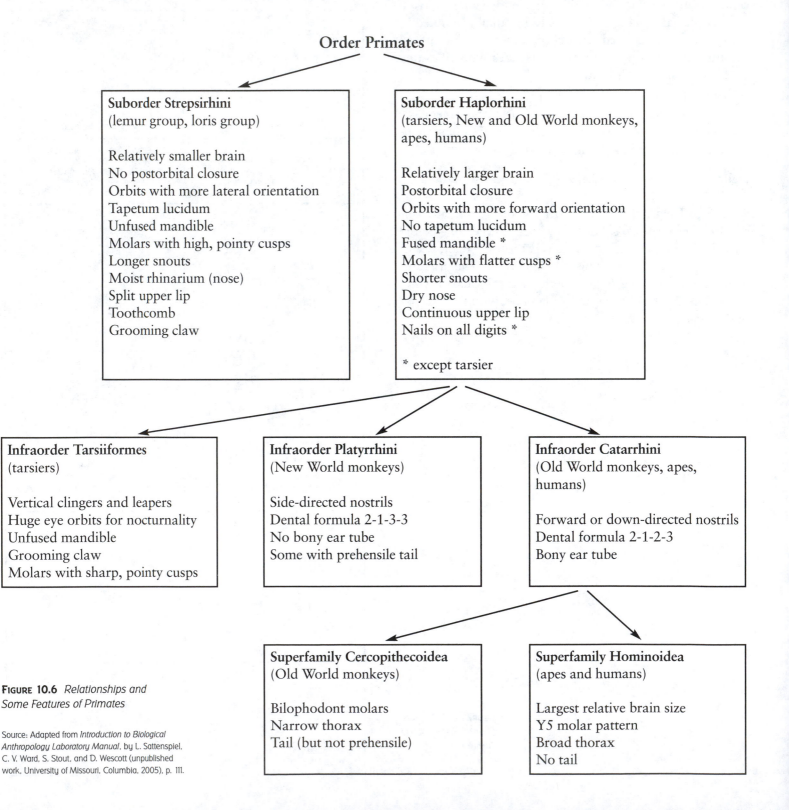

Order Primates

Suborder Strepsirhini
(lemur group, loris group)

Relatively smaller brain
No postorbital closure
Orbits with more lateral orientation
Tapetum lucidum
Unfused mandible
Molars with high, pointy cusps
Longer snouts
Moist rhinarium (nose)
Split upper lip
Toothcomb
Grooming claw

Suborder Haplorhini
(tarsiers, New and Old World monkeys, apes, humans)

Relatively larger brain
Postorbital closure
Orbits with more forward orientation
No tapetum lucidum
Fused mandible *
Molars with flatter cusps *
Shorter snouts
Dry nose
Continuous upper lip
Nails on all digits *

* except tarsier

Infraorder Tarsiiformes
(tarsiers)

Vertical clingers and leapers
Huge eye orbits for nocturnality
Unfused mandible
Grooming claw
Molars with sharp, pointy cusps

Infraorder Platyrrhini
(New World monkeys)

Side-directed nostrils
Dental formula 2-1-3-3
No bony ear tube
Some with prehensile tail

Infraorder Catarrhini
(Old World monkeys, apes, humans)

Forward or down-directed nostrils
Dental formula 2-1-2-3
Bony ear tube

Superfamily Cercopithecoidea
(Old World monkeys)

Bilophodont molars
Narrow thorax
Tail (but not prehensile)

Superfamily Hominoidea
(apes and humans)

Largest relative brain size
Y5 molar pattern
Broad thorax
No tail

FIGURE 10.6 *Relationships and Some Features of Primates*

Source: Adapted from *Introduction to Biological Anthropology Laboratory Manual*, by L. Sattenspiel, C. V. Ward, S. Stout, and D. Wescott (unpublished work, University of Missouri, Columbia, 2005), p. 111.

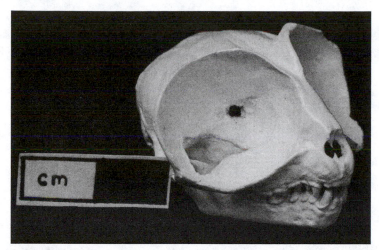

PHOTO 10.1 *Tarsier skull*

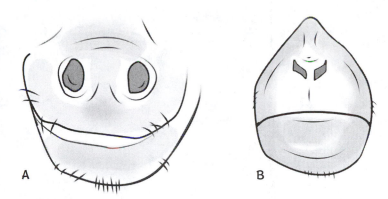

FIGURE 10.7 *Nose Shape and Nostril Orientation in Platyrrhines and Catarrhines*

PHOTO 10.2 *(A) Platyrrhine and (B) catarrhine ear region.*

bony ear tube

Superfamily Level As we move down to lower levels in the biological classification system, members of the taxa share more features. We will continue to focus on the haplorhines, keeping in mind that the strepsirhines also have taxonomic sub-groupings.

Within the Platyrrhini, there is only one superfamily of New World monkeys, the **Ceboidea.** We will not classify the lower levels within the Ceboidea. Examples of New World monkeys include spider monkeys, capuchins, squirrel monkeys, marmosets, and tamarins.

Within the Catarrhini, there are two superfamilies: the **Cercopithecoidea** (Old World monkeys) and the **Hominoidea** (ape and human group). Some differences between the two superfamilies are given in Figure 10.6 and are observable in Figure 10.8.

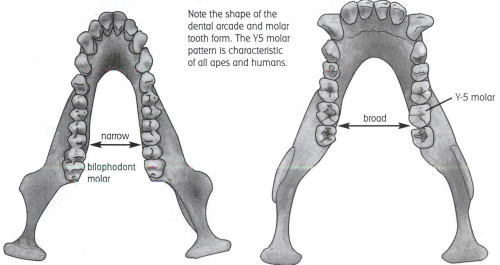

Note the shape of the dental arcade and molar tooth form. The Y5 molar pattern is characteristic of all apes and humans.

narrow

bilophodont molar

Y-5 molar

broad

FIGURE 10.8 *Examples of Differences Between (A) a Cercopithecoid and (B) a Hominoid.*

LAB EXERCISE 10.3

NAME _____ SECTION _____ DATE _____

1. Using Figure 10.5 as guide, decide which of the specimens in photos A–E on page 190 are strepsirhines and which are haplorhines. List them below.

   Strepsirhines:

   Haplorhines:

2. Fill out the chart with reference to the photos A–E, shown below:

Specimen	Size of orbits relative to brain size (small or large)	Fused mandibular symphysis?	Fully enclosed orbits?	Dental formula (if observable)	Bony ear tube? (if observable)
A					
B					
C					
D					
E					

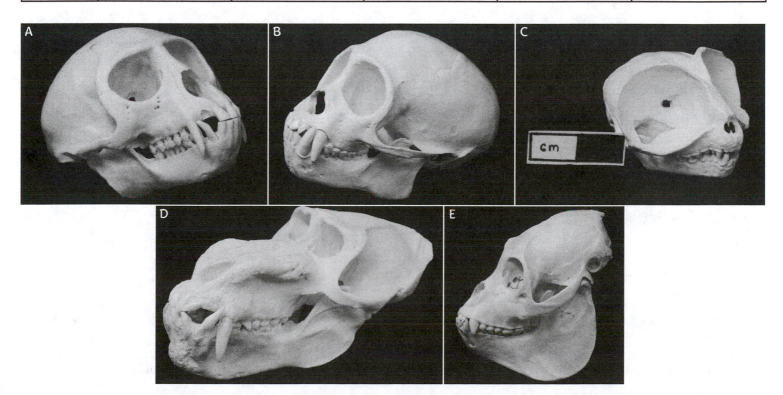

3. Which of the specimens are haplorhines? _____

   Which are strepsirhines? _____

4. Is one of these specimens a tarsier? _____ If so, which one? _____

5. Which are platyrrhines _____, and which are catarrhines? _____

6. Using the last set of photos below, answer these questions for each. Be careful to use characteristics that are *distinguishing for that group* at that *specific level in the taxonomic hierarchy*! For example, if deciding whether an animal is a platyrrhine or a catarrhine, be sure to name features that distinguish members of Platyrrhini from Catarrhini.

Photo A

1. Is this a primate? Why or why not?

2. Is this a strepsirhine or a haplorhine? _____How do you know?

3. If a haplorhine, is it a tarsier, a platyrrhine or a catarrhine? _____. How do you know?

Photo B

1. Is this a primate? _____ Why or why not?

2. Is this a strepsirhine or a haplorhine? _____ How do you know?

3. If a haplorhine, is it a tarsier, a platyrrhine or a catarrhine? _____
How do you know?

Photo C

1. Is this a primate? _____ Why or why not?

2. Is this a strepsirhine or a haplorhine? _____ How do you know?

3. If a haplorhine, is it a tarsier, platyrrhine or catarrhine? _____. How do you know?

S E L F - T E S T   1 0 . 1

NAME _____ SECTION _____ DATE _____

1. Would you say the following represent examples of a homology or an analogy? Why?

    a. bird humerus and bat humerus

    b. vertebral column of a fish and vertebral column of a cat

    c. butterfly wing and bird wing

2. What is an important difference between evolutionary taxonomists and cladists in the way the living organisms are classified?

3. Which charactersistics are the most useful to use for classification, primitive or derived?

4. What is a binomen? _____

   Give an example:

5. Match the following characteristics with the correct taxon.

    _____ 1. no tail   A. Catarrhini

    _____ 2. laterally-directed nostrils   B. Hominoidea

    _____ 3. bony ear tube   C. Platyrrhini

    _____ 4. some have prehensile tails   D. Strepsirhini

    _____ 5. two-part mandible   E. Cercopithecoidea

6. Name two strepsirhine characteristics that differentiate them from haplorhines.

   a.

   b.

7. Name two catarrhine characteristics that differentiate them from platyrrhines.

   a.

   b.

8. Name two haplorhine characteristics (that differentiate them from strepsirhines).

   a.

   b.

9. Name two platyrrhine characteristics (that differentiate them from catarrhines).

   a.

   b.

10. Name two differences between hominoids and cercopithecoids.

    a.

    b.

11. Observing the Behavior of Living Primates

OBJECTIVES

- Learn to identify major groups of living (extant) primates on the basis of their observable physical features

- Become familiar with the main techniques of data collection in animal behavior

- Become familiar with species-specific behavior of some primate species

- Learn which methods are more suitable for different types of studies or for different species

"Have you ever wondered...?"

✋ What *did* Jane Goodall do out there in the forest for all those years?

✋ What is involved in actually observing primates?

In the introduction to the study of primate behavior in this chapter, armed with the knowledge of the basic primate groups, you will actually observe some live representatives of the primate order. You probably will come away from this lab with a different perspective on nonhuman primates than you held previously.

The study of animal behavior involves attempting to quantify phenomena that are observed, and striving to collect data in the most unbiased and objective manner possible. Data collected on captive primates is intrinsically interesting, as these data also can be useful in dealing with zoo management issues such as gauging the effects of a new enclosure or new cagemates.

You will learn some specific techniques today. In lieu of an accessible zoo or other facility with at least two primate species, a video may be substituted. (Videos and accompanying exercises for the instructor are suggested on the Instructor Manual Web site).

Captive Primates

Captive primates exhibit a somewhat different range of behaviors than they would in their natural habitat. They are provisioned with food regularly, and their diet is different from what their wild counterparts would be eating; they move about on different substrates than they would in nature; and they are not free to migrate from one group to another. Thus, their ability to express choice in mates is more limited than it would be in the wild. Still, behaviors specific to each species distinguish them from all others, whether in the wild or in a captive setting. From captive primates, observers can obtain a good sense of the behavioral characteristics of different species.

Preparation

Success in conducting this research depends upon closely following instructions. Careful organization allows you to easily assemble your report and will make for more feasible evaluation of your work by your instructor. Read over the entire lab to be sure the instructions are clear before you begin observing and collecting data.

You will need the following items at the zoo:

- classification sheet with physical characteristics of primates from Figure 10.6 in Chapter 10
- blank paper (graph paper or lined paper)
- clipboard or notebook
- watch (preferably digital)

Optional:

- ruler (particularly if you don't have graph paper)
- binoculars or opera glasses (primates may be housed a distance away—for example, on an island)
- camera or videocamera
- tape recorder

Please follow all instructions posted at the zoo; don't feed or interact with the animals. You will be attempting to obtain the most natural behavior you can retrieve in this setting. Always treat the animals with respect.

You will differentiate the various types of primates at the zoo and record some basic information on their physical and behavioral features, as well as facts on ecology and distribution from the zoo signs (supplemented by information from other sources as needed). You will use basic observational techniques to collect data.

L A B   E X E R C I S E   **11.1**

NAME _____   SECTION _____   DATE _____

List up to eight primate species at the zoo for which you may record information. This lab can be feasibly conducted even if only two or three primate species are present.

Common Name   **Scientific Name**

1. _____   _____

2. _____   _____

3. _____   _____

4. _____   _____

5. _____   _____

6. _____   _____

7. _____   _____

8. _____   _____

Classification of Primates, Characteristics, Geographical Distribution

For at least four species of *primate* at the zoo (this number may be modified at the instructor's discretion), fill out A through D below. For sections A, B, and C, additional information may be necessary to look up in a text or on the Internet. Be sure to cite any sources used. Figure 10.6 in Chapter 10 will be useful here.

A. Common name and scientific name of primate

Below, write the common name and the scientific name. The proper way to write a scientific name is to either *italicize* (if using the computer) or underline *both the genus and species* names (and subspecies if it has one), capitalizing only the first letter of the genus name (for example, *Saguinus oedipus*).

_____   _____

B. Classification

1. To which suborder does the primate belong (Strepsirhini or Haplorhini)? _____

   How can you tell which suborder, *by looking at the individuals before you*? (What features are observable to *you* that indicate its classification?)

2. To what infraorder does the species belong? _____

3. To which superfamily does the species belong? _____

C. Habitats, geographical distribution

1. In what kind of habitat is the primate found? (e.g., savanna, rainforest)

2. Where is the primate found geographically? (continent, region)

D. Observed features and behaviors

1. What is the primate's body size? (Compare it to commonly seen animals, or approximate body weight, if known.)

2. Look at its hands. Is there anything unusual about the fingers or thumb? How similar or different do they appear compared to our hands? (*Hint*: Look at fingernails and opposability of thumb.)

3. Does this primate have a tail? If so, is it prehensile (grasping)? What does the tail do, even if nonprehensile? How long is the tail in relation to its body length?

4. What is its primary mode of locomotion (how does it move around)?

5. How many individuals are in the exhibit, and how old do they appear to be? How many males and how many females?

6. Is this a sexually dimorphic species? (In **sexual dimorphism**, males and females may have different body sizes.)

7. Describe the primate's pelage (coat).

8. Are the primates feeding? If so, what are they eating?

9. Observe the animals in the exhibit for about five minutes, and describe some behaviors you see.

Primate Behavioral Observations

Now you will learn some common animal observational techniques. You will choose one species of primate at the zoo and apply three different data collection techniques to that species: **ad libitum, instantaneous sampling,** and **scan sampling.** An important objective is to learn to distinguish which sampling methods are best for which species and/or situations.

If possible, choose species that are visible in their exhibit so you can collect data successfully. In the ad libitum, or "diary approach," record all behaviors for all animals (Altmann, 1974; Martin and Bateson, 1993).

Ad Libitum Sampling

On the "*Ad Libitum Sampling*" sheet, record your chosen primate species.

You will spend *one-half hour* collecting data on the study species, keeping a detailed running list of *all behaviors performed by all animals*, including references to the time. For example:

> From 11:32 to 11:35, the female groomed her own leg.
>
> At 11:35, she got up, quadrupedally walked over to the male, and sat down one foot away from him."

Detail is important. If your animals are inactive, even more specificity is needed. For example, instead of "The male sat for 10 minutes, and the female stood nearby," you might write something like:

> Beginning at 3:27, the male sat still on his haunches on the ground, looking forward; licked lips, rolled eyes.
>
> At 3:29 he closed his eyes and rested for 2 minutes, at times twitching his left little finger. At the same time, the female was standing quadrupedally, watching me.

LAB EXERCISE 11.2

NAME _____ SECTION _____ DATE _____

Ad Libitum Sampling

Species: _____   Date: _____

Conditions: _____   Starting time: _____

Focal Animal Instantaneous Sampling

The focal animal instantaneous sampling method is really a combination of two different techniques that are useful for the collection (and later analysis) of data on a number of variables at once.

1. In **instantaneous sampling** (Altmann, 1974; Martin and Bateson, 1993), data are recorded at *predetermined intervals* (e.g., every 30 seconds, or every 2 minutes).

2. **Focal animal sampling** allows the observer to concentrate and collect data more accurately on the behavior of *one individual at a time* (Altmann, 1974; Martin and Bateson, 1993).

This lab has two options, depending upon time constraints and your instructor's directions.

Option 1:   Create your own data sheet, or

Option 2:   Use the data sheet "Focal Animal Instantaneous Sampling."

Normally you would spend some time observing your animals to obtain an idea of their general behavior. Because you have just watched them and recorded their behavior, this step isn't necessary.

Option 1: Ethogram and Data Sheet Preparation

An ethogram (also called a behavioral taxonomy; Lehner, 1987) is a catalogue of the behaviors in the behavioral repertoire of a species.

1. After spending at least 20 additional minutes observing the animals, *list all* of the *behaviors* you see.

2. Immediately afterward, while this is still fresh in your mind, *define* each behavior descriptively. For example:

> quadrupedal stand: position in which all four limbs are approximately perpendicular to the torso.

It can be on any substrate as long as the body is approximately parallel to the ground. Each behavior should be *mutually exclusive*. This means that each behavior should be defined so it is distinguishable from all other behaviors, because you will be recording only one behavior at a time. For example, if an animal is sitting *and* grooming, you must decide whether to record "sitting" and "grooming" or separately devise a category that takes into account both sitting and grooming. You must be clear in your definitions, then consistent in your data collection.

3. Categorize the various types of behaviors, such as
> *locomotor behaviors* (run, walk, leap),
> *social behaviors* (groom, wrestle, hug),
> and so on.

4. Compose your data checksheet. See the sample data sheet for Focal Animal Instantaneous Sampling, along with the codes. Using the categories from your ethogram, make a similar data sheet and codes. Include only the behaviors that you actually observed. Again, take care to make your behavioral categories mutually exclusive.

Option 2: Use of Prepared Data Sheet

Focal Animal Instantaneous Sampling Use the Focal Animal Instantaneous Sampling sheet (page 209) and continue below. You may modify the data sheet to include behaviors you noted during your preliminary observations.

1. For the focal animal instantaneous sampling method, collect data for at least one-half hour, using either the data checksheet provided or one you devised. Collect data at 2-minute intervals. This is your *time interval*. Before you begin, you may refer to the example on the back of the lab.

2. Choose your focal animal. Data collection is more interesting and instructive if you choose one that is exhibiting some behavior other than sleeping.

3. If you have a watch that can be set to beep at 2-minute intervals, set it now. Fill in the information at the top of the data sheet, note the starting time, then wait for the 2-minute interval.

4. Exactly 2 minutes *after* the starting time, jot down on the data sheet what your focal animal is doing, along with the code for the observed behavior. This will have been your first *sample point*. Continue for at least another 28 minutes.

Keep in mind that in this method you will *not* be listing *all* behaviors during the entire sample interval, only that which occurs at the instant of the sample point. Thus, only *one* behavior is listed at every sample. (This is one reason for making categories mutually exclusive.) If a behavior you observe is not listed, may add it to the data sheet and to the codes.

Scan Sampling

In scan sampling (Altmann, 1974; Martin and Bateson, 1993), the general activity for all animals in the exhibit is recorded simultaneously, at predetermined intervals. This method is used to record either general categories of behavior or to focus attention on only one or two specific types of behavior to the exclusion of all others.

As in focal animal instantaneous sampling, you'll be taking data only *at the sample point* between the sampling intervals. Use 2-minute samples for this technique as well. An example is provided at the back of the data sheet.

LAB EXERCISE 11.3

NAME _____ SECTION _____ DATE _____

Focal Animal Instantaneous Sampling
(use 2-minute intervals and the accompanying codes)

Species: _____   Date: _____

Conditions: _____   Focal animal description:

Description: _____

Starting time: _____

Time	Context (general activity)	Position	Social Behavior	Substrate	Food Type (if feeding)	Comments

Codes for Focal Animal Instantaneous Sampling

Feed: includes foraging (searching for food), ingesting (getting food into mouth), and chewing

R   Rest: in a stationary posture for at least 10 seconds after time interval begins

T   Travel: moving from one area of the exhibit to another

S   Social: interacting with another individual of its species

Positions:

Si	Sit
St – b	Stand bipedally
St – q	Quadrupedally
Li	Lie
Clg	Cling
Qw	Quadrupedal walk
R	Run
Le	Leap
Clb	Climb
O	Other (then specify)

Social behaviors:

P	Sit in close proximity (w/in 1 meter)
H	Hug
Gr	Groom (other)
Pl	Play (specify how)
T	Threaten
C	Chase
M	Mounting
O	Other

Substrate:

Br	Branch
Sh	Shelf
G	Ground
F	Fence
O	Other

Focal Animal Instantaneous Sampling

(use 2-minute intervals and the accompanying codes)

Species: __Lemur catta__   Date: __9/23/05__

Conditions: __sunny, warm__   Focal animal description:

__adult female__

Starting time: __2:12__

Time	Context (general activity)	Position	Social Behavior	Substrate	Food Type (if feeding)	Comments
2:12	F	Si	P	Br	apple	
2:14	F	Si		Br	potato	
2:16	R	Li	P	Sh		Had threatened a female
2:18						

Lab Exercise 11.4

NAME _____ SECTION _____ DATE _____

Scan Sampling Data Checksheet
(use 2-minute intervals)

At each sample point, note down the number of individuals in the group that are feeding, those that are resting, traveling, or engaging in social behavior.

Species: _____   Date: _____

Conditions: _____   Starting time: _____

Time	# Feeding	# Resting	# Traveling	# Social	Total
Total					

Example: Scan Sampling Data Checksheet

(2-minute intervals)

At each sample point, note down the number of individuals in the group that are feeding, those that are resting, traveling, or engaging in social behavior.

Species: __Macaca mulatta__   Date: __9/23/05__

Conditions: __cloudy, cool, construction noise__   Starting time: __2:32 p.m.__

Time	# Feeding	# Resting	# Traveling	# Social	Total
2:32	/ / /		/ / / /		7
2:34		/ / / / /	/ /		7
2:36	/ / /	/ /		/ /	7
2:38		/ / / / /		/ /	7
Total	6	12	6	4	21

Completing the Lab

Use your observations and completed forms to complete the lab.

1. Based on the *ad libitum* observations, make a statement about the amount of time your primates spent in various activities.

2. Do the same for the *focal animal instantaneous sampling* method. With the number of observations as your sample size, figure out the percentages of time spent (or, rather, samples observed) for each different behavior. You may write this out in a simple list as shown here, or you may make a table for the results if you wish—for example:

feeding	22%
sitting	10%
grooming	16%
etc.	

3. Figure out totals for the *scan sampling* technique.

> These techniques can be modified to best answer your research questions and allow you to acquire the most accurate data. The data sheets included here are offered for your use or as models for your own. Whatever technique is used, researchers must state their methodology clearly so other researchers can usefully compare the results to their own data.

SELF-TEST 11.1

NAME _____ SECTION _____ DATE _____

1. On a separate paper, write approximately a page comparing the three methods of data collection you used. For each method, list advantages and disadvantages, considering the following:

   What might be a situation that calls for ad libitum data collection?

   For focal animal sampling?

   For scan sampling?

   Might one method work better for some species than others, or for some behaviors rather than others? Why?

   Which seems more objective, and which more subjective?

2. What are some cues that were useful to you in distinguishing among different individuals of the same species in the zoo?

3. What are some reasons for studying primates in captivity?

12. Early Primates from the Paleocene through the Miocene

"Have you ever wondered...?"

✋ The first primates were from Africa, right?

This chapter focuses on primate evolution, which leads up to the evolution of our own family, the Hominidae. Before studying our human ancestors, we will investigate the primates that preceded us so we can put human evolution into the context of primate evolution as a whole. The focus here is on identifying the main fossil groups and the features that distinguish them from one another.

We study earth's history from the fossil record. Defined broadly, a fossil is anything that remains to document life of the past. It can take the form of an imprint or cast, or something that actually has gone through the process of **fossilization** (see Figure 12.1). When an animal dies and is buried, minerals from the sediment in which it lies replaces the organic material in bone, particle by particle. This is a slow process, and the time it takes depends upon the sediment and its mineral content, as well as the ambient temperature at which the process occurs.

Geological Time Scale

A **geological time scale** is shown in Table 12.1. This table covers only the time range of the **Phanerozoic Eon**. Previous to the Phanerozoic Eon was the **Precambrian Eon**, which lasted from the time of earth's formation through 542 million years ago (mya). In this chapter we will focus primarily on the **Cenozoic Era**, because this is the portion of time during which the primates evolved. The geological time scale is a hierarchical system of classifying time (similar to biological classification), with larger blocks of time divided into smaller ones (eons divided into eras, eras into periods, and periods into epochs). Scientists have divided up these blocks of time in accordance with the rise and fall of major groups of organisms.

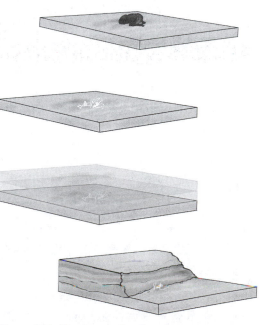

FIGURE 12.1 *Fossilization Process*

TABLE 12.1: Geological Time Scale within the Phanerozoic Eon

Era	Period	Epoch
Cenozoic Era (65 mya to the present	Quaternary (1.8 mya to the present) Tertiary (65–1.8 mya)	Holocene (10,000 years ago to the present) Pleistocene (1.8 mya–10,000 ya) Pliocene (5 – 1.8 mya) Miocene (24 – 5 mya) Oligocene (38 – 24 mya) Eocene (55 – 38 mya) Paleocene (65 – 55 mya)
Mesozoic Era (251 – 65 mya)	Cretaceous (146 – 65 mya) Jurassic (205 – 146 mya) Triassic (251 – 205 mya)	
Paleozoic Era (542 – 251 mya)	Permian (299 – 251 mya) Carboniferous (359 – 299 mya) Devonian (416 – 359 mya) Silurian (444 – 416 mya) Ordivician (488 – 444 mya) Cambrian (542 – 488 mya)	mya = million years ago ya = years ago

Plate Tectonics

The earth's plates that underlie the continents are in motion. This is known as **plate tectonics,** or **continental drift.** The position of the continents influences the geographical distribution patterns of all living things, including the primates. The **paleoclimate** has changed considerably through time, and this has influenced the type of habitats and, thus, survivability of the flora and fauna within it. Over the entire Cenozoic Era, the primary trend has been one of cooling and drying, but with many fluctuations within.

Primate Beginnings in the Paleocene Epoch (65 mya to 55 mya)

The earliest known primates were from a seemingly unlikely place: North America! Keep in mind that the earth looked quite different 65 million years ago, back in the **Paleocene** epoch (65 mya to 55 mya). North America, Europe, and Asia were joined in one huge landmass, called **Laurasia.** In the southern hemisphere, another landmass, **Gondwanaland,** was in the process of splitting apart into what would be Africa, South America, Antarctica, and Australia. India was an island continent and hadn't "docked" at Asia, so the Himalayas didn't yet exist. Much of the globe was warm and humid, with little difference between the northern and southern latitudes. From Minnesota to Argentina, tropical rainforests dominated. England had alligator-filled swamps, and the Ozarks were a vast, low, forested plain with slow streams and swamps.

Primates were an early branch of the mammalian tree, very near the trunk. Soon after early mammals began to diverge into distinct groups, primates and primate-like creatures were already present, by 63 million years ago. An extinct taxonomic group called the **Plesiadapiformes** (G *plesi*: near, recent; L *adapi*: rabbit) consists of early mammals with certain primate-like characteristics.

Some researchers consider Plesiadapiformes to be primates because of their petrosal bulla, more rounded molar cusps, and arboreal features of the postcranial skeleton (Szalay and Delson, 1979; Szalay, 1981). Others disagree and would place this group in a different but closely related mammalian order (e.g., Rasmussen, 2002). This interpretation, in turn, was challenged by scientists who again support the idea of Plesiadapiformes as primates (Bloch and Silcox, 2006). Whatever they were, they existed in North America and Europe, with a few in China.

Although the fossil evidence doesn't allow us to confidently answer questions about the origin of Plesidapiformes and their specific relationships with modern primates, we do know that they were a diverse group of about 75 species, ranging from the size of a small mouse to that of a medium house cat. Some groups had more primate-like features than others. Two examples from this group are the genera *Purgatorius* (early Paleocene of North America) and *Plesiadapis* (Paleocene to early Eocene, widespread in North America and Europe) (Figure. 12.2; *Atlas* p. 260; br. ed. p. 32).

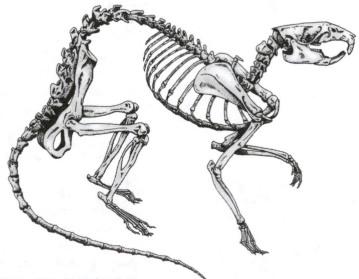

Figure 12.2 *Plesiadapis*

TABLE 12.2: Plesiadapiforms Compared to Primates

Plesiadapiform features	Primate features
Small brain size	Large relative brain size
No postorbital bar	Postorbital bar
Laterally-facing eye orbits	Forward-facing eye orbits
Prognathic (forward-protuding) face	Shortened snout
Possible petrosal bulla	Petrosal bulla
Large, ever-growing incisors	Canine usually largest tooth
Lack of opposable big toe	Opposable big toe
Claws on digits	Nails on digits

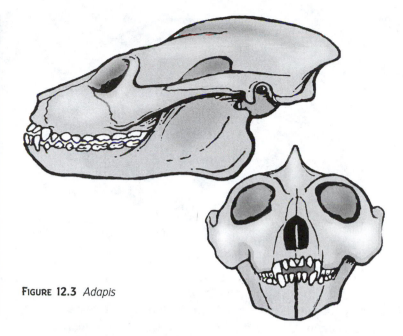

FIGURE 12.3 *Adapis*

Some plesiadapiform features are listed in Table 12.2 in comparison to primate characteristics. Some of the primate features you are familiar with can be observed as well in fossils.

Some of the Plesiadapiformes lasted through much of the following epoch, the Eocene, then became extinct. Their extinction may have been brought about by competition with rodents, which were fast becoming the most numerous mammalian species (Van Valen and Sloan, 1966).

The "True" Primates of the Eocene Epoch (55 to 34 mya)

During the **Eocene** the earth did not undergo drastic changes, but the main tectonic event of importance for primate distribution was the increasing separation of North America from Europe as the Laurasian landmass broke apart. By the end of the epoch, the two were parts of separate landmasses. At around this time, a severe drop in temperature also influenced the ecology and distribution of many species.

Primates of the Eocene epoch were present in North America, Europe, Asia, and Africa. In the Eocene epoch, Europe had more than 200 primate species—comparable to the total number of primate species alive today. The two best-known and best-represented groups that inhabited North America and Europe were the taxonomic superfamilies **Adapoidea** (Adapoids) and **Omomoyidea** (Omomyoids). All of the primate features with which you are now familiar also were present in these early primates.

Adapoids: Ancestors of Strepsirhine

One of the main Eocene groups includes the probable ancestors of the strepsirhines. These adapoids, having more than

80 different species, ranged in size from a large rat to a large housecat. There is widespread agreement that members of this group gave rise to the strepsirhines (including, among others, the lemurs and lorises of today). Among the best known of these primates are the genera **Cantius** (North America and Europe), **Notharctus** (North America), and **Adapis** (Europe) (see Figure 12.3; *Atlas* pp. 264–265; br. ed. pp. 36–37). A few representatives also are found in Africa and Asia.

Omomyoids: Possible Ancestors of Haplorhines

Similar in appearance to the modern tarsier, the omomyoids are even more numerous than the adapoids, with more 90 species. Like the adapoids, the omoyoids are best known from North America and Europe, but some representatives were present in Asia and possibly in Africa. It is from the Omomyoidea that the ancestral haplorhine may have arisen. Thus, the shared common ancestor of the tarsier and the groups that include monkeys, apes, and humans lie within this fossil taxon.

Omomyoids were typically smaller in body size, on average, than adapoids. Some of the better-known omomyoids are **Necrolemur** (Europe), **Tetonius** (North America), and **Rooneyia** (North America) (see Figure 12.4; *Atlas* pp. 263, 267, 270; br. ed. pp. 35, 39, 42).

Other Eocene Primates from Africa and Asia

Although all of the known fossils from North America and Europe from the Eocene epoch fit relatively neatly into either the Omomyoidea or the Adapoidea, such is not the case for Eocene fossil primates from Asia and Africa. Representatives of the omomyoids and adapoids are found in Asia and Africa,

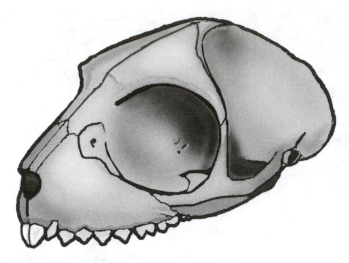

FIGURE 12.4 *Necrolemur*

but some fossils are quite distinct from them. An excellent example from Asia is *Eosimias* (Figure 12.5), a tiny late Eocene primate from China that exhibits features of the **anthropoids** (the group that includes monkeys, apes and humans) before their divergence into platyrrhines and catarrhines (Gebo et al., 2000).

Other Eocene Asian primates that also may represent early anthropoids are *Amphipithecus* and *Pondaungia* (Fleagle, 1999). In Africa, the very late Eocene *Catopithecus* (*Atlas* p. 271; br. ed. p. 43) is clearly an anthropoid and even possesses catarrhine features (Simons and Rasmussen, 1996). It is one of the members of a fossil primate family from a site in Egypt (described next).

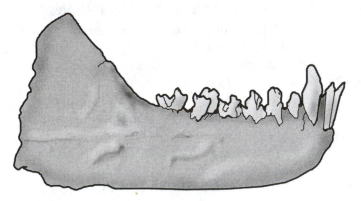

FIGURE 12.5 *Eosimias*

The Oligocene Primates (34 to 24 mya)

As a result of the extreme drop in temperature at the end of the Eocene epoch, what had been appropriate primate habitat in the northern hemisphere became inhospitable to the tropically adapted primates. This virtually eliminated them from the region. Primates in North America and Europe either became extinct or migrated southward, most suffering the former fate. Thus, there are very few fossil primates worldwide in the **Oligocene** epoch. The primary exception consists

of the rich fossil deposits in the Egyptian **Fayum Depression,** a region that was a lush gallery (riverine) forest during the Oligocene epoch. Time-wise, the lower Fayum deposits are near the boundary between the Eocene and the Oligocene (about 24 mya), extending up through the earliest part of the Miocene (Fleagle, 1999).

The continents were active, causing a great deal of tectonic and volcanic activity. Africa and Europe crowded around an existing inland sea, enclosing it into what we now call the Mediterranean Sea. India had begun its collision course with Asia, starting the uplift we now know as the Himalayas. Australia and South America separated from Antarctica so that all became island continents.

During the Oligocene, two fossil primate families were present at the site:

1. **Parapithecidae:** *Apidium* is a primary example of this family. This anthropoid, from about 36 million ago, has some similarities to New World monkeys, which you will see when you compare the figure with a platyrrhine specimen (see Figure 12.6; *Atlas* p. 272; br. ed. p. 44). Thus, some researchers think a creature with features similar to *Apidium* may be an ancestor of the platyrrhines and catarrhines. *Apidium* was about the size of a squirrel monkey (or a large squirrel).

2. **Propliopithecidae:** *Aegyptopithecus,* the best-known representative of this family, dates from about 33 mya (Photo 12.1; *Atlas* p. 273; br. ed. pp. 44–45). This howler monkey-sized primate is most likely an early catarrhine and may have given rise to both the cercopithecoid (Old World monkey) and hominoid (ape/human group) lines. *Aegyptopithecus* is a good candidate for ancestry for the both of these groups of Old World anthropoids because it is generalized enough to have given rise to both groups rather than exhibiting specific features of either one.

The teeth actually are more comparable to those of hominoids and are the first in the fossil record to exhibit the **Y5 molar cusp pattern** (*Atlas* p. 67, Figure. 3.65). The tooth pattern of the Old World monkey (bilophodonty) appears after the hominoid molar pattern.

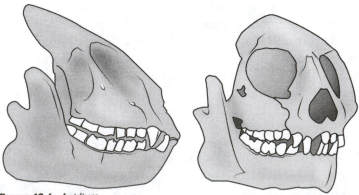

FIGURE 12.6 *Apidium*

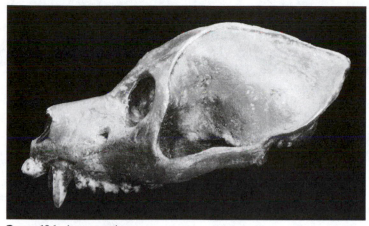

PHOTO 12.1 *Aegyptopithecus*

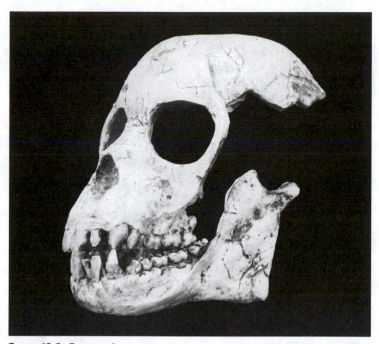

PHOTO 12.2 *Proconsul*

Miocene Hominoids (24 to 5 mya)

In the **Miocene** epoch, the previous cooling trend reversed temporarily and the world experienced warmer temperatures for a time. Geological processes were hard at work forming the earth's surface much as we know it today. For example, the tectonic activity that brought India into place along the Asian continent continued and the Himalayas rose dramatically.

A variety of catarrhine primates of the superfamily Hominoidea existed in Africa, Asia, and Europe during the Miocene. These apes, most of which were small-bodied compared to their modern relatives, are termed the **Miocene hominoids.** They were primarily arboreal, with ape-like heads and a body with a mixture of ape-like and monkey-like features. As in the modern hominoids, they had no tail. In contrast to the relatively few apes now (only four or five genera), the Miocene epoch yielded about 30 genera!

African Forms

The earliest of these genera was ***Proconsul*** (Photo 12.2), first discovered in Kenya in 1948. Its relationship to modern apes was quickly assumed, and it was named in reference to its presumed ancestry of chimpanzees. A famous pipe-smoking chimpanzee named Consul (Photo 12.3) had resided at the Belle Vue Zoo in England, so the fossil form was named as its progenitor. Four species of *Proconsul* existed between 22 and 14 million years ago in East Africa, ranging from cocker spaniel-sized to chimp-sized. In addition to *Proconsul*, about 18 genera of ape existed in Africa during the Miocene.

During the early part of the Miocene epoch, Africa was an island continent. The previous isolation of Antarctica from South America and Australia brought about a change in ocean currents such that the warm tropical waters and cold polar waters mixed less. This had the effect of lowering the circum-polar temperatures and leading to a buildup of the Antarctic ice cap. Although the Miocene was generally warmer than the Oligocene, the cold polar temperatures caused much seawater to be trapped in ice, which lowered

PHOTO 12.3 *Consul, the performing chimpanzee*

the sea levels. This had an important consequence for primate distribution, because it opened up a land bridge from Africa to Europe 17 to 18 million years ago. After this connection between the continents, we begin to see Miocene hominoids in Europe and Asia, presumably descendants of the African forms.

Asian Forms

The Asian hominoid ***Sivapithecus*** (Photo 12.4; *Atlas* pp. 277–280; br. ed. pp. 49–52), from India and Pakistan, appeared about 15 million years ago. You will be comparing it to living apes to determine its possible relationships.

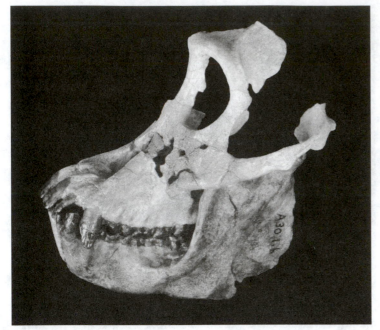

PHOTO 12.4 *Sivapithecus*

Another important and fascinating Asian hominoid, related to *Sivapithecus*, was **Gigantopithecus**, one species of which appeared in India and Pakistan in the late Miocene (about 9 mya). Another, larger, species of *Gigantopithecus* persisted until less than a million years ago in China and Vietnam, and even co-existed with *Homo erectus*. Although known only from its jaws and teeth, this clearly was the largest primate that ever lived, with a larger dentition than even the gorilla (see Figure 12.7). Representatives of about five other genera existed during the Miocene of Asia.

European Forms

About eight genera of European ape existed between 13 and 8 million years ago. The most famous of these is **Dryopithecus** (see Figure 12.8; *Atlas* p. 276; br. ed. p. 48), which was the size of a large monkey (or a small golden retriever). About nine additional genera of Miocene ape lived in Europe, including the newly discovered **Pierolapithecus catalaunicus**. Discoverers of *Pierolapithecus* interpreted it to be a member of the group that gave rise to the great apes and humans (Moya-Sola et al., 2004). Alternatively, it may be an early representative of the group that gave rise to the African ape/human line (Begun and Ward, 2005).

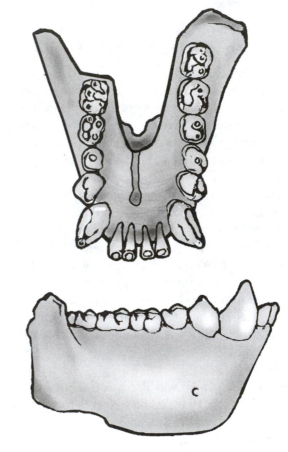

FIGURE 12.8 *Dryopithecus Mandible*

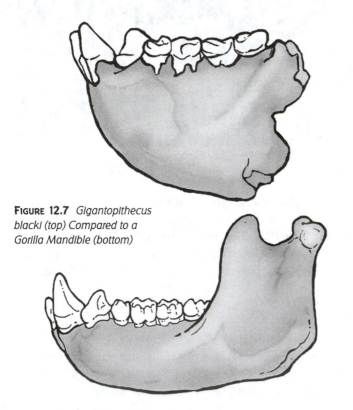

FIGURE 12.7 *Gigantopithecus blacki (top) Compared to a Gorilla Mandible (bottom)*

LAB EXERCISE 12.1

NAME _____ SECTION _____ DATE _____

1. Compare the illustration of a Plesiadapiform primate (*Plesiadapis*) (*Atlas* p. 260; br. ed. p. 32) with the skull (or the photo) of a strepsirhine (*Atlas* p. 102; br. ed. p. 8).

2. a. Fill out the chart below. Refer to Table 12.2 for body parts that are not shown in the accompanying illustration or photo.

Skull Features	Plesiadapiform	Strepsirhine
Postorbital bar		
Position of orbits: lateral or forward-facing?		
Relative size of braincase (compared with face)		
Prognathism: length of snout relative to cranium		
Fused versus unfused mandibular symphysis (mandible made up of one or two bones?)		
Form of incisors and incisor size relative to canines and molars		
Postcranial Features		
Nails versus claws*		
Opposable big toe?*		

*not observable from photos

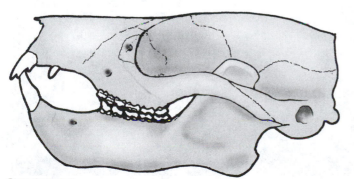

Plesiadapis skull

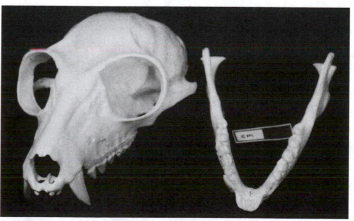

Ring-tailed lemur

b. Why are plesiadapiformes considered by some researchers to be members of the primate order?

c. Which of the plesiadapiform features are decidedly unlike those of primates?

2. a. Compare the fossil and living forms listed below, using a combination of specimens and accompanying illustrations and photos on this page and the next. (*Adapis: Atlas* p. 265, br. ed. p. 37; Ring-tailed lemur: *Atlas* pp. 102; *Necrolemur: Atlas* p. 267, br. ed. p. 39; Tarsier: *Atlas* pp. 112–113). If you can't determine a particular feature, put a "not obs" (not observable) in the blank.

Skull Feature	*Adapis* (Adapoid)	Lemur *(Lemur)*	*Necrolemur* (Omomyoid)	Tarsier *(Tarsius)*	*Eosimias*
Postorbital bar?					
Postorbital closure?					
Position of orbits					
Relative size of braincase					
Snout length relative to cranium					
Fused mandibular symphysis?					
Size of anterior versus posterior dentition					

*Other strepsirhine skulls may be substituted for the lemur.

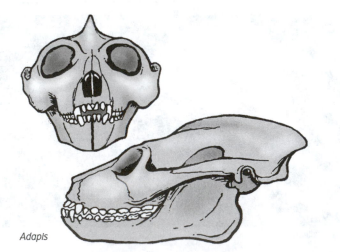

Adapis

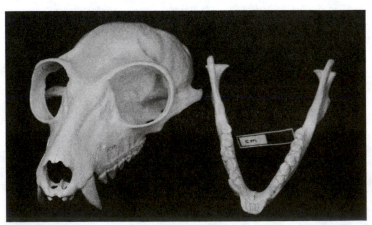

Ring-tailed lemur

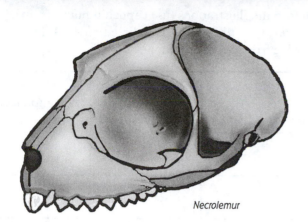

Necrolemur

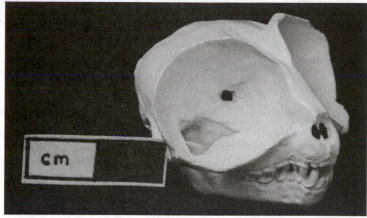

Tarsier

Eosimias

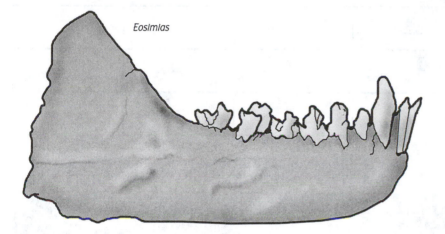

b. Using lab specimens or the accompanying photos, look
at the relative size of orbits of the tarsier versus those of
a monkey and a lemur (see photo from question #1).
What can we tell about the activity patterns (diurnal versus
nocturnal) from fossilized remains?

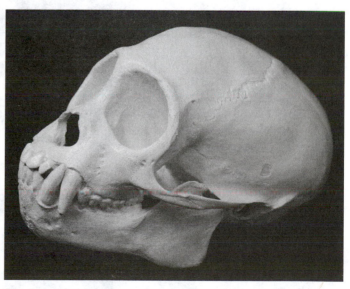

Capuchin monkey

c. Adapoids are thought to be ancestral to what?

d. Omomyoids may be ancestral to what?

3. Compare the skulls of the Fayum primates *Apidium* and *Aegyptopithecus* to a New World monkey, an Old World monkey, and an African ape.

   a. Fill out the chart below using specimens or the accompanying photos and illustrations (use capuchin photo from previous question) (*Apidium*: *Atlas* p. 272, br. ed. p. 44; *Aegyptopithecus*: *Atlas* p. 272–273, br. ed. p. 44-45; chimpanzee: *Atlas* pp. 140-142). Again, not all features will be visible from the photos alone.

Skull Features	*Apidium*	Capuchin Monkey (or Other New World monkey)	*Aegyptopithecus*	Vervet (or Other Old World Monkey)	Chimpanzee (or Gorilla)
Postorbital closure					
Dental formula					
Length of snout					
Molar form* (bilophodont versus Y5 pattern)	NA	NA			
Form of ear region (bony tube?)					

*If actual specimen is available

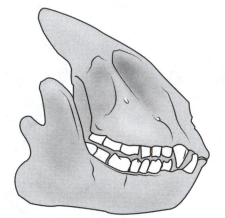

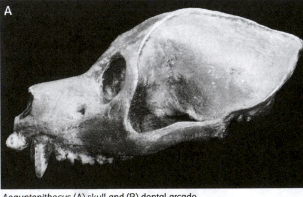

Aegyptopithecus (A) skull and (B) dental arcade

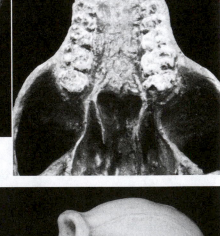

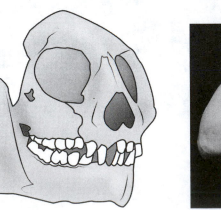

Apidium

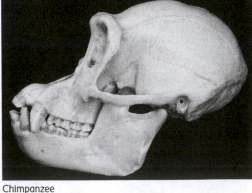

Vervet monkey

Chimpanzee

b. In which features is *Apidium* similar to a capuchin?

c. In which features is *Aegyptopithecus* similar to the Old World monkey?

To the chimpanzee (or gorilla)?

4. Examine skulls, accompanying photos or and/or figures to make the following comparisons (*Dryopithecus*: *Atlas* p. 276, br. ed. p. 48; Chimpanzee: *Atlas* p. 140–142; see chimpanzee and vervet skull photos from previous question and on next page). Keep in mind that for some specimens or species, a feature may be unobservable or unknown (particularly if a post-cranial feature).   *Another Old World monkey skull may be substituted for a vervet, and a gorilla may be substituted for a chimpanzee.

	Proconsul	*Dryopithecus*	Chimpanzee	Vervet (or other Old World monkey)
Shape of dental arcade				*
Relative brain size (compared to face)		*		
Molar form (bilophodont versus Y5 pattern)				
Tail?*				

*Not observable from photos

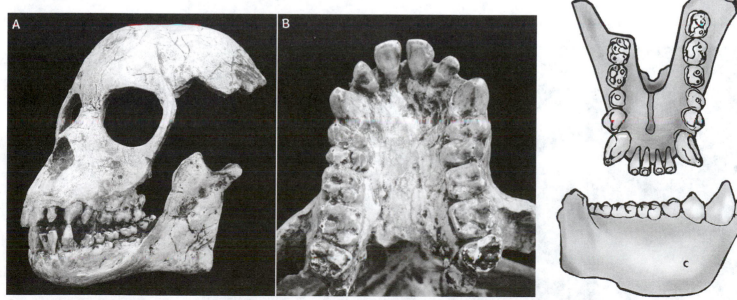

Proconsul (A) skull and (B) dental arcade

Dryopithecus mandible

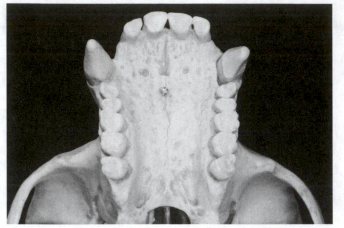

Chimpanzee dental arcade

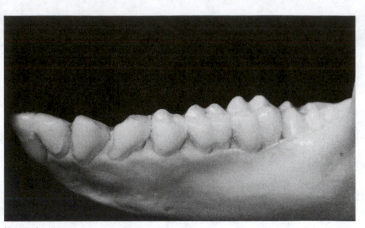

Vervet dentition

5. a. Compare *Sivapithecus* (below) to the photos of an orangutan and an African ape on the following page (*Sivapithecus*: *Atlas* pp. 277–280, br. ed. p. 49–52; Orangutan: *Atlas* pp. 136–139; Chimpanzee: pp. 140–142), and fill out the chart.

	Sivapithecus	Orangutan	Gorilla (or chimpanzee)
Interorbital distance (greater versus smaller?)			
Shape of orbits			
Size and shape of zygomatic arch			
Relative size of central versus lateral incisors			
Size of supraorbital ridge			
Shape of subnasal region (alveolar prognathism?)			

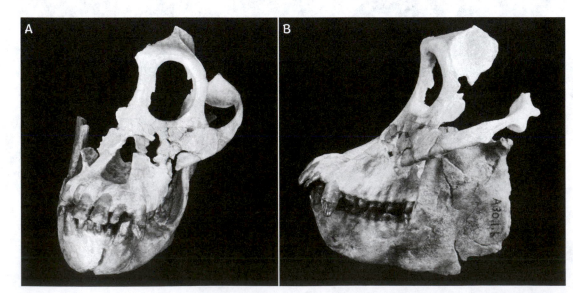

Sivapithecus (A) anterior and (B) lateral view

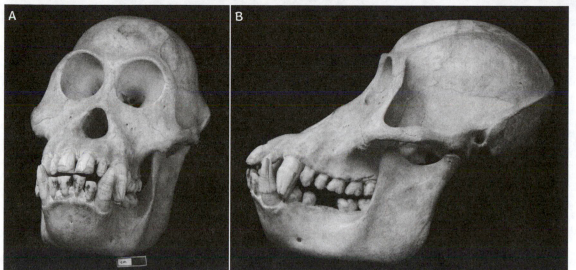

Orangutan (A) anterior
and (B) lateral view

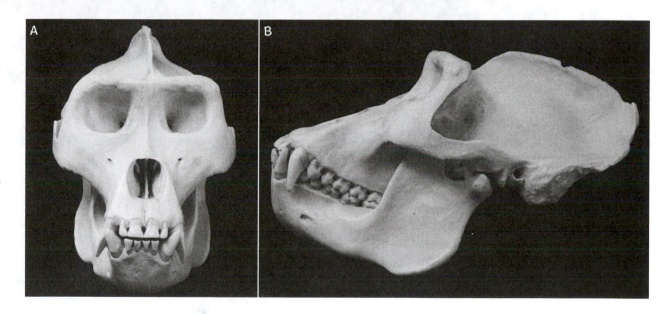

Gorilla (A) anterior
and (B) lateral view

b. *Sivapithecus* is most similar to which of the modern apes? In what features?

SELF-TEST 12.1

NAME _____ SECTION _____ DATE _____

1. What are five primate features that would be apparent from fossils?

2. Based upon which features are the Plesiadapiformes considered primates? What about them is not primate-like?

3. For the Oligocene primates:

   a. *Apidium* and *Parapithecus* have the dental formula of 2-1-3-3. What kinds of living primate have this dental formula?

   b. *Aegyptopithecus* has a dental formula of 2-1-2-3. What kinds of living primate have this dental formula?

   c. All of the Oligocene primates have no bony ear tube (ectotympanic tube). What primate group is this similar to?

4. a. Of the features you have observed, which features does *Aegyptopithecus* share with other anthropoids? List two.

   b. With other catarrhines? Name one.

   c. With hominoids? Name one.

5. If you find a fossil sample made up of numerous adult individuals of the same species, some having a larger body size and larger canines, what might this indicate? What would this imply about the mating system of this species?

6. Which occurred earlier in time, *Proconsul* or *Dryopithecus*?

   Where was each found?

   Why is the timing of their existence significant in terms of the possible evolutionary relationship between the two?

7. Compare the *Gigantopithecus* specimen to a gorilla mandible. How is it similar?

   Different?

13. Who's in Our Family?

"Have you ever wondered...?"

✋ Why didn't the apes keep evolving?

✋ Who was Lucy?

Our taxonomic family, the **Hominidae**, shares a common ancestor with our closest living relatives, the African apes (chimpanzee and gorilla). Our hominid ancestors and other relatives share an adaptation to **bipedalism** that occurred after the split from the African apes. We can determine the mode of locomotion of our extinct relatives by observing the morphology of the fossilized postcrania we find. All hominids exhibit anatomical correlates of bipedalism.

The Comparative Basis

To assess fossils and place them in a taxonomic scheme, we must have some comparative basis. For fossil hominids, we must be familiar with human locomotor adaptations as well as those of our closest living relatives, the African apes. We would expect an extinct common ancestor of humans and the African apes to have shared homologous features with both living groups, but evidence certainly supports the idea that living African apes are more similar anatomically to that common ancestor than are modern humans (see Figure 13.1). Apes didn't "stop evolving," but many more obvious changes accumulated on the human branch of the evolutionary tree. Thus, although it is easy to differentiate modern humans from modern African apes on the basis of anatomical characteristics, it gets more difficult to compare early members of the human family with apes or our ape-like ancestors. The earliest hominids were quite ape-like.

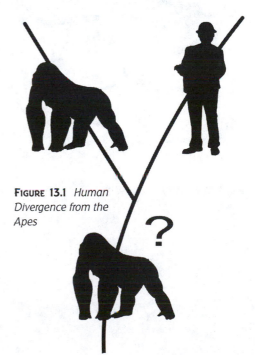

FIGURE 13.1 *Human Divergence from the Apes*

In this chapter we will compare the anatomy of African apes and humans in the cranial and postcranial skeleton, with special reference to the anatomical adaptations for humans to bipedal locomotion.

Bipedalism: the Hallmark of Humanity

Although there are many four-legged runners, climbers, and so on, humans are the only ones to walk upright on two legs habitually. Our mode of locomotion has advantages and disadvantages, but presumably the advantages provided more survival value than the disadvantages were detrimental. We display many unique features of muscle and bone related to bipedalism, and while modern African apes are capable of walking bipedally, they do not exhibit the anatomical adaptations for doing so. African apes are known as **knuckle-walkers**, a type of quadruped.

Human bipedalism is unique in its **striding gait.** Although most of us walk every day, we rarely think about the "mechanics" as we are doing so. In bipedalism, the walking cycle has two phases :

1. In the **stance phase,** the foot is in contact with the substrate and supports the weight. This phase has three parts: the heel strike, the flat foot (or midstance), and the toe-off (leaving the ground for the next step) (Figure 13.2).

2. In the **swing phase,** the foot comes off the substrate and is being repositioned for the next stance phase (Figure 13.3). Here, the leg comes forward and around toward

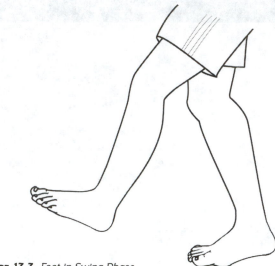

Figure 13.3 *Foot in Swing Phase*

the center (called *adduction*). In humans, some of the gluteal muscles are positioned on the side; these act as stabilizers for the contralateral side so we don't fall over to the side when one foot is off the ground. Our legs come in at the knees so the center of gravity doesn't have to be shifted laterally back and forth much while walking.

Compared to most other animals, humans are "unbalanced" in locomotion. Think about it: We are balancing all of our weight on just one leg about half the time we are walking! This causes balance problems that are dealt with by our having redistributed (during our evolutionary past) the orientation and function of various muscles and their associated skeletal supporting structures.

Three main aspects of our locomotion are

1. *propulsion* (push-off),
2. *stabilization* (so we don't fall over trying to balance on one leg), and
3. *adduction* (our leg swings around to the center with each step).

Certain muscle groups allow each of these actions, and we will see the differences in the hip and leg bones in humans versus apes resulting from this difference in muscle function.

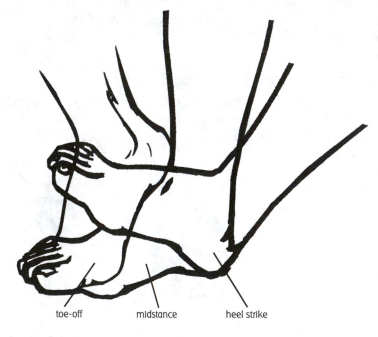

toe-off   midstance   heel strike

Figure 13.2 *Foot in Stance Phase*

LAB EXERCISE 13.1

NAME _____ SECTION _____ DATE _____

1. Stand up. In slow motion, lift one leg, take a step forward, and place your foot on the ground in the same way you do when you walk. Continuing slowly, take another step. In what area of your body do you feel your muscles tense when you lift your leg to first take that step? (Where are the muscles located?)

2. Just before you put your foot down on the heel and transfer the weight to your forward foot, what is your other leg doing? (What area in your other leg feels tense?)

3. Take several steps at a normal pace. Notice how your leg swings naturally around to the center before you put your leg down, enabling you to walk a straight line. Where do you think the muscle group that causes this is found?

   As mentioned, humans have balance problems that our quadrupedal relatives do not, because of our mode of locomotion.

4. Remain standing, and pretend that you are about to cross a log lying across a deep gorge between two cliffs. How would you position yourself to best avoid a fall? What if you expect someone to try to push you over? How will your body position change?

   In the quadrupedal locomotion of a chimpanzee, the legs don't adduct naturally toward the center as ours do and instead move along two parallel (parasagittal) planes. When a chimp walks upright, its center of gravity shifts with each step so that its upper body shifts as well.

5. Walk like an upright chimp. Don't adduct your legs as you walk. Keep them parallel to each other. Describe what your upper body does naturally as a result. Does it shift from side to side?

6. Males and females have slightly different centers of gravity caused by a difference in body proportion. Squat on the ground, and have someone place a marker (such as a dry erase marker) on its end 8 to 10 inches out in front of you, between your feet. Put your hands behind your back. Lean down and attempt to knock over the marker with your nose.

Who is more successful at knocking over the marker?

What does this say about the location of the center of gravity in males and females?

Ape-Human Anatomical Comparisons

We assume that gorillas and chimpanzees are more similar than are humans to the common ancestor of African apes and humans, but what was the ancestral locomotor pattern? Although some researchers support the idea of knuckle-walking as the ancestral condition, additional fossil evidence will answer the question more satisfactorily.

Adaptations to Bipedalism

The many differences between an ape's and a human's post-cranial skeleton result from many generations of selection for the most efficient locomotion for each (Figure 13.4). Our important first step will be to learn about a few of the many such differences, in order to make inferences about the features of our fossil relatives. The features we point out here will all be familiar to you from Chapter 7.

Vertebral Column

The characteristic curves you observed in the human vertebral column (Figure 7.9 and *Atlas* p. 184, Figure 5.74) are absent in the apes. The difference in size between cervical and lumbar vertebrae are more marked in humans because the difference in the amount of weight born by the cervical vertebrae (the head) differs from the lumbar vertebrae (the entire upper body). Apes have a less marked difference because all four limbs share in weight-bearing. Therefore, the lumbar vertebrae don't have to be as large.

The ape ilia are more posterior, so they are closer to each other and the intervening sacrum is thus thinner. In the human, because the ilia are out to the sides, the bones are farther apart, spanned by the wider sacrum.

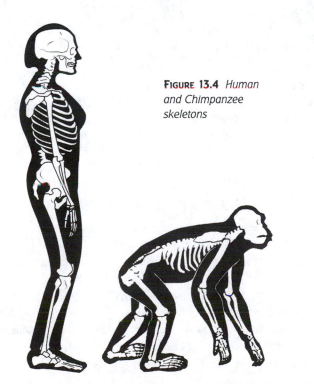

FIGURE 13.4 *Human and Chimpanzee skeletons*

Pelvis

On the ape pelvis the ilium is long and skinny (*Atlas* p. 184, Figure 5.72) and the gluteal muscles function as powerful hip extensors. In humans the gluteal muscles act as stabilizers for the hip, so there has been selection for shifting these muscles toward the sides as their function changed. The bony support, the ilium, now has a lateral orientation (Figure 13.5 and *Atlas* p. 184, Figure 5.73 A and B).

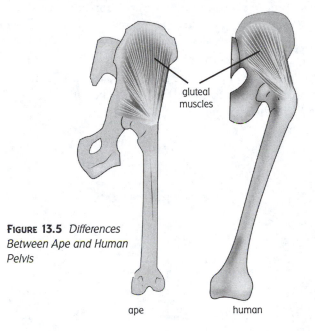

FIGURE 13.5 *Differences Between Ape and Human Pelvis*

A major muscle of propulsion in humans is the *rectus femoris* of the quadriceps muscle group. The rectus femoris is not significant in apes, but the origin of this muscle on the human pelvis causes a large projection, the *anterior inferior iliac spine* (Figure 13.6). This feature is very small on an ape innominate. The muscle actually crosses two joints, its action producing movement at both the hip and the knee. It inserts on the *anterior tibial tuberosity*, which is also large in humans and small in apes. If you stand up, lift your leg (flex leg at hip), then straighten your knee (extend leg at knee), you will experience the rectus femoris in action.

anterior inferior iliac spine

rectus femoris muscle

FIGURE 13.6 *Attachment of Rectus Femoris Muscle in Humans*

Femur

The pulling of the leg around toward the center as you step forward is caused by the adductor muscle group, muscles of which run from your posterior pelvis to the linea aspera on your posterior femur (Figure 13.7). The muscle is relatively weak in apes, so the linea aspera is small compared to the marked one observed on a human femur.

If you look in a mirror, or at your classmates when they're in a standing position (anatomical position), you'll see that the legs come in toward the center, from hip to knee. At the hip they're farther apart, but our knees are close together. This is a result of the articulations at the hip and the knee, caused by the shape of the joint surfaces. The femur thus creates an angle with the tibia upon which it rests, called the *bicondylar angle* (also called the carrying angle; Figure 13.8).

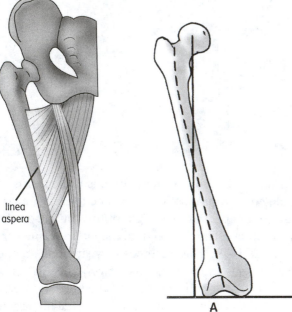

FIGURE 13.7 *Adductor Muscles Inserting onto a Human Posterior Femur at Linea Aspera*

FIGURE 13.8 *Orientation of Femur in (A) Humans and (B) Apes*

Feet

Human feet are well designed for terrestrial distance walking, with toes all in a line, the most medial of which is greatly developed to absorb forces and assist in propulsion, and ligaments bind our foot bones into arches to serve as shock absorbers. Our heel strike, in which all of our body weight is transmitted through the calcaneus, has selected for a large such bone in humans (Figure 13.9 and *Atlas* p. 194, Figure 5.100B) compared to an ape calcaneus.

Apes retain an arboreally adapted grasping toe, not so different in size from the other toes, and a longitudinal arch is not necessary. Ape toes are longer, and metatarsals and

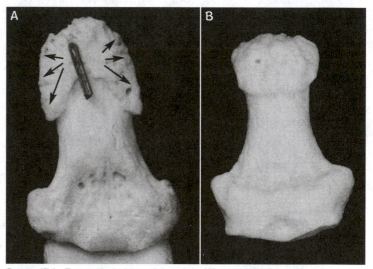

FIGURE 13.9 *(A) An Ape Foot and (B) a Human Foot*

phalanges are more curved than ours, another arboreal adaptation.

Hands

Similar to the differences between human and ape foot bones, our metatarsals and phalanges are straighter and those of apes are more curved. The terminal phalanx of the thumb provides an expanded area for muscle attachment in humans (Photo 13.1A). This is not the case in apes, in which the thumb tip is thinner and lacks the extensive muscle attachment sites (Photo 13.1B).

PHOTO 13.1 *Terminal phalanx of thumb in (A) ape and (B) human*

Cranial and Dental Differences Between Humans and Apes

Although adaptations to bipedalism were some of the earliest apparent changes from the common ancestor of humans and African apes, dental and cranial features changed as well and are visible in fossils of early hominids. The key, again, is to use our comparative base of living apes and humans to see differences in skulls and dentition. The basic knowledge of ape and human cranial and dental differences and similarities is essential to interpret the fossil record, which is made up largely of jaws and teeth! The numerous distinguishing features of ape versus human skulls and teeth are far too numerous to detail here, but we'll highlight some of the major ones.

Cranium

The position of the foramen magnum is the only cranial feature indicating body posture, because it is the entry point for the spinal cord. The foramen magnum is more anterior in humans (Photo 13.2A; *Atlas* p. 87, Figure 4.16), and more posterior in apes (Photo 13.2B; *Atlas* p. 142, Figure 4.164).

The much greater cranial capacity of humans influences cranial shape such that our skull is higher, with the maximum breadth high on the parietals (Photo 13.3; *Atlas* p. 88, Figure 4.20). Humans exhibit virtually no postorbital constric-

tion compared to the apes (Photo 13.4; *Atlas* p. 85, Figure 4.12A, p. 142, Figure 4.163), because the human brain fills the space behind the orbits.

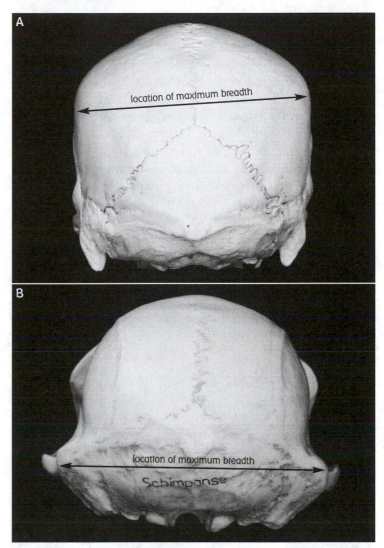

PHOTO 13.3 *Posterior view of (A) human skull and (B) chimpanzee skull*

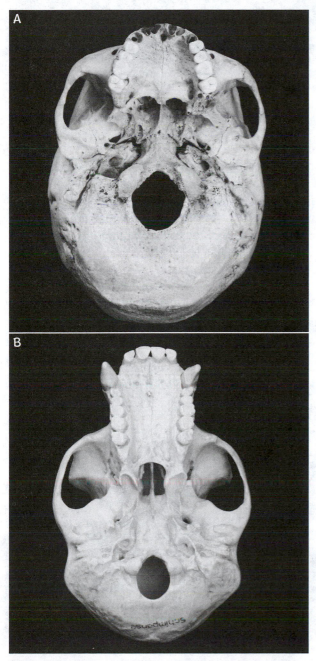

PHOTO 13.2 *Ventral view of (A) human skull and (B) chimpanzee skull*

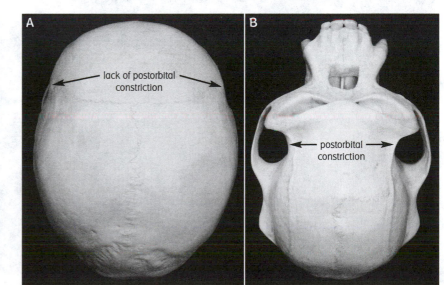

PHOTO 13.4 *Superior view of (A) human skull and (B) chimpanzee skull*

Face and Jaws

We are **orthognathic**. Our face is quite vertical, as opposed to the **prognathic** appearance of the apes, with their forward-jutting jaw (Photo 13.5). Our dental arcade is **parabolic** (*see* Photo 13.2; *Atlas* p. 87, Figure 4.16) as opposed to the rectangular shape observable in the ape tooth rows (*Atlas* p. 147, Figure 4.175). The human mandible is gracile, and chewing forces are buttressed by the bony anterior projection of the chin. The apes' mandible is robust, and chewing forces are buttressed on the internal aspect of the mandible, with a **simian shelf** (Photo 13.6).

Also related to chewing force is the development of a sagittal crest in gorillas and some male chimpanzees (*Atlas* p. 146), and the flaring of the zygomatic arches. Both of these features are related to extensive development of the temporalis muscle.

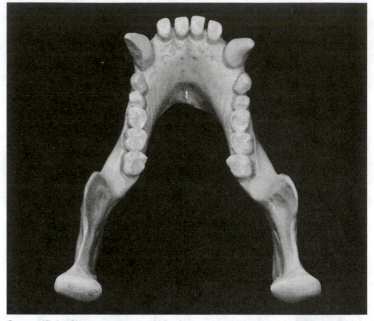

Photo 13.6 *Chimpanzee mandible demonstrating simian shelf*
1. simian shelf

Teeth

The large canines of apes are part of a functional complex called a **canine shearing complex, or honing triad** (Photo 13.7). In addition to large canines are spaces (each is a **diastema**) in which it fits in the upper and lower tooth rows, and a lower premolar just posterior to the bottom space that is sharpened as it sharpens the upper canine. This tooth is called the **sectorial P$_3$**. While it is the first premolar in the tooth row, P$_1$ and P$_2$ have been lost through evolutionary time; the remaining premolars in catarrhines are P$_3$ and P$_4$ (*Atlas* p. 67, Figures 3.65, 3.66; p. 71, Figure. 3.72). The size relationship of molars differs in apes and humans such that in apes, molar size increases somewhat toward the back (M3>M2>M1). In humans, molar size decreases toward the back (M1>M2>M3).

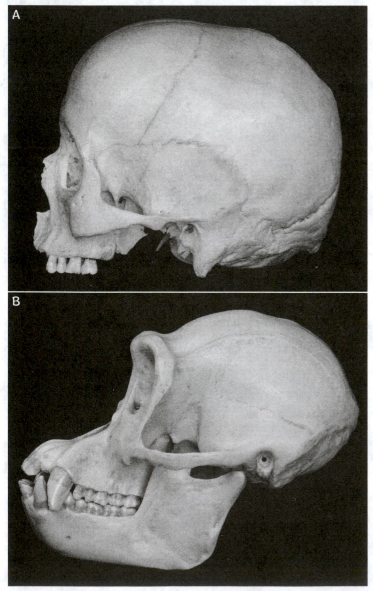

Photo 13.5 *Lateral view of (A) human and (B) chimpanzee skull*

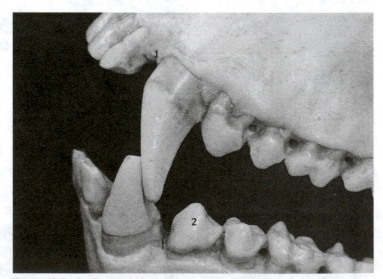

Photo 13.7 *Gorilla mandible demonstrating canine shearing complex*
1. diastema   2. sectorial P$_3$

LAB EXERCISE 13.2

NAME _____ SECTION _____ DATE _____

1. It is useful to observe the skulls of young individuals of different species. How do the chimp infant and fetal human skull shown here look more or less similar to one another than do adults of the two species? (*Atlas* p. 96, Figure 4.38; p. 143, Figure 4.166)

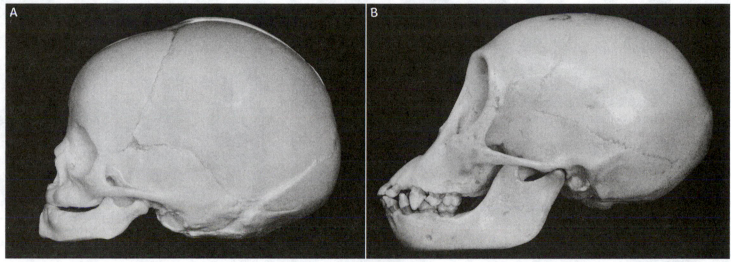

(A) Human fetal skull and (B) chimpanzee infant skull

2. Examine Figures 13.5, 13.6, 13.8, and 13.9, and the photos on the next page (or your lab specimens). Describe your observed differences between ape and human with regard to differences related to bipedalism (*Atlas* p. 184, Figure 5.72; p.192.

	Chimpanzee	Human
Pelvis Ilium shape, length		
Orientation of iliac blades (posterior versus lateral)		
Size of anterior inferior iliac spine		
Femur Bicondylar angle?		
Orientation of femoral head, height of greater trochanter		
Size of linea aspera		
Foot Position of big toe		
Size of calcaneus		
Relative thickness of big toe to other toes		

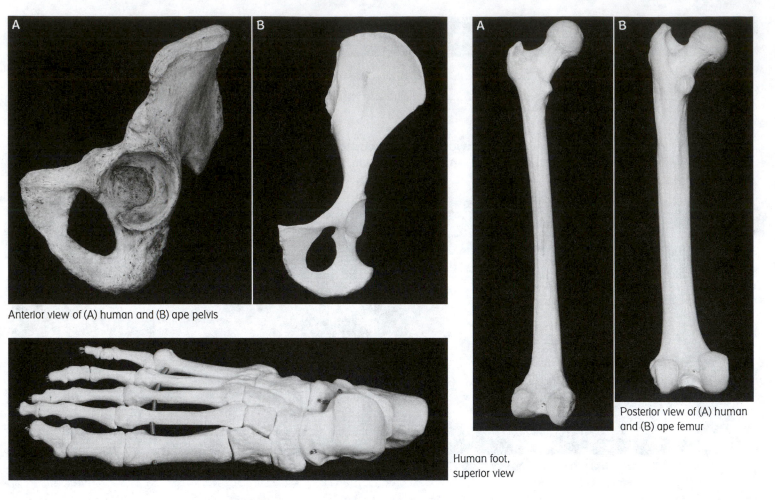

Anterior view of (A) human and (B) ape pelvis

Human foot, superior view

Posterior view of (A) human and (B) ape femur

3. Compare the cranial and dental features of an ape and a human, and fill out the chart, using lab specimens or photos 13.2 through 13.7.

	Chimpanzee	Human
Position of foramen magnum		
Shape of dental arcade		
Relative size of molars: M1, M2, M3		
Location of maximum skull breadth (viewed from back)		
Degree of postorbital constriction		
Cranial capacity (cranium size relative to facial skull)		
Degree of prognathism		
Canine shearing complex: Canine size Diastema Shape of P_3		
Chin versus receding mandibular symphysis		

Introducing the Australopiths

The human fossil record now contains a dazzling array of fossilized bone, stone tools, and other evidence from our evolutionary history. The last several years alone have yielded unprecedented numbers of fossils, far exceeding our expectations. One of the most recent finds is that of *Sahelanthropus tchadensis* (*Atlas* p. 282; br. ed. p. 54), found in Chad (Brunet et al., 2002). Some researchers have interpreted this fossil to represent the earliest known hominid to split from the ape line. As the record has become more complete, however, it becomes more difficult to "connect the dots" and link the various hominid forms to one another through time.

In this chapter we will not go into the various classification schemes that have been interpreted from the fossil evidence. We will only point out some of the best-known fossil forms and their features. In our attempt to make sense of the past, different researchers may use knowledge to classify and categorize in ways that everyone does not necessarily agreed upon. This is the nature of science. Here, the goal is to present the material in a way that will enhance learning of the basics, particularly emphasizing the empirical aspects: the morphology of the specimens themselves. We will follow the traditional classification of separating humans and our ancestors from our ape relatives from the point of the split with our shared common ancestor.

Previously we defined this group as the Hominidae. Subdividing the Hominidae can be accomplished most conveniently by grouping together the earlier forms, many of which are placed in the genus *Australopithecus*, from the later hominids, which share more similarities with modern humans. We thus follow the path of least resistance and consider fossils of our extinct relatives as members of either (1) the **australopiths,** or (2) the genus *Homo*.

"Lucy," the most famous of the australopiths, is a member of the species *Australopithecus afarensis*. In the remainder of this chapter, we'll focus on the australopiths, particularly the best-known examples (such as Lucy's species), and see where they fit relative to chimpanzees and humans in terms of locomotor adaptations and cranial/dental features.

The approximately 11 australopith species in five (or six) genera are found only in Africa. They have in common a relatively small brain and ape-like head, perched upon a rather human-like body. Because there are so many species (see Online Instructor's Manual for a more complete list and time range), it is convenient to learn about them in groups whenever possible. Many of them can be placed feasibly into one of three fossil australopith groups:

1. **primitive,**
2. **gracile,** and
3. **robust.**

Australopithecus afarensis is our representative of the primitive group, and *Australopithecus africanus* is the gracile form. The robust group is composed of three species. Although some researchers place members of this group into their own genus (*Paranthropus*), we will use the more conservative genus of *Australopithecus*: *Australopithecus robustus, A. boisei,* and *A. aethiopicus.* We will focus on a few well-known representatives of each of the three groups, with the understanding that several others species exist, and that not all fossils fit so neatly within one of the three groups. Rather than our pointing out the differences between these fossils now, you will discover them for yourself in Lab Exercise #3.

LAB EXERCISE 13.3

NAME _____ SECTION _____ DATE _____

1. Observe lab specimens and the photos in this and the previous lab exercise. Compare postcranial bones of *Australopithecus afarensis* (Lucy) to those of a chimpanzee and a human (*Atlas* p. 287, Figures 8.66, 8.67; br. ed. p. 59, Figures. 3.66, 3.77), and fill out the chart below. Answer from a comparative perspective. For example, for orientation of iliac blades, you might say, "more laterally placed" (for *A. afarensis* compared to a chimpanzee) and "slightly more posteriorly placed" (for *A. afarensis* compared to a human). See next page for *A. afarensis* proximal femur.

	A. afarensis compared to a Chimpanzee	*A. afarensis* compared to a Human
Vertebral column Width of sacrum		
Pelvis Ilium shape, length		
Orientation of iliac blades		
Size of anterior inferior iliac spine		
Femur Bicondylar angle?		
Orientation of femoral head, height of greater trochanter		
Size of linea aspera		

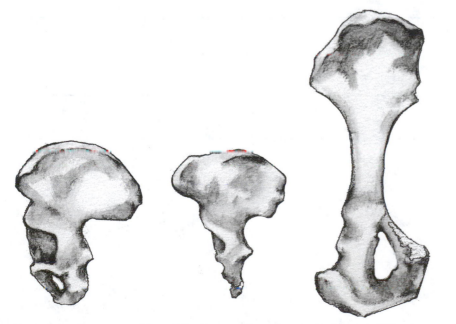

Comparison of Innominate Bone of (A) a Human, (B) an Australopithecine, and (C) an Ape

A. afarensis pelvis, anterior view

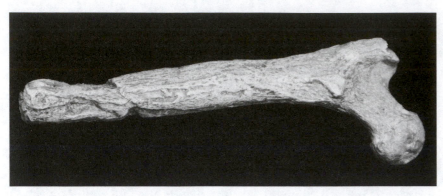

Proximal femur of *A afarensis,*
posterior view

2. In the chart, describe the cranial and dental features of *A. afarensis* compared to a chimp and to a human, using the lab specimens and photos 13.2 through 13.5, and on the following page (*see also Atlas* pp. 286–287; br. ed. pp. 58–59).

	A. afarensis compared to a Chimpanzee	*A. afarensis* compared to a Human
Position of foramen magnum		
Shape of dental arcade		
Relative size of molars: M1, M2, M3		
Location of maximum skull breadth (viewed from back)		
Degree of postorbital constriction		
Cranial capacity (cranium size relative to facial skull)		
Degree of prognathism		
Canine shearing complex: Canine size Diastema Shape of P_3		
Chin versus receding mandibular symphysis		

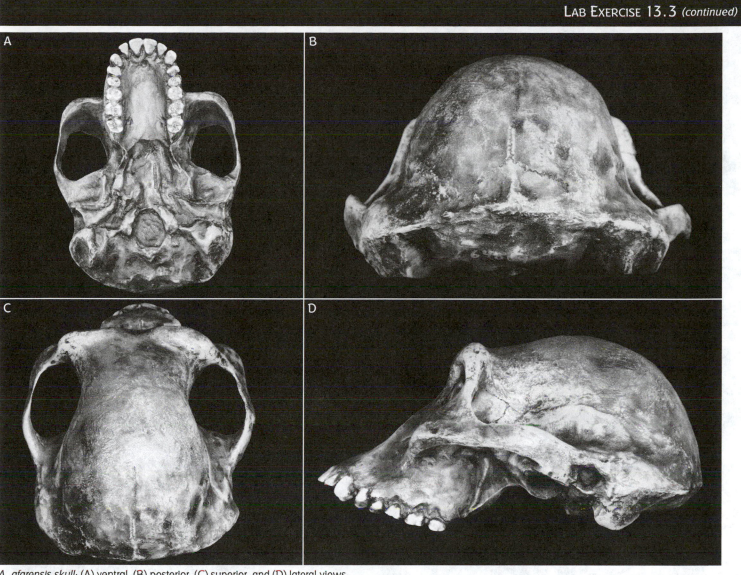

A. afarensis skull: (A) ventral, (B) posterior, (C) superior, and (D) lateral views

3. For the following exercise on cranial and dental features, observe representatives of the gracile and robust group from the photos here (*Atlas* pp. 288–293; br. ed. pp. 60–65) and compare them to the specimens or photos of *A. afarensis*, a chimp, and a human. Fill out the chart on page 249.

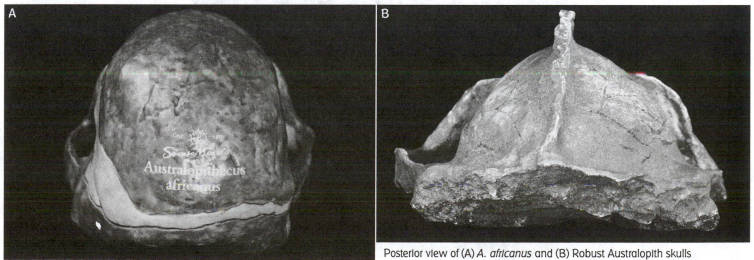

Posterior view of (A) *A. africanus* and (B) Robust Australopith skulls

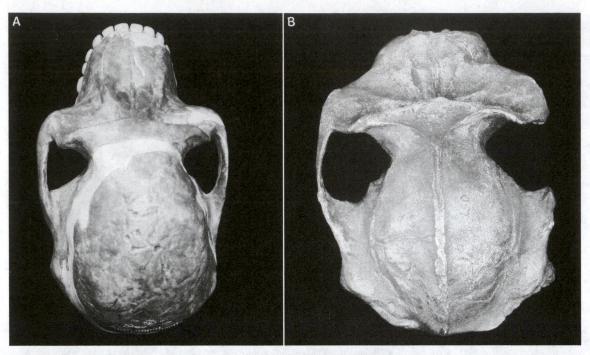

Superior View of (A) *A. africanus* and (B) Robust Australopith skulls

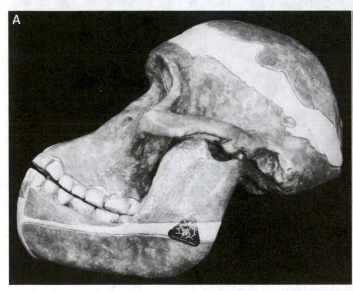

Lateral View of (A) *A. africanus* and (B) Robust Australopith Skulls

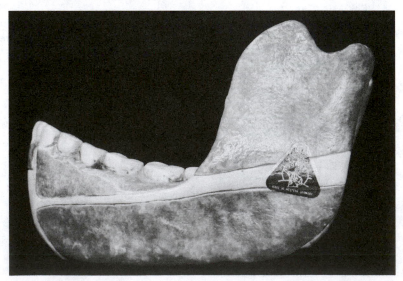

A. africanus mandible

	Chimp	*A. afarensis*	*A. africanus*	Robust australopith	Human
Location of maximum skull breadth					
Degree of postorbital constriction					
Degree of zygomatic flare					
Cranium size relative to facial skull					
Degree of prognathism					
Facial profile shape					
Sagittal crest?					
Shape of occipital and nuchal region					
Canine shearing complex: Canine size Diastema Shape of P_3					
Chin versus retreating mandibular symphysis					

4. Regarding the robust australopiths, how would you interpret the molar tooth form and size, degree of zygomatic flare, and presence of sagittal crest?

What do these three features have to do with each other?

5. The relative size of the anterior and posterior dentition changes through time. Tooth proportions can be measured to track that change. Measure the width of one of the central upper incisors, and the width of an upper second molar from the same side. Then calculate an index to obtain a ratio of incisor-to-molar width.

$$\frac{\text{Incisor width}}{\text{Molar width}} \times 100$$

	Incisor width	M$_2$ width	Index
Chimpanzee			
A. *afarensis*			
A. *africanus*			
Robustus australopith			
Modern human			

6. Which specimen is most similar to which other specimen?

   Do you observe any trends in changes of tooth proportion over time?

7. Compare the photo of the Taung child (*Atlas* p. 288, Figure 8.69; br. ed. p. 60, Figure. 3.69), *Australopithecus africanus*, with the modern fetal human skull and that of the baby chimp in Exercise 13.2. Why do you think the discoverer of the Taung child, Raymond Dart, insisted that the Taung skull was that of a hominid, not an ape? What features led him to this conclusion?

8. Look at the size of the molars. Keeping in mind that this was a very young individual (3 to 4 years old), what does it indicate about the teeth of an adult of this species? Can we definitely assign this youngster to either a gracile or a robust australopithecine species?

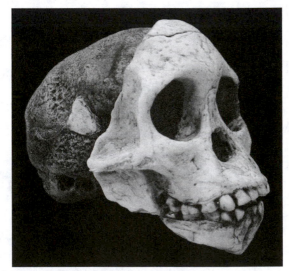

Taung child skull, mandible, and endocast

SELF-TEST 13.1

NAME _____ SECTION _____ DATE _____

1. What are at least three skeletal differences between apes and humans that relate to locomotion?

   a.

   b.

   c.

2. What are at least three cranial or dental differences between apes and humans?

   a.

   b.

   c.

3. What are the two phases of the walking cycle? Briefly describe each.

   a.

   b.

4. What defines the family Hominidae?

5. What are the two main groups within the family Hominidae?

   a.

   b.

6. What is an example of a fossil species representing the primitive group of australopiths?

   The gracile group?

   The robust group?

7. Why was it important for robust australopithecines to have such huge molars? (What are they good for?) related: sagittal crest, flaring zygomatics

8. What are two features that differ between primitive, robust, and gracile australopiths? Describe the feature for each group.

9. a. Overall, does the skull of an *A. afarensis* look more ape-like or more human-like?

   b. What features play a primary role in causing this overall appearance?

10. Why is *A. afarensis* considered a hominid?

11. a. Does the australopith pelvis look more ape-like or more human-like?

   b. What features are primarily responsible for this overall appearance?

14. The Genus *Homo*

"Have you ever wondered...?"

✋ So, did they ever find the "Missing Link?"

Early members of the genus *Homo* have been found in both East Africa and South Africa. They range in time from about 2.4 to 1.4 million years ago.

Early Homo

The earliest known member of our genus was found by Mary and Louis Leakey. Formally named by Louis Leakey, Philip Tobias, and John Napier, its scientific name was suggested to Louis Leakey by Raymond Dart, the South African paleontologist who discovered the Taung child fossil, among many others.

Homo habilis, which roughly translates from the Latin as "handy man," was named because of its presumed association with stone tools. Though it was similar to *Australopithecus africanus* in many ways, its brain was significantly larger and its face and dentition smaller. Compared to *A. africanus*, features of *Homo habilis* are the following.

1. Cranium size:
   a. Higher cranium
   b. Larger cranial capacity: average of 650 cc (25%–40% larger than australopiths); largest was ~775 cc
   c. Less postorbital constriction
   d. More rounded cranium
   e. Face smaller relative to cranium

2. Diet and chewing:
   a. More vertical face (less prognathic, more orthognathic)
   b. Smaller, thinner mandible
   c. Mandible more parabolic and less V-shaped
   d. Shortened length of posterior tooth row
   e. Teeth more human-shaped: premolars and molars smaller, incisors larger

Many researchers think two species of early *Homo* existed, because the range of variation seems to be too wide to be contained within just one species. The fossils fall into two groups that differ from each other in cranial and postcranial features, and may indicate two species: *Homo habilis* and *Homo rudolfensis* (Photo 14.1; *Atlas* p. 295; br. ed. p. 67). Some distinguishing features are listed in Table 14.1.

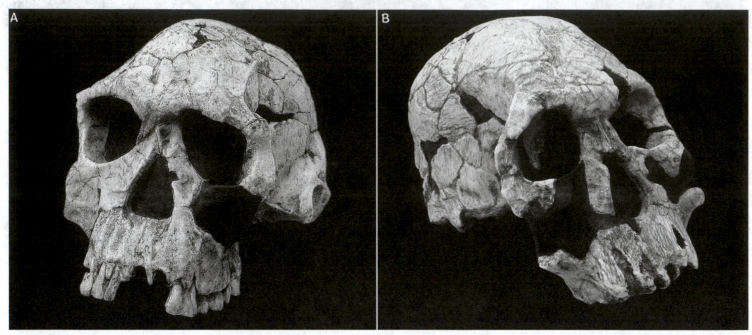

PHOTO 14.1 *Early Homo: Homo habilis (A) and H. rudolfensis (B)*

TABLE 14.1: Features of *Homo rudolfensis* and *Homo habilis*	
H rudolfensis (2.4–1.6 mya – E. Africa)	**H. habilis (2.0–1.6 mya – E. & S. Africa)**
Larger body size; 1.5 m tall	Smaller body size
Larger absolute, but smaller relative cranial capacity	Larger supraorbital ridge
Smaller supraorbital ridge	Facial bones smaller, nose more developed
More robust facial features	More gracile facial features
More orthognathic	More prognathic
Large palate	Smaller palate
More robust mandible	Thinner jaw
Larger posterior teeth (but narrow molars)	Smaller molars
More human-like femur	Postcranium more primitive; relatively long arms

Use Source (Wood, 1991; McKee et al., 2005)??

The tools associated with *Homo habilis* are referred to as **Olduwan** (see Figure 14.1), after the site in Tanzania (Olduvai Gorge) at which they were first discovered.

Homo erectus

Homo erectus closely followed early populations of *Homo habilis* in time and existed over a long period, dating from almost 2 million years ago up to at least as recently as 250,000 years ago in the Far East. *Homo erectus* was first found by Eugene Dubois, a Dutch doctor who traveled to the Dutch East Indies precisely to find "The Missing Link!" After much searching at various sites, Dubois eventually found a skullcap and femur of *Homo erectus* on the Indo-

nesian island of Java, but his assumption that any single fossil would represent the missing link was mistaken.

Like any family tree, the human evolutionary past is represented by many branches, so the idea of a single half-human half-ape form is a myth. After the Dubois find in the late 1800s, many more *Homo erectus* fossils were found in Asia and in Africa.

Similar to the case for *Homo habilis*, the variation of fossils attributed to *Homo erectus*, as well as its time range and geographical distribution, make us doubt that all such fossils belong to only one wide-ranging species. Now they are often split into two species: *Homo erectus* and *Homo ergaster* (Photo 14.2; *Atlas* pp. 296–297, 303; br. ed. pp.

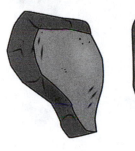
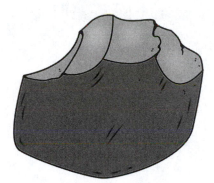

FIGURE 14.1 *Examples of Olduwan Tools*

68–69, 75). *Homo erectus* is the Asian species, and some researchers think it represents an evolutionary dead-end. *Homo ergaster* is found in Africa and may represent the ancestor of later humans. Numerous similarities exist between these two species, and features of both, compared to *Homo habilis/H. rudolphensis*, include:

- thicker bone
- long, low skull
- cranial capacity of 850–1100 cc
- sagittal keel
- large supraorbital torus (larger than *H. habilis*)
- shorter face
- less postorbital constriction
- receding forehead
- sharp nuchal torus, set high on occipital, V-shaped
- maximum breadth near base of skull
- projecting nasal region

- vertical or receding mandibular symphysis (no chin)
- taller at adulthood
- less sexual dimorphism
- basically modern postcrania; more muscled and robust than modern humans

Why were these hominids so important? Some member of this group was presumably the first to leave Africa. In addition, they were the first known to control fire. Their stone tool type, better-developed than Olduwan, is known as the **Acheulean.** A typical Acheulean tool is a large, bifaced, and often tear-drop shaped tool, the **hand axe** (Photo 14.3). Hand axes are found in Africa and in Europe but not in eastern Asia. Experiments show that they probably were used on meat, bone, wood, and hides. These ubiquitous hand axes have been referred to as the "Swiss Army knife of the Lower Paleolithic."

We'll now make some comparisons involving these earlier members of our genus and their stone tools.

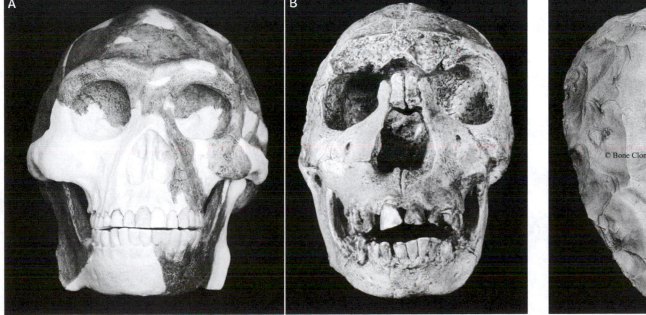

PHOTO 14.2 *(A) Homo erectus and (B) Homo ergaster*

PHOTO 14.3 *Example of Acheulean tool*

L A B   E X E R C I S E   1 4 . 1

NAME _____ SECTION _____ DATE _____

1. Take a look at Olduwan tools (refer to Figure 14.1).

   a. What would make you think they are tools and not just a couple of rocks?

   b. In what specific ways do these tools differ from Acheulean tools? It may be helpful to draw them as part of your answer.

2. Compare the earlier members of the genus *Homo* with a predecessor as well as a modern human to highlight changes occurring over time. Use the photos on the next pages and from Chapter 13, pages 247–248 (also see *Atlas* pp. 289, 290, 295–298, 303; br. ed. p. 61, 62, 67–70, 75) or fossil casts. Many of your descriptions may be in relative terms (larger, smaller, etc.).

	A. africanus	*H. habilis* or *H. rudolfensis*	*H. erectus* or *H. ergaster*	Modern human
Shape of dental arcade				
Size of front teeth relative to back				
Relative size of molars: M1, M2, M3				
Sagittal keel?				
Location of maximum skull breadth				
Degree of postorbital constriction				
Cranial shape (height versus length				
Cranium size relative to facial skull				
Supraorbital ridge size				
Degree of prognathism				
Shape of occipital and nuchal region (nuchal torus?				
Mandibular symphysis form (receding, vertical, chin)				

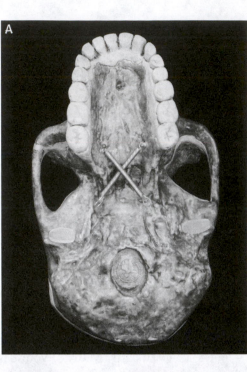

Australpithecus africanus,
ventral view

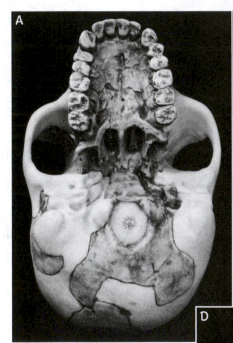

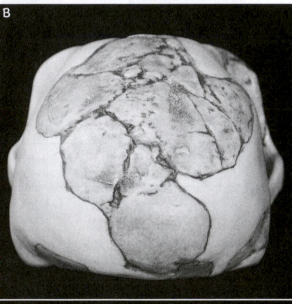

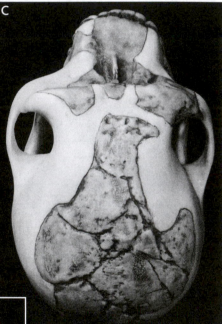

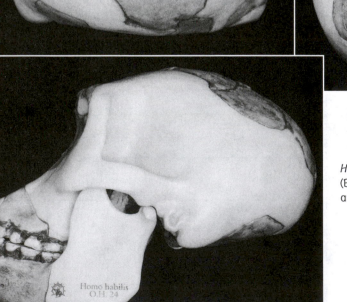

Homo habilis: (A) ventral,
(B) posterior, (C) superior,
and (D) lateral views

A

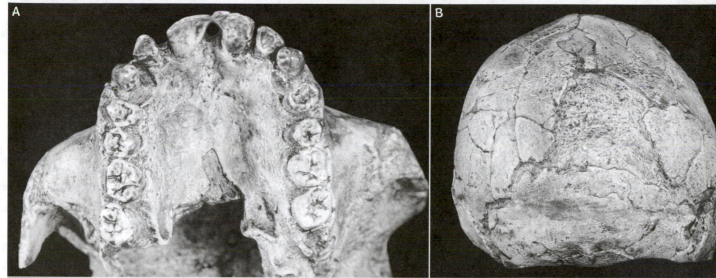

B

C

D

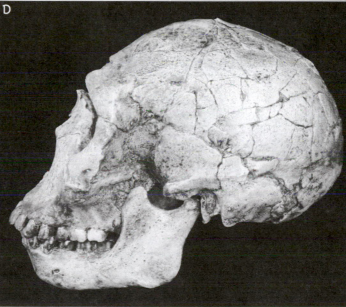

Homo ergaster: (A) ventral,
(B) posterior, (C) superior,
and (D) lateral views

Modern human dental arcade
(see also Photos 13.2 and 13.5)

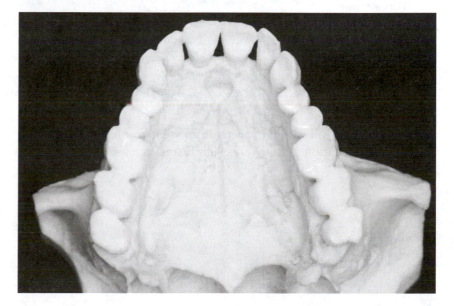

3. You've observed several cranial features. Which ones are directly related to (or appear to be a result of) increased cranial capacity?

4. Although bigger brains are known to be related to higher intelligence in a general sense, bigger individuals within a species that obviously that have a bigger body size and head size aren't smarter than their smaller-headed companions. Brain size has intraspecific (within species) variation. When comparing various species, a significant aspect to study is *relative brain size*—brain size compared to body size.

   To determine the significance of this correlation, we can gauge the ratio of brain size to body size. The chart below provides you with data on average cranial capacity (cc) and average body weight for several species. It is up to you to calculate the ratio by dividing the cranial capacity by body weight. Obviously, a species with a value of .05 has a smaller relative brain size than one with a 0.12 value.

$$\frac{\text{cranial capacity (in cubic cm)}}{\text{body weight (in kg)}} = \text{brain/body size ratio}$$

Fill out the chart for the following species listed.

Species	Cranial Capacity (cc)	Average Approximate Body Weight (kg)	Brain/Body Size Ratio
Chimpanzee	395[1]	54[3]	
Gorilla	506[1]	120[3]	
A. afarensis	438	37[5]	
A. africanus	440	35[5]	
Robust australopiths	515[2]	39[2]	
H. habilis	631	42[5]	
H. erectus	985[2]	56[4]	
H. sapiens	1325[1]	63[4]	

Adapted from Sattenspiel, L., C. V. Ward, S. Stout, and D. Wescott. *Introduction to Biological Anthropology Laboratory Manual* (unpublished work, University of Missouri, Columbia, 2001, p. 130).

Data obtained:

[1] Jurmain, R., H. Nelson, L. Kilgore, and W. Trevathan. 2003. *Introduction to Physical Anthropology*, 8th ed. Belmont, CA: Wadsworth/Thomson Learning.

[2] Park, M. A. 2005. *Biological Anthropology*. New York: McGraw-Hill.

[3] Fleagle, J. G. F. 1999. *Primate Adaptation and Evolution*, 2nd ed. New York. Academic Press.

[4] Stanford, C., J. S. Allen, and S. C. Anton. 2006. *Biological Anthropology*. Upper Saddle River, NJ: Pearson Prentice Hall.

[5] McHenry, H. 1992. Body size and proportions in early hominids. *Am. J. Phys. Anthropol.* 87:407–431.

5. Is this what you would expect? From what you have found among the hominids species listed above, at what point in human evolution did the most significant increase in relative brain size occur?

Later *Homo*: "Archaic" *Homo sapiens*

By 800,000 years ago, other human forms appeared with a mix of *Homo erectus* and *Homo sapiens* features. These were widespread in Africa, Asia, Europe. Their lack of a consistent set of features and their wide geographical range make it clear that they represented more than one species, but they traditionally have been referred to as **"archaic" *Homo sapiens*,** or **transitional forms** (Photo 14.4; *Atlas* pp. 307–312; br. ed. pp. 79–84).

Because any human appearing during this time is thrown into this group, this is sometimes also referred to as the "garbage pail group." Many of these forms in Europe may have belonged to the species *Homo heidelbergensis*, named after the German city near the site at which one of these forms was first discovered. There are numerous interpretations of the number of species and their appropriate scientific names. Further information on the assignment of specific fossils to species is found in the Online Instructor's Manual.

Relative to *Homo erectus*, some features the "archaic" *Homo sapiens* exhibited were:

- ☙ larger cranial capacity
- ☙ decreased postorbital constriction
- ☙ higher skull, shorter skull (front to back)
- ☙ occipital more rounded (less angular)
- ☙ forehead more rounded
- ☙ smaller teeth and jaws

Compared to modern humans, some features are:

- ☙ heavier face
- ☙ larger teeth

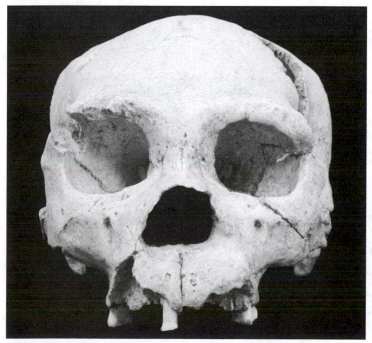

PHOTO 14.4 *"Archaic" Homo sapiens (from Atapuerca, Spain)*

- ☙ lower, longer skulls
- ☙ large supraorbital ridge, varied, often not continuous across frontal bone, but arched over each eye

"Archaic" *Homo sapiens* were culturally more diverse than *H. erectus*, with advances including new and more varied tools, some primitive shelters, and more efficient hunting techniques. While use of Acheulean tools continued for a time, they began to be interspersed with new tool-making techniques, particularly one undertaken to create **Levalloisian** flake tools. In this technique, the core was modified to produce more predictable sizes and shapes of flakes. The hafting of points onto shafts for spears also occurred during this time.

The "Archaic" *Homo sapiens* group frequently is divided into two subgroups, based on time of occurrence. The first consists of fossils referred to as **early "archaics,"** which lived between 400,000 and approximately 150,000 years ago. Around the time of their disappearance, two groups of people appeared. One was the **late "archaics,"** which include the well-known and interesting **Neanderthals,** and the other was our own "brand" of people, the **anatomically modern humans.**

Special Case of the Neanderthals

The first discovery of a fossil that was recognized as human at the time of its discovery was of a Neanderthal partial skeleton, found near Dusseldorf, Germany in the mid-1800s. First thought to be the bones of a cave bear, a high school science teacher recognized them as human.

Neanderthals existed in the Middle East and Europe from about 130,000 years ago until about 30,000 years ago. The most distinctive specimens are those that first appeared about 75,000 years ago in Europe, during the height of the Pleistocene ice ages. These are referred to as "classic" Neanderthals, and are best exemplified by specimens such as those pictured (Photo 14.5; *Atlas* pp. 314–319; br. ed. pp. 86–89), and by the features listed on page 262. The Neanderthals frequently inhabited caves and were efficient game hunters. Their stone tools were more complex and varied than previous tools, using a tool technology referred to as the **Mousterian** industry (Photo 14.6).

The place of the Neanderthals in our evolutionary history —or whether they even *had* a place in our history—continue to be debated! Some researchers see Neanderthals as a defunct side branch and an evolutionary dead-end. Others are convinced that some Neanderthal traits are present in modern human populations. Mitochondrial DNA taken from the humerus of a Neanderthal was interpreted to indicate a split between anatomically modern humans and Neanderthals between 550,000 and 690,000 years ago, too long ago for any shared gene pool (Krings et al., 1997).

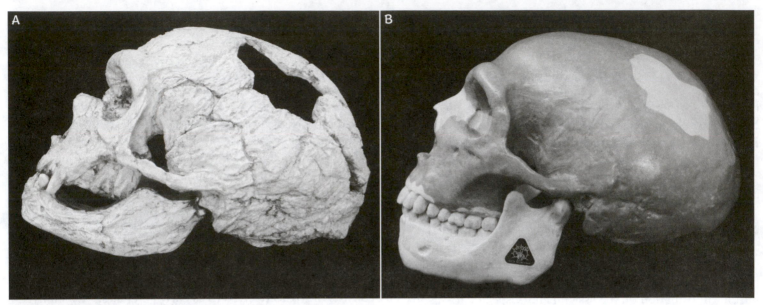

Photo 14.5 *Neanderthal specimens*

Photo 14.6 *Examples of Mousterian tools*

Neanderthal features relative to modern humans are:

👋 long, low skull

👋 average cranial capacity 1520 cc

👋 maximum breadth midway down skull

👋 occipital bun

👋 large supraorbital ridge

👋 rounded orbits

👋 midfacial prognathism ("puffy" maxillary region, which houses the maxillary sinuses)

👋 more rounded ("swept back") zygomatic arches

👋 broad nasal aperture

👋 retromolar space (space posterior to the lower third molar, anterior to the ascending ramus of the mandible)

👋 vertical mandibular symphysis (no chin)

👋 massive limbs

Anatomically Modern Humans

Anatomically modern humans (Photo 14.7; *Atlas* pp. 320–322; br. ed. p. 92–94) first appeared in Africa about 150,000 years ago and reached Europe by about 35,000 years ago. Dates on their arrival in Asia are less clear, but certainly by 25,000 years ago and possibly by 40,000 years ago. These earliest Africans of our species were from what is now Ethiopia, South Africa, and Tanzania. The very earliest, discovered quite recently, is from Ethiopia, and dates from between 160,000 and 154,000 years ago (White et al., 2003).

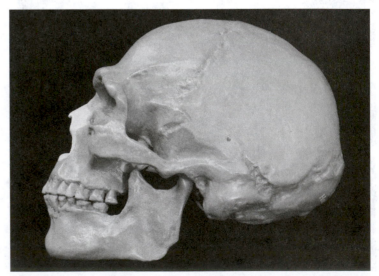

Photo 14.7 *Anatomically modern human (Predmöst, Czechoslovakia)*

By about 100,000 years ago, these humans already had migrated to Israel.

The best known of the anatomically modern humans of Europe, ***Homo sapiens sapiens***, was from the French site of **Cro Magnon,** a term that came to be synonymous with the earliest Europeans. These humans used a variety of Upper Paleolithic tools, which comprised the tool technologies referred to as Aurignacian, Gravettian, Solutrean, Magdalenian, and Perigordian. Their new tools included the atlatl (spear thrower), spears, javelins, harpoons for fishing, clubs, stone missiles, boomerangs, bolas (stones tied together, probably to snare birds), and burins (a wood-working tool). Their tools were made from a wide variety of raw materials, such as bone, antler, and wood. From these materials they made awls, needles, pins, fasteners, and fish hooks.

Features of anatomically modern humans compared to Neanderthals include:

- shorter, higher skull
- 1200–1700 cc (avg. 1325)
- more vertical forehead
- small supraorbital ridge
- maximum breadth high on parietals
- more angular orbits
- more squared-off zygomatic arches
- narrow nasal aperture
- chin (mental protuberance)
- smaller teeth, jaws
- skeleton more slightly built

Obviously, our story does not end here, but from this point on, technological changes have transformed our species to a much greater degree than have anatomical ones. Our differences from one another, though they may be noticeable, are very superficial compared with the vast changes we have undertaken over our evolutionary history.

LAB EXERCISE 14.2

NAME _____ SECTION _____ DATE _____

1. Compare various human forms, using lab specimens or photos 14.4 through 14.7, and those shown on the next pages (*Atlas* pp. 307–312, 314–319, 320-322; br. ed. p. 79–84, 86-89, 92–94).

	"Archaic" *H. sapiens*	Neanderthal	Early Anat. Modern Human	Modern Human
Size of front teeth relative to back				
Dentition/teeth size relative to face size				
Location of maximum skull breadth				
Degree of postorbital constriction				
Cranial shape (height versus length				
Cranium size relative to facial skull				
Supraorbital ridge size				
Degree of prognathism				
Form of midfacial region (prognathic?)				
Shape of occipital and nuchal region (bun? torus?)				
Mandibular symphysis form (receding, vertical, chin)				
Retromolar space?*				

*Not observable from photos

A

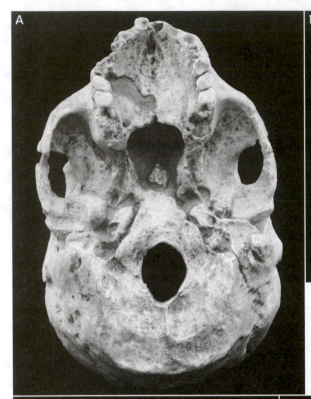

B

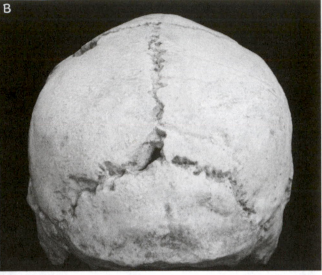

"Archaic" *Homo sapiens:* (A) ventral, (B) posterior, (C) superior, and (D) lateral views

C

D

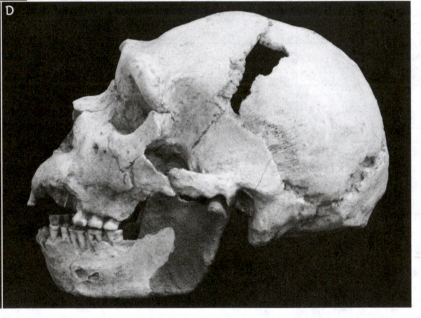

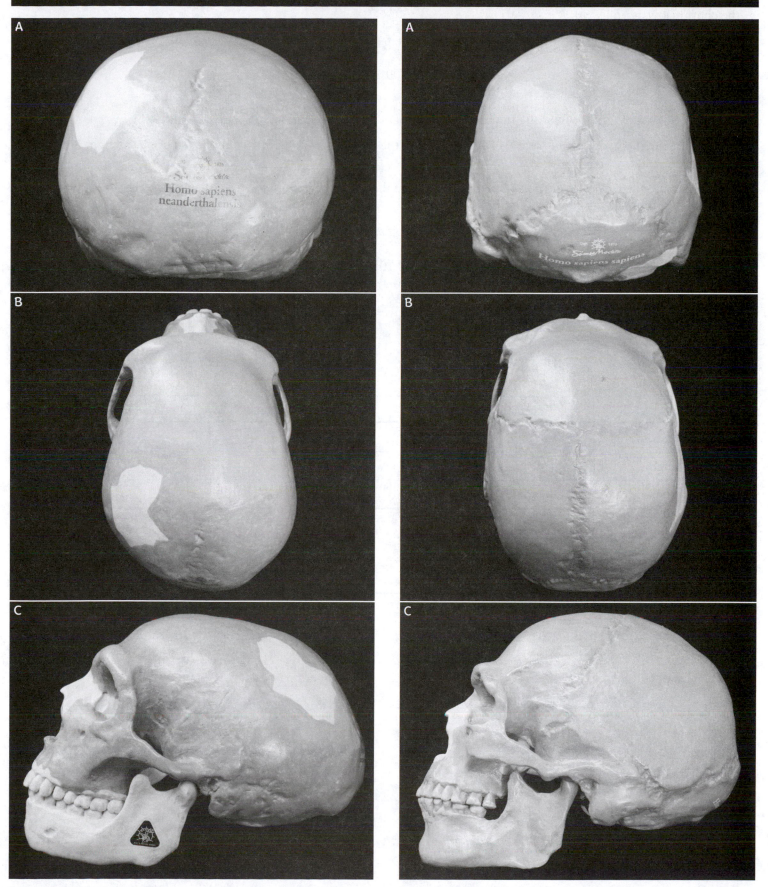

Neanderthal: (A) posterior, (B) superior, and (C) lateral views

Anatomically modern human: (A) posterior, (B) superior, and (C) lateral views

2. If skulls are available, you will conduct some quantitative comparisons of Neanderthals with modern humans. Measure and calculate indices for the following: a Neanderthal, an early anatomically modern, and a recent human skull. Fill out the chart below as you work.

a. Calculate the cranial index. (You learned the technique in Chapter 8):

$$\frac{\text{cranial breadth}}{\text{cranial length}} \times 100 = \text{cranial index}$$

b. Use the sliding calipers to measure the comparative length of the anterior and posterior tooth rows.

— Measure the width of the *anterior tooth row* from the outside (buccal/labial side) of canines on the right and left sides.

— Measure the length of the *posterior tooth row* from the mesial surface of the first premolar to the distal surface of the third molar.

— Calculate an index to represent the ratio of the two parts of the dental arcade.

$$\frac{\text{anterior tooth row}}{\text{posterior tooth row}} \times 100$$

c. Compare tooth proportions: central incisor width relative to second molar width, using the same technique as that used in Chapter 13.

$$\frac{\text{central incisor width}}{\text{second molar width}} \times 100$$

	Neanderthal	Early a.m. Human	Modern Human
Cranial breadth			
Cranial length			
Cranial index			
Anterior tooth row			
Posterior tooth row			
Index			

3. Based on your measurements, what can you say about the differences between Neanderthals and modern humans in terms of:

Cranial shape?

Anterior versus posterior teeth?

Tooth proportions?

SELF-TEST 14.1

NAME _____ SECTION _____ DATE _____

1. What are at least four changes in the cranium or dentition that occurred between the australopithecines and early members of the genus *Homo*?

    a.

    b.

    c.

    d.

2. Name (without looking at your chart, if possible) two characteristics of *Homo erectus* that are not observed in the other species studied so far.

    a.

    b.

3. What are at least four characteristics that appear to unite all members of the species *Homo sapiens*?

    a.

    b.

    c.

    d.

4. Which of the following "inventions" was first used by which hominid?

   a. Walking bipedally _____

   b. Burying their dead _____

   c. Use of Acheulean tools _____

   d. Control of fire _____

   e. Use of Olduwan tools _____

   f. Use of Mousterian tools _____

   g. Use of Upper Paleolithic tools _____

   h. Building nuclear reactors _____

5. Name and explain three *trends* that occurred *over the course of human evolution*. These could have to do with skull shape, facial morphology, or tooth and jaw proportions. Describe how each trend showed continual change over time, and include descriptive examples of which fossil forms had which form of each trait you discuss.

   a.

   b.

   c.

6. What is the "Missing Link," and has it been found?

Concluding Comments

The topics covered in this lab manual, as we mentioned at the beginning, are tied together by the thread of an underlying evolutionary framework. Evolution works in populations to cause significant changes over time, such as those we have studied in human evolutionary history. All four evolutionary forces have contributed to these changes, with both random and nonrandom factors acting to change gene frequencies from generation to generation (as we saw in our toothpick "populations").

You've learned about the genetic basis for evolution: the structure of the genetic material, how genetic material is passed on through the generations and results in physical characteristics (the phenotype), and how genetic variation is produced (mutations) and reshuffled (in gamete production) to create innumerable combinations of genotypes. You've studied the outcome of this genetic variation, particularly in terms of the skeletal variations exhibited within the human species, and how natural selection results in a diverse range of adaptations according to various environmental pressures over time.

Chromosomes in a Dividing Cell

(for use in Lab Exercise 4.1, number 2)

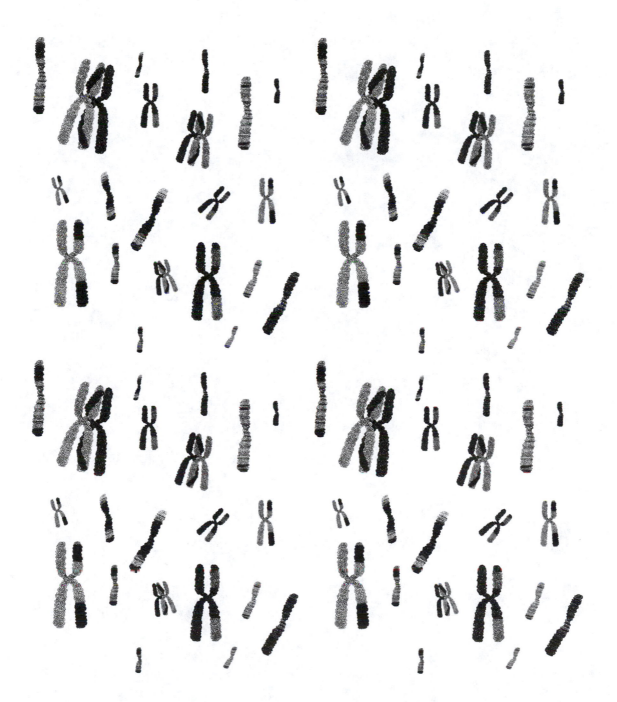

Latin and Greek Roots
for Selected Anatomical Terms

Root	Language	Meaning	Feature (or Bone)
coron	L	crown	coronal suture
cribr	L	sieve	cribriform plate
crist	L	crest	crista galli
foram	L	opening	foramen, foramina
foss	L	ditch, trench	fossa
gall	L	rooster	crista galli
glab	L	smooth	glabella
lambd	G	similar to Greek letter *lambda*	lambdoidal suture
magn	L	large	foramen magnum
mand	L	chew	mandible
mandibul	L	jaw	mandible
metop	G	forehead	metopic suture
nas	L	nose	nasal, nasion
orbi	F	circle	orbit
parie	L	wall	parietal
sagitt	L	arrow	sagittal sutur
sell	L	saddle	sella turcica
stape	L	stirrup	stapes
tympan	G	drum	tympanum (eardrum)
zyg	G	yoke	zygomatic

Various Mammalian Postcranial Bones

(for use in Lab Exercise 9.2, number 2)

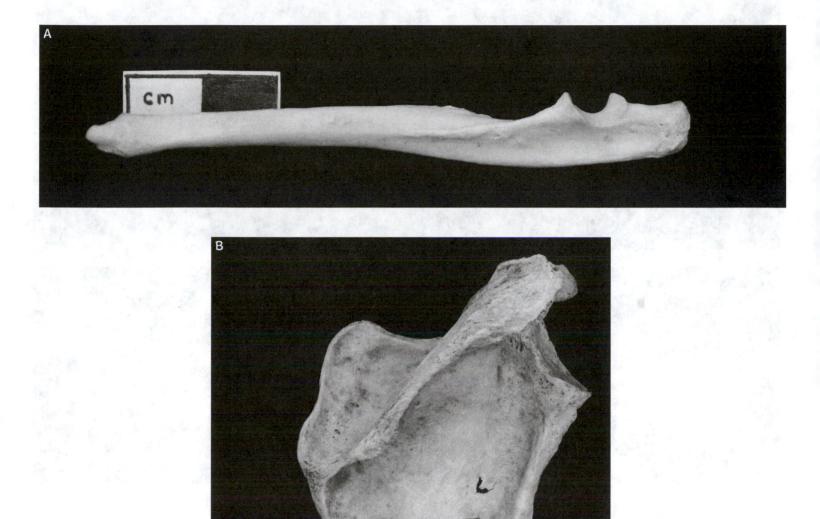

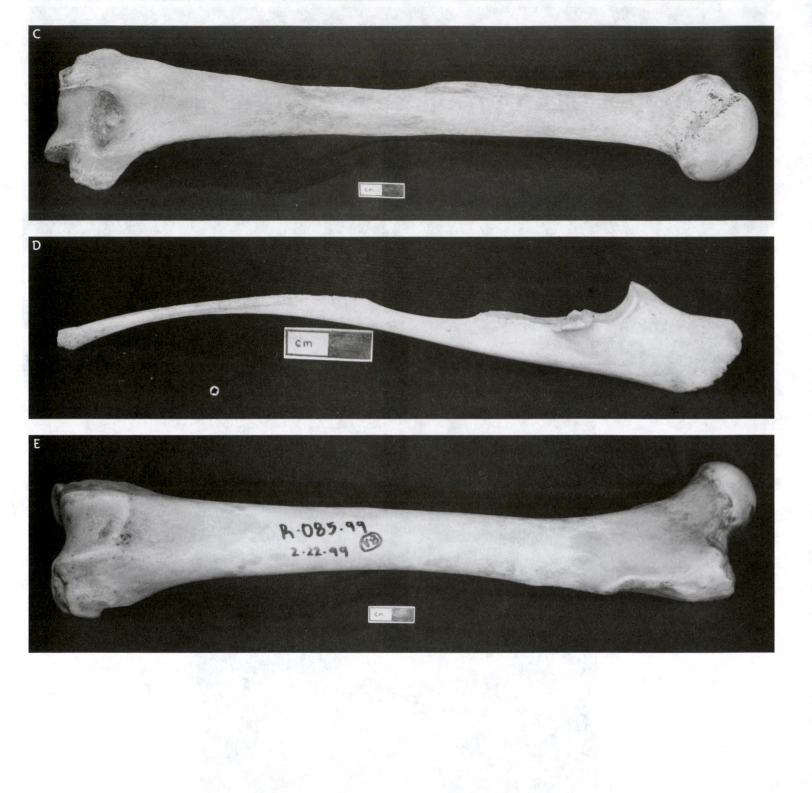

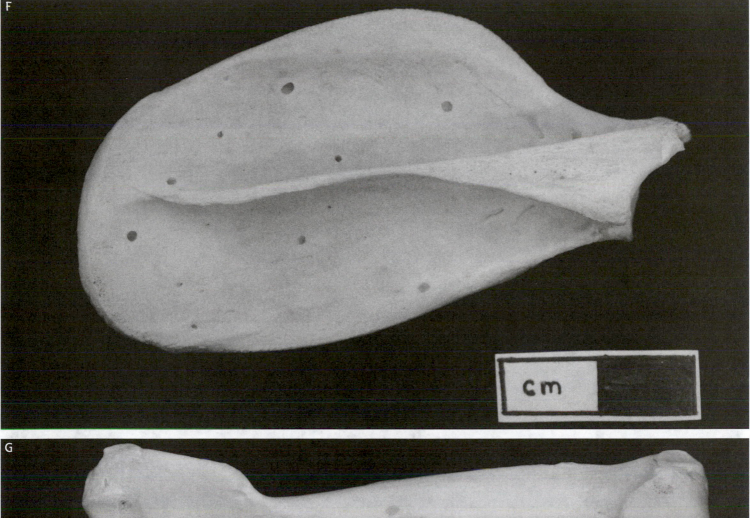

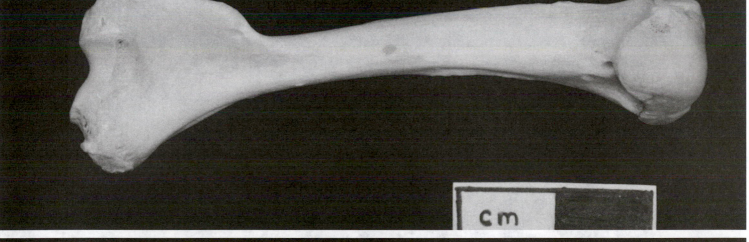

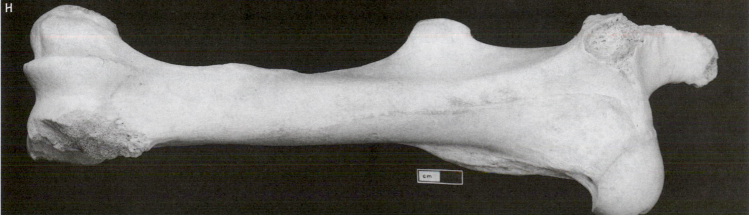

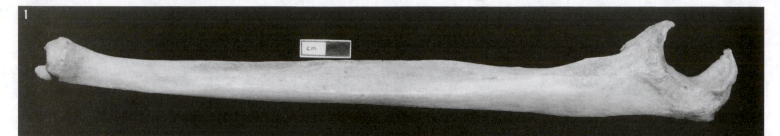

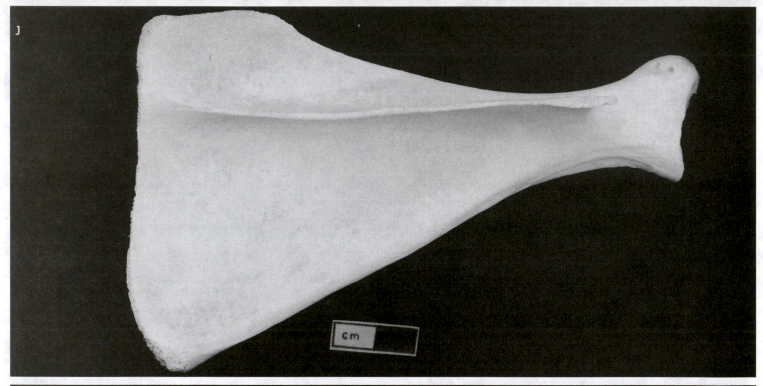

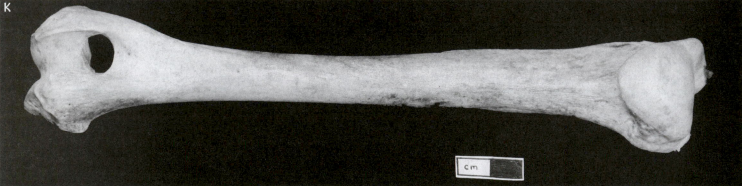

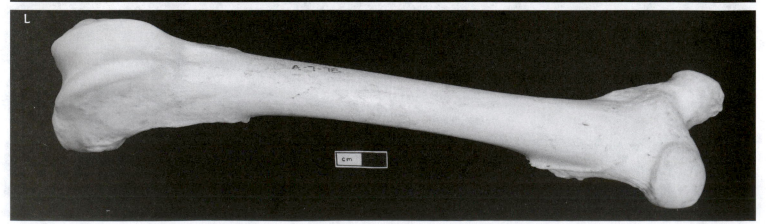

Bibliography

Adams, M. D., et al. 2000. The genome sequence of *Drosophila melanogaster*. *Science* 287:2185–2195.

Altmann, J. 1974. Observational study of behavior: sampling methods. *Behaviour* 49:227–267.

Ayers, J., R. L. Jantz, and P. H. Moore-Jansen. 1990. Giles & Elliot race discriminant functions revisited: a test using recent forensic cases. In: G. W. Gill and J. S. Rhine (eds.) *Skeletal Attribution of Race: Methods for Forensic Anthropology*. Albuquerque, NM: Maxwell Museum of Anthropology Papers No. 4, pp. 65–71.

Bartoshuk L. M., V. B. Duffy, and I. J. Miller. 1994. PTC/PROP tasting: anatomy, psychophysics, and sex effects. *Physiol Behav.* 56:1165–1171.

Bartoshuk L. M., V. B. Duffy, L. A. Succhina, J. Prutkin, and K. Fast. 1998. PROP (6-n-propylthiouracil) supertasters and the saltiness of NaCl. *Ann NY Acad Sci.* 855:793–796.

Bass, W. M. 1995. *Human Osteology: A Laboratory and Field Manual*, 4th ed. Columbia: Missouri Archaeological Society Special Publication No. 2.

Begun, D. R., and C. V. Ward. 2005. Comment on "*Pierolapithecus catalaunicus*, a new Middle Miocene great ape from Spain." *Science* 308:203.

Blattner, F. R., G. Plunkett III, C. A. Bloch, N. T. Perna, V. Burland, M. Riley, J. Collado-Vides, J. D. Glasner, C. K. Rode, G. F. Mayhew, J. Gregor, N. W. Davis, H. A. Kirkpatrick, M. A. Goeden, D. J. Rose, B. Mau, and Y. Shao. 1997. The complete genome sequence of *Escherichia coli* K–12. *Science* 277:1453–1462.

Bloch, J. I., and M. T. Silcox. 2006. Cranial anatomy of the Paleocene plesiadapiform *Carpolestes simpsoni* (Mammalia, Primates) using ultra high-resolution X-ray computed tomography, and the relationships of plesiadapiforms to Euprimates. *J. Hum. Evol.* 50:1–35.

Brothwell, D. R. 1981. *Digging Up Bones*, 3rd ed. New York: Cornell University Press.

Brunet, M., F. Guy, D. Pilbeam, H. T. Mackaye, A. Likius, D. Ahounta, A. Beauvailain, C. Blondel, H. Bocherens, J-R. Boisserie, L. De Bonis, Y. Coppens, J. Dejax, C. Denys, P. Duringer, V. Eisenmann, G. Fanone, P. Fronty, and D. Geraads. 2002. A new hominid from the Upper Miocene of Chad, Central Africa. *Nature* 418:145–151.

Buikstra, J. E., and Ubelaker, D. H. 1994. *Standards for Data Collection from Human Skeletal Remains*. Fayetteville: Arkansas Archeological Survey.

Bukovsky A., M. R. Caudle, M. Svetlikova, J. Wimalasena, M. E. Ayala, and R. Dominguez. 2005. *Endocrine* 26:301–316.

Byers, S. 2005. *Introduction to Forensic Anthropology : A Textbook*, 2nd ed. Boston: Allyn and Bacon.

Fleagle, J. G. F. 1999. *Primate Adaptation and Evolution*, 2nd ed. New York. Academic Press.

France, D. L. 1986. Osteometry at muscle origin and insertion in sex determination. *Am. J. Phys. Anthropol.* 76:515–526.

Gadsby, P. 2000. Tourist in a taste lab. *Discover* 21:70–75.

Gebo, D. L., M. Dagosto, K. C. Beard, T. Qi, and J. Wang. 2000. The oldest known anthropoid postcranial fossils and the early evolution of higher primates. *Nature* 404:276–278.

Giles, E., and O. Elliot. 1963. Sex determination by discriminant function analysis of crania. *Am J. Phys. Anthropol.* 21:53–68.

Hardy, G. H. 1908. Mendelian proportions in a mixed population. *Science* 28:49–50.

Hinkes, M. J. 1990. Shovel-shaped incisors in human identification. *Skeletal Attribution of Race: Methods for Forensic Anthropology*. Albuquerque, NM: Maxwell Museum of Anthropology Papers No. 4, pp. 21–26.

Hrdlicka, A. 1920. Shovel-shaped teeth. *Am J. Phys. Anthropol.* 3:429–465.

Johnson J., M. Skaznik-Wikiel, H. J. Lee, Y. Kiikura, J. C. Tilly, and J.L. Tilly. 2006. Setting the record straight on data supporting postnatal oogenesis in female mammals. *Cell Cycle*, Nov. 20; 4(11) (e-pub ahead of print)

Jurmain, R., H. Nelson, L. Kilgore, and W. Trevathan. 2003. *Introduction to Physical Anthropology*, 8th ed. Belmont, CA: Wadsworth/ Thompson Learning.

Katz, D., and J. M. Suchey. 1986. Age determination of the male *Os pubis*. *Am. J. Phys. Anthropol.* 69:427–435.

Krings, M. A., A. Stone, R. Schmitz, H. Kraintzi, M. Stoneking, and S. Paabo. 1997. Neanderthal DNA sequences and the origin of modern humans. *Cell* 90:19–30.

Krogman W. M., and M. Y. Iscan. 1986. *The Human Skeleton in Forensic Medicine*, 2nd ed. Springfield, IL: Charles C Thomas.

Lehner, P. N. 1987. Design and execution of animal behavior research: an overview. *Journal of Animal Science* 65:1213–1219.

Malthus, T. R. 1826. *An Essay on the Principle of Population as It Affects the Future Improvement of Society*, 6th ed. London: J. Johnson.

Mange, E. J., and A. P. Mange. 1994. *Basic Human Genetics*. Sunderland, MA: Sinauer.

Martin, N. G. 1975. No evidence for a genetic basis of tongue rolling or hand clasping. *J. Hered.* 66:179–180.

Martin, P., and P. Bateson. 1993. *Measuring Behaviour: An Introductory Guide*, 2nd ed. Cambridge, MA: Cambridge University Press,

McHenry, H. 1992. Body size and proportions in early hominids. *Am. J. Phys. Anthropol.* 87:407–431.

McKern, T. W., and T. D. Stewart. 1957. Skeletal age changes in young American males. *U.S. Army Quartermaster Research and Development Command, Technical Report EP-45.*

McKey, J. K., F. E. Poirier, and W. S. McGraw. 2005. *Understanding Human Evolution*, 5th ed. Upper Saddle River, NJ: Pearson Prentice Hall.

Moya-Sola, S., M. Köhler, D. M. Alba, I. Casanovas-Vilar, and J. Galindo. 2004. *Pierolapithecus catalaunicus*, a new Middle Miocene great ape from Spain. *Science* 306:1339–1344.

National Institute of Child Health and Human Development. Turners page: http://turners.nichd.nih.gov/ClinFrIntro.html. Klinefelter's page: http://www.nichd.nih.gov/publications/pubs/klinefelter.htm#xwhat

Park, M. A. 2005. *Biological Anthropology*. New York: McGraw-Hill.

Phenice, T. W. 1969. A newly developed visual method for sexing the *Os pubis*. *Am. J. Phys. Anthropol.* 30:297–302.

Rasmussen, D. T. 2002. Early catarrhines of the African Eocone and Oligocene. In *The Primate Fossil Record*. W. C. Hartwig, ed. Cambridge, MA: Cambridge University Press, pp. 203–220.

Rat Genome Sequencing Project Consortium. 2004. Genome sequence of the Brown Norway rat yields insights into mammalian evolution. *Nature* 428: 493–521.

Rhine, S. 1990. Non-metric skull racing. *Skeletal Attribution of Race: Methods for Forensic Anthropology*. Albuquerque, NM: Maxwell Museum of Anthropology Papers No. 4, pp. 9–20.

Sattenspiel, L., C. V. Ward, S. Stout, and D. Wescott. *Introduction to Biological Anthropology Laboratory Manual* (unpublished work, University of Missouri, Columbia, 2001, pp. 111 and 130).

Scientific American Frontiers Archives: http://www.pbs.org/safarchive/4_class/45_pguides/pguide_904/4494_peppers.html#act2

Shahbake, M., I. Hutchinson, D. G. Laing, and A. L. Jinks. 2005. Rapid quantitative assessment of fungiform papillae density in the human tongue. *Brain Res.* 1052:196–201.

Simons, E. L., and D. T. Rasmussen. 1996. Skull of *Catopithecus browni*, an early tertiary catarrhine. *Am. J. Phys. Anth.* 100:261–292.

Stanford, C. J. S. Allen, and S. C. Anton. 2006. *Biological Anthropology*. Upper Saddle River, NJ: Pearson Prentice Hall.

Szalay, F. S. 1981. Phylogeny and the problem of adaptive significance: the case of the earliest primates. *Folia Primatol.* 36:157–182.

Szalay, F. S., and E. Delson. 1979. *Evolutionary History of the Primates*. New York: Academic Press.

Todd, T. W. 1920. Age changes in the pubic bone I: The male white pubis. *Am. J. Phys. Anthropol.* 3:285–334.

Todd, T. W. 1921. Age changes in the pubic bone II: The pubis of the male negro–white hybrid; III: The pubis of the white female; IV: The pubis of the female white–negro hybrid. *Am. J. Phys. Anthropol.* 4:1–70.

Trotter, M. 1970. Estimation of stature from intact long limb bones. In: T. D. Stewart (ed.) *Personal Identification in Mass Disasters*. Washington, DC: National Museum of Natural History.

Ubelaker, D. H. 1978. *Human Skeletal Remains: Excavation, Analysis, Interpretation*. Chicago: Aldine.

Ubelaker, D. H. 1999. *Human Skeletal Remains: Excavation, Analysis, Interpretation*, 2nd ed. Chicago: Aldine.

Van Valen, L., and R. Sloan. 1965. The earliest primates. *Science* 150:743–745.

Watson, J. D., and F. H. C. Crick. 1953. Molecular structure of nucleic acids: a structure for deoxyribose nucleic acid. *Nature* 171:737–738.

Weinberg, W. 1908. Über den nachweis der vererbung beim menshcen. Jahresh. Wuertt. *Ver. vaterl. Natkd.* 64:369–382.

White, T., B. Asfaw, D. DeGusta, H. Gilbert, G. D. Richards, G. Suwa, and F. C. Howell. 2003. Pleistocene *Homo sapiens* from Middle Awash, Ethiopia. *Nature* 423:742–747.

Whitehead, P. F., W. K. Sacco, and S. B. Hochgraf. 2005. *A Photographic Atlas for Physical Anthropology*. Englewood, CO: Morton.

Wood, B. A. 1991. *Koobi Fora Research Project. Vol. 4: The Hominid Cranial Remains*. Oxford, England. Clarendon Press.

Glossary

A

ABO blood group: A blood type system coded for by alleles at a locus on chromosome 9; three primary alleles (I^A, I^B, I^O) determine blood type (A, B, O, or AB).

Acheulean: Refers to a tool kit associated with *Homo erectus* in Africa and early "archaic" *Homo sapiens* in Europe; classified as Lower Paleolithic tools.

ad libitum: Sampling technique in which all observed behaviors are recorded on all visible animals.

Adapis: Member of extinct superfamily Adapoidea from the Eocene of Europe.

Adapoidea: Superfamily of Eocene primates, within which lie the likely ancestors of strepsirhines; most occurred in North America and Europe.

adaptation: An evolutionary shift in a population in response to environmental change; a feature that acts to increase survival or reproductive success in individuals and is a result of natural selection.

adenine: One of the four bases in DNA and RNA.

Aegyptopithecus: Best-known representative of extinct family Propliopithecidae from the Oligocene of Egypt; an early catarrhine that may have given rise to the Old World monkey and ape/human lines.

agglutination: Clumping effect of serum antibodies with antigens of red blood cells of a different blood type.

Agnathans: Members of the extinct Class Agnatha; these fish were the earliest vertebrates.

allele: Alternative form of a specific gene; different alleles code for different forms of a trait.

amino acids: The subunits making up proteins; 20 common types are found in most proteins.

Amphipithecus: Eocene primate from Asia; may represent an early anthropoid.

analogy / analogous features: Similar features in different taxonomic groups arising independently under similar evolutionary pressures.

anaphase: The stage of cell division in which the chromosomes migrate to opposite poles of the cell.

anatomical position: In a human, a standing position with the arms down at the sides and the palms of the hands facing forward, thumbs out to the sides.

anatomical terminology: Words used to describe directions and position of bodies and body parts.

anatomically modern humans: Taxonomic designation *Homo sapiens sapiens*, denoting our own species and subspecies; first appeared in Africa about 150,000 years ago.

anemia: A condition in which red blood cells fail to deliver oxygen to the body's tissues.

aneuploidy: The condition of having an incorrect number of chromosomes.

anterior: A direction term meaning toward the front of the body

anterior dentition: Teeth at the front of the dental arcade: incisors and canines.

Anthropoidea: One of the two suborders of Order Primates in the traditional classification scheme; consists of monkeys, apes, and humans.

Anthropoids: Group that includes monkeys, apes, and humans; traditionally a formal taxonomic suborder of primates.

anthropometry: The measurement of humans.

anthroposcopy: Qualitative examination of human features.

antibodies: Proteins formed by the body's immune system in response to specific invading antigens.

anticodon: Triplet of three exposed bases on a tRNA molecule; complementary to mRNA **codon.**

antigens: Molecules that provoke an immune response (antibody production).

Apidium: Member of extinct family Parapithecidae from the Oligocene of Egypt; exhibit similarities to New World monkeys.

appendicular skeleton: Portion of the skeleton that develops later; consists of limb bones and bones of the pelvic and pectoral girdles.

arboreal: Means tree-living.

"archaic" *Homo sapiens:* Fossil specimens distributed in Africa, Asia, and Europe from about 800,000 years ago to about 30,000 years ago; known also as **transitional forms** because they exhibit a combination of *Homo erectus* and anatomically modern human features.

arms: On a chromosome, the portions extending from the centromere.

articular cartilage: Layer of cartilage covering the epiphyseal ends of long bones.

artificial selection: The process whereby humans select for specific traits in domesticated plants or animals; selective breeding.

Australopithecus aethiopicus: Oldest member of the robust australopith group; found in East Africa.

Australopithecus afarensis: East African hominid species of the primitive australopith group; species includes "Lucy" specimen.

Australopithecus africanus: African early hominid species, also referred to as the "gracile" form of australopith.

Australopithecus boisei: Member of robust australopith group having the most massive teeth and jaws; found in East Africa.

Australopithecus robustus: Member of robust australopith group; found in South Africa.

australopiths: Group of early hominids from Africa that exhibit many primitive features, composed of approximately 11 species.

autosomal dominant: Mode of inheritance in which an allele is expressed whenever it is present.

autosomal recessive: Mode of inheritance in which an allele must have been inherited by both parents to be expressed.

autosomal trait: Trait coded-for by a gene on a chromosome numbered 1–22.

autosomes: All chromosomes except the sex chromosomes.

axial skeleton: Portion of the skeleton that develops first; consists of midline structures such as skull, vertebral column, rib cage, sternum, and hyoid.

B

base: One of four types of chemical substances bonded to the sugar molecules in DNA and RNA nucleotides; DNA bases are adenine, cytosine, guanine, and thymine, and RNA bases are adenine, cytosine, guanine, and uracil.

base of support: Area between the supporting body parts in contact with the substrate.

base pairs: Bases occurring in pairs along the DNA molecule, making up the "rungs" of the DNA double helix (adenine bonds with thymine, cytosine with guanine).

bilophodont: Refers to molar teeth in which two crests connect the pairs of cusps in a mediolateral direction; typical of Old World monkeys.

binomen: Refers to the combination of genus and species as part of the Latin binomial classification scheme used worldwide; scientific name.

binomial nomenclature: Classificatory system for organisms devised by Carl Linnaeus featuring the binomen (genus and species).

bipedal/bipedalism: Adaptations to habitual upright walking on two legs.

C

cancellous (spongy) bone: Bone usually found deep within bone, surrounding the marrow cavity and within the ends of long bones; contains many large spaces filled with mostly red marrow.

canine shearing complex: Also called the **honing triad**; a combination of three features found in apes: large canines, **diastema**, and **sectorial P₃**.

Cantius: Member of extinct primate superfamily Adapoidea, from the Eocene of North America and Europe.

carrier: An individual who possesses a recessive allele for a genetic trait disorder but is unaffected himself or herself.

Catarrhini: Infraorder of haplorhine primates that includes Old World monkeys, apes, and humans.

Catopithecus: Early catarrhine from the late Eocene of Egypt.

caudal: Term meaning closer to the tip of the tail.

Ceboidea: Superfamily of platyrrhine primates; New World monkeys.

cell: Basic structural and functional unit of living things.

Cenozoic Era: Most recent era of Phanerozoic Eon; time range from 65 million years ago to present.

center of gravity: The point at which an object's mass is concentrated.

centriole: Organelle composed of microtubules; organizes the cytoskeleton for cell division.

centromere: Portion of the chromosome found at junction of arms; consists of tightly coiled DNA.

cephalic: Refers to the skull or head.

Cercopithecoidea: Superfamily of catarrhines consisting of Old World monkeys.

chromatid: One of the two sides of a chromosome in its doubled state after replication of its DNA.

chromatin: Condition of genetic material during interphase portion of cell cycle when cell is not dividing.

chromosomal anomaly: Having too many or too few chromosomes (also called **chromosomal aberration**).

chromosomal mutations: Mistakes that result in an extra or missing piece of chromosome, entire chromosome, or set of chromosomes.

chromosomes: Nuclear bodies made of the genetic material DNA, coiled around various proteins.

circumvallate: V-shaped row of **papillae** at the back of the tongue.

cladistics: School of thought about taxonomy and classification that emphasizes recency of common ancestry for establishing evolutionary relationships.

codominant: Describes the condition when a heterozygote's two alleles for a given locus are both expressed in the phenotype.

codon: Triplet of three bases on an mRNA strand read by ribosomes during protein synthesis; each codon determines a specific amino acid.

compact (dense) bone: Bone usually found in more superficial portions of bone, thickest in diaphysis of long bones; provides protection and support and resists stress.

continental drift: *See* **plate tectonics.**

convergent evolution: Features in distantly related groups that become more similar over time because of selective forces acting in similar ways.

coronal (frontal) plane: Imaginary plane dividing the body into front and back portions.

cranial: Refers to the skull or head.

cytoplasm: Watery, jelly-like substance within a cell but outside of the nucleus.

Cro Magnon: Fossil site in France of an early anatomically modern human; term referring to early anatomically modern humans in Europe.

crossing over: Exchange of portions of maternally and paternally derived chromosomes of a homologous pair; occurs during Prophase I of meiosis.

cytosine: One of the four bases in DNA and RNA.

cytoskeleton: Network of microtubules and microfilaments; dispersed in cytoplasm to provide a structural framework for cell division.

D

deep: Refers to position away from body's surface; internal.

degenerative changes: Modifications occurring as a result of age, wear, and disease.

deletion: Type of mutation in which one (or more) nucleotides is removed from the DNA molecule.

dense (compact) bone: Bone usually found in more superficial portions of bone, thickest in diaphysis of long bones; provides protection and support; resists stress.

dental formula: Number of teeth in an upper and lower quadrant of mammalian jaw.

deoxyribonucleic acid (DNA): A nucleic acid in the form of a long, linear molecule composed of bases, sugar, and phosphate molecules; the genetic material of all organisms.

deoxyribose: The specific type of sugar molecule in DNA.

derived features: Features that have undergone change from the ancestral form, as differentiated from **primitive features.**

diaphysis: Shaft of a long bone; portion between epiphyseal plates.

diastema: A space in the tooth row; in the canine shearing complex, the space in the lower tooth row for the upper canine to fit, and vice versa.

differential reproductive success: The condition in which individuals within a population reproduce at different rates; a result of natural selection.

differentiation: Embryological process dictated by the DNA that results in differential development of stem cells into various cellular types.

diploë: Porous portion of flat bones of skull.

diploid: Term that describes the number of chromosomes in somatic cells.

disomy: Normal condition in which the set of chromosomes in a human zygote includes 23 homologous pairs.

disjunction: Separation of chromosome pairs or sister **chromatids** during **anaphase** of cell division.

distal: Position on the limbs relatively farther from attachment of limb to trunk of body.

dominant: An allele that is always expressed when present.

dorsal: Position on body closer to the back; term used more frequently for quadrupeds.

double helix: Common manner of referring to the double-stranded, helical (twisted) nature of DNA's structure.

Down syndrome: The condition produced by having an extra chromosome 21 (**Trisomy 21**).

Dryopithecus: European Miocene ape.

E

early "archaics": Fossil hominid specimens occurring between about 800,000 years ago and 150,000 years ago.

egg cells: Gametes present in females, originating in the ovaries; human egg cells have 23 chromsomes.

endoplasmic reticulum: Membranous network of channels in cytoplasm, continuous with nuclear membrane, that forms a pathway for transporting substances within the cell and stores synthesized molecules.

enzyme: Class of proteins that speed up chemical reactions in cells.

Eocene: Epoch within Cenozoic Era in which the first "true" primates appeared and diversified; time range from 55 to 38 million years ago.

Eosimias: Tiny late Eocene primate from China, a likely early representative of anthropoids.

epiphyseal line: Remnant of epiphyseal plate.

epiphyseal plate: Portion at end of diaphysis where bone growth occurs as cartilaginous cells divide, to be replaced later by bone cells (same portion as metaphysis).

epiphyses: Portions at ends of a bone; the last to fuse (ossify); separated from rest of bone by epiphyseal plate during development.

essential amino acids: Amino acids not produced by the body and must be taken in as protein. *See also* **amino acids.**

eukaryotes: Organisms whose genetic material is enclosed within a nuclear membrane within the cell.

euploidy: Having the correct number of chromosomes.

evolution: A change in gene frequency within a population over time, caused by one or more of the **evolutionary forces.**

evolutionary forces: Four factors that cause gene frequencies to change in a population: natural selection, mutation, migration, and genetic drift.

evolutionary taxonomy: School of thought about taxonomy and classification that regards the amount of divergence from a common ancestor as a valid criterion for classification.

F

facets: Smooth areas on bone where articulation occurs.

Fayum Depression: Geological formation in Egypt that yields many known primate fossils from the late Eocene and Oligocene epochs.

features: Characteristics of bone related to function and muscle development.

filiform: Thread-like papillae (structures that house taste buds) near the back of the tongue; contain nerve endings sensitive to touch.

fitness: Degree of reproductive success of an individual relative to other members of the population.

flat bones: Bones of cranium, shoulder, pelvis, and rib cage.

focal animal sampling: Animal behavior technique that uses observations of one individual at a time.

foliate: Ridged papillae (structures that house taste buds) near the back and on the lateral borders of the tongue.

fontanels: Spaces between bones on infant skull that allow room for growth; also called "soft spots."

form of a trait: The specific appearance of a characteristic, for example, brown hair; **phenotype.**

formative changes: Bony modifications occurring during the process of growth and development.

form–function: Relationship between the morphology of a feature to the manner in which the feature is used.

fossilization: Process by which organic material in hard parts (bone, teeth, shell) is replaced, particle by particle, by minerals in the sediment; premineralization.

founder effect: A form of genetic drift in which a small sub-population is reproductively isolated from the main population, "founding" a new population.

frameshift mutation: An insertion or deletion mutation that results in a shift in the "reading frame" of all the rest of the codons on an mRNA strand.

frequency: Rate of occurrence in a population; expressed as a percent.

frontal (coronal) plane: Imaginary plane dividing body into front and back portions.

functional complexes: A holistic view of an adaptation: anatomy and associated use of a feature.

fungiform: Mushroom-shaped papillae (structures that house taste buds) throughout the tongue.

G

gametes: **Haploid** cells that pass on genetic material to offspring at fertilization; sperm and egg cells.

gene: A segment of DNA coding for a specific polypeptide (or protein).

gene flow (migration): Movement of genes from one population's gene pool to another, causing change in gene frequencies of both former and new gene pools.

gene frequency: Within a population, the percent of each type of gene that exists for a specific trait.

gene pool: All the genes in a population at a specific point in time.

genetic code: The specific amino acids determined by each type of codon of mRNA.

genetic drift (random genetic drift): Random fluctuations in gene frequency of a population between generations; particularly in a small population, gene frequencies do not accurately represent those of the parental population.

genotype: The allele pair present for a specific locus in an individual.

genotypic ratio: Number of homozygous dominant to heterozygous to homozygous genotypes for a particular parental cross.

genus (pl: genera): Taxonomic level above the species and below the subfamily; a group of closely related species.

geological time scale: Hierarchical classification of time on earth into eons, eras, periods, and epochs based upon the rise and fall of major groups of organisms.

Gigantopithecus: Genus of ape originating in the Miocene but existing until well into the Pleistocene; largest known primate.

Golgi body and vesicles: Delivery system of cell, which collects, modifies, packages, and distributes molecules that are synthesized at one location and used at another.

Gondwanaland: Landmass in the southern hemisphere that consisted of what would become Africa, South America, Antarctica, and Australia.

gracile australopiths: The more slender form of early hominid; primarily *Australopithecus africanus.*

guanine: One of the four bases in both DNA and RNA.

H

hair follicle: Small, sac-like pocket in the epidermis that houses the base (bulb and root) of each hair.

hand axe: Bifaced, teardrop-shaped stone tool; the most common and widely distributed tool in the Acheulean tool kit.

haploid: Term that describes the number of chromosomes in gametes; one-half the full chromosomal complement, or one set of chromosomes (1n).

Haplorhini: Primate suborder that includes tarsiers, monkeys, apes, and humans.

Hardy-Weinberg formula: Mathematical formula used to express the relationship between allele and genotype frequency of a population; $p^2 + 2pq + q^2 = 1$, where *p* represents the dominant allele, *q* the recessive allele, and the number 1 the entire population (100%).

Hardy-Weinberg law: A mathematical relationship existing between allele frequency and genotype frequency such that the frequencies of particular genotypes can be predicted from allele frequencies; allele and genotype frequencies will remain constant from one generation to the next (in equilibrium) if mating is random and there is no action of the evolutionary forces.

hemizygous: The condition of males for an X-linked trait; because males have only one X chromosome, they cannot be homozygous or heterozygous for X-linked traits.

hemoglobin: Protein in red blood cells that carries oxygen from the lungs to the body's tissues.

heterodont: The situation of having teeth within the jaw differentiated into different types to serve various functions.

heterozygous: The condition of having inherited two different alleles at a particular locus.

Hominidae: The taxonomic group defined variously as modern humans and our extinct relatives after the split from the African apes, or humans plus our extinct relatives *and* the African apes.

Hominoidea: Superfamily of the catarrhine infraorder composed of apes and humans.

Homo: Members of the human genus; exhibits derived dental and cranial features relative to the common ancestor of African apes and humans.

Homo erectus: Species of early members of genus *Homo* characterized by large brain; the first such species to be found outside Africa; may combine two species, *H. erectus* (from Asia) and *H. ergaster* (from Africa).

Homo ergaster: Species designation for fossil specimens that co-existed with and were similar to *H. erectus.*

Homo habilis: Earliest named members of the genus *Homo;* may consist of members of two species, *H. habilis* and *H. rudolfensis.*

homology / homologous feature: A characteristic that is similar in various groups of organisms because of their origin from a common ancestor possessing that characteristic.

Homo rudolfensis: Species designation of some early members of the genus *Homo;* distinguishable from *Homo habilis* by a number of cranial and postcranial features.

Homo sapiens sapiens: Taxonomic designation of our own species and subspecies; first appeared in Africa about 150,000 years ago.

homologous pairs: Chromosomal couples of each type of chromosome (pair number 1, 2, etc.).

Homonoid: Member of superfamily **Hominoidea.**

homozygous: The condition of having inherited the same two alleles from the parents at a specific locus.

homozygous dominant: The condition in which two alleles inherited at a specific locus both code for the dominant form of the trait.

homozygous recessive: The condition in which two alleles inherited at a specific locus both code for the recessive form of the trait.

honing triad: Also called **canine shearing complex;** combination of three features found in apes: large canines, **diastema,** and **sectorial P₃.**

horizontal plane: Imaginary plane dividing the body into upper and lower parts.

hydrogen bond: Weak linkage between two negatively charged atoms that share a hydrogen atom.

hypothesis: A statement proposed to explain some phenomenon; framed to be testable/falsifiable.

I

independent assortment: Random distribution of each pair of chromosomes into daughter cells during **meiosis.**

inferior: Refers to portion of body closer to bottom of feet.

ingestion: Getting the food into the mouth.

insertion (muscle): Site at which muscle tendon attaches to the bone that is movable relative to the other bone; usually located on the more distal bone.

insertion (mutation): Type of mutation in which one (or more) nucleotides is mistakenly added to the DNA molecule.

instantaneous sampling: A technique of time sampling in which behavior is sampled periodically at sample points between a set time interval.

interphase: Stage of the cell cycle in which cell division is not occurring; cell growth, DNA replication, and organelle replication are in progress.

irregular bones: Category of bone that includes vertebrae, facial bones, and some wrist and ankle bones.

K

karyotype: The chromosomal complement of an individual; also, an organized arrangement of an individual's chromosomes.

knuckle-walker: Specialized mode of quadrupedal locomotion in the African apes, in which the weight of the front of the body is borne by the knuckles.

L

landmarks: Sites on the skull that serve as points for measurement and allow for consistent measurements to be taken on various individuals.

late "archaics": Fossil hominid specimens occurring between about 125,000 years ago and about 30,000 years ago; a primary group was the Neanderthals.

lateral: Refers to position on the body farther from median plane.

Laurasia: Landmass made up of northern continents consisting of North America, Europe, and Asia.

law: A statement of fact meant to describe, in concise terms, an action or set of actions generally accepted to be true and universal.

Levalloisian: Describes prepared core technique used by later "archaic" *Homo sapiens* that produced flakes of a predictable size and shape

locomotion: Body position involving displacement of the body's mass; movement.

locus: The position of a gene on a chromosome, consistent for genes on chromosomes for all individuals of a species.

long bones: Category of bone that includes limb bones, finger and toe bones.

"Lucy": Well-known specimen of a 40% complete female *Australopithecus afarensis*, found in Ethiopia.

lysosome: Sac-like attachment to cell membrane that digests unneeded molecules; formed from vesicles of Golgi body.

M

mechanical digestion: First part of the digestive process, carried out by action of the teeth to break down food into smaller pieces for easier breakdown by digestive enzymes.

medial: Position on body closer to the median plane.

median (midsagittal) plane: Imaginary plane dividing the body into equal left and right halves.

medullary (marrow) cavity: Space along the inside of the diaphysis containing yellow marrow (in adults), which consists mostly of fat cells and scattered blood cells.

meiosis: The type of cell division occurring in the testes of males and ovaries of females whereby a specialized somatic (diploid) cell divides and produces daughter cells that develop into gametes.

Meiosis I: The first meiotic division, in which the number of chromosomes is reduced from 46 to 23; homologous chromosomes are separated into different daughter cells.

Meiosis II: The second meiotic division, in which the sister chromatids of each chromosome are separated from each other.

Mendelian traits: Genetically simple traits determined by alleles at a single gene locus.

messenger RNA (mRNA): Type of RNA strand synthesized by using a DNA gene as a template; carries the "message" of the DNA sequence of a gene from the nucleus to the cytoplasm during protein synthesis.

metaphase: Stage of cell division in which the chromosomes line up along the equator of the cell in preparation for separating to opposite poles of the cell.

metaphysis: Region in mature bone where diaphysis meets epiphysis; formed the epiphyseal plate before the cartilage was replaced by bone.

midsagittal (median) plane: Imaginary line dividing the body into equal left and right halves.

migration (gene flow): Movement of individuals between populations, altering gene frequencies of both original and new populations.

Miocene: Epoch within the Cenozoic Era in which apes (Miocene hominoids) diversified and spread geographically; time range from 24 to 5 million years ago.

Miocene hominoids: Term used to refer to the approximately 30 genera of early apes occurring between 20 and 5 million years ago; primarily arboreal with a mix of ape-like and monkey-like features but no tail.

missense mutation: A substitution mutation in which the mistakenly replaced nucleotide causes a different amino acid to be coded for.

mitochondria: Oblong organelle where adenosine triphosphate (ATP) production occurs for cellular energy; possesses its own DNA, called mitochondrial DNA.

mitosis: The type of cell division whereby a somatic cell divides and produces two identical daughter cells.

monogenic: Describes a trait whose gene expression is controlled by alleles at a single locus.

monosomy: Situation in which one of a homologous pair of chromosomes is missing.

Mousterian: Designates tool kit associated with Neanderthals; classified as Middle Paleolithic tools.

mutagens: Environmental factors that cause mutation to occur.

mutation: Inherited change in the DNA sequence; the only evolutionary force to introduce new variation into the gene pool.

N

nasal: Refers to the nose.

natural selection: A primary factor causing evolutionary change in populations, in which individuals whose inherited traits allow them to better survive and/or reproduce contribute more offspring to the subsequent generation.

Neanderthals: Fossils classified variously as either *Homo sapiens neandertalensis* or *Homo neandertalensis*; relatively specialized group of robustly built early humans occurring between 75,000 and 35,000 years ago.

Necrolemur: Member of extinct superfamily Omomyoidea from Europe.

nondisjunction: Failure of chromosomes to separate before moving to opposite poles of the cell during anaphase; results in wrong number of chromosomes in the daughter cells after cell division is complete.

nonsense mutation: A substitution mutation resulting in formation of a **stop codon** where there previously was none; causes premature halting of translation and a truncated polypeptide length.

Notharctus: Member of extinct superfamily Adapoidea from the Eocene of North America.

nuclear membrane: Double-layered structure composed of phospholipids and protein molecules that controls passage of material into and out of nucleus.

nucleic acid: Acidic substance found in all cells: DNA and RNA.

nucleolus: Mass of proteins and ribosomal RNA in the nucleus; site of ribosome production.

nucleotide: The most basic unit of both DNA and RNA; consists of one phosphate molecule, one sugar molecule, and one base.

nucleus: Structure that contains the genetic material (DNA); separated from the rest of the cell by a **nuclear membrane.**

O

occlusal surface: Portion of the tooth that comes into contact with the teeth of the opposite tooth row.

Olduwan tools: Earliest of the stone tools, the tool kit associated with *Homo habilis*; classified as Lower Paleolithic tools.

Oligocene: Epoch within the Cenozoic Era during which ancestors of New World monkeys and hominoids evolved; time range from 38 to 24 million years ago.

Omomyoidea: Extinct primate superfamily from the Eocene; most representatives are from Europe and North America.

opsin: Proteins in cone cells of retina that enable perception of color; bind to visual pigments in the red-sensitive cones, green-sensitive cones or blue-sensitive cones, making the visual pigment/opsin complex sensitive to light of a specific wavelength.

organ: A structure formed by two or more cellular tissues; carries out a specific function in the body.

organelles: Components of a cell within the cytoplasm.

organism: A single living entity.

organ systems: A group of organs working together to perform a bodily function or set of functions.

origin: Site from which a muscle arises; usually on the "fixed" bone and more proximal than the insertion.

orthognathic: Describes the vertical orientation of the human face.

orthograde: Upright **bipedal** animals (e.g., humans).

ossification: The process of becoming bone.

osteometry: Subcategory of anthropometry that deals with measurement of the skeleton.

P

Paleocene: Epoch within the Cenozoic Era in which primates first evolved; time range from 65 to 55 million years ago.

paleoclimate: Earth's climatic conditions of the past; important in interpreting and analyzing extinct species' adaptations and distribution patterns.

papillae: Bumps on the tongue that house the receptor cells (taste buds).

parabolic: Refers to the **U-shaped,** or **rounded,** form of the **dental arcade**

Parapithecidae: Extinct primate family from the Oligocene of Egypt; members share similarities to New World monkeys.

pedigree: A diagram that delineates the genetic relationships of family members over two or more generations; used to observe patterns of inheritance.

peptide bonds: Chemical connection holding amino acids together.

periosteum: Connective tissue covering bone in places where there is no articular cartilage.

Phanerozoic Eon: More recent of the two largest blocks of geological time, from which many evident life forms evolved; time range from 542 million years ago to the present.

phenotype: Outwardly observable traits and features of an individual; may be physical or behavioral.

phenotypic ratio: Number of offspring from a parental cross potentially expressing the dominant form of trait relative to the number expressing the recessive form.

phosphate molecule: Component of DNA and RNA that, together with sugar molecules, makes up the "backbone" of the strands.

Pierolapithecus catalaunicus: Recently discovered European ape from the Miocene epoch that may represent an ancestral form either to the African ape/human line or to the great ape and human line.

plasma membrane: Double-layered structure surrounding a cell, composed of phospholipids and protein molecules, that controls passage of material into and out of the cell.

plate tectonics: Movement of the continental plates making up the earth's surface.

Platyrrhini: Infraorder of haplorhine primates composed of the superfamily Ceboidea, or New World monkeys.

Plesiadapiformes: Diverse group of early mammals from the Paleocene of North America and Europe; may represent the earliest primates.

Plesiadapis: Member of extinct mammalian group Plesiadapiformes from the Paleocene; found in North America and Europe.

point mutation: Type of mutation in which one or up to a few bases is/are mistakenly out of place in the DNA.

polygenic: A trait whose gene expression is controlled by alleles at more than one locus.

polymorphic: Describes the condition in which when a genetically determined trait has more than one form in a population (a gene with more than one allele); a **polymorphism.**

polynucleotide chain: String of nucleotides of DNA or RNA; two such chains make up the DNA molecule.

polypeptide (polypeptide chain): String of amino acids linked end to end by peptide bonds .

Pondaungia: Eocene primate from Asia; may represent an early anthropoid.

population bottleneck: Form of genetic drift in which a drastic reduction in the number of individuals in a population results in great differences between gene frequencies of the original and the newly reduced population

positional behavior: Spatial relationship between the body mass of an individual and its environment.

postcranial skeleton: Part of the skeleton from the cervical (neck) vertebrae inferiorly.

posterior: Refers to position on body more toward the back.

posterior dentition: Teeth at the back of the dental arcade: premolars and molars.

posture: Body position that does not involve displacement of the body's mass.

Precambrian eon: Largest portion of geological time scale, from the earth's formation to the beginning of the Phanerozoic Eon 542 million years ago.

prehensile: Ability to grasp.

primary oocyte: Type of cell that undergoes meiosis in the female; found in the ovaries.

primary spermatocytes: Type of cell that undergoes meiosis in the male; found in the testes.

Primates: Taxonomic mammalian group at the level of the order; includes prosimians, monkeys, apes, and humans.

primitive: Features that are similar in form to that of an ancestor (by contrast, see **derived**).

primitive australopith: Group of the earliest form of hominid, made up of several species that include *A. afarensis*; members possess numerous features of the ape-human ancestor.

principle of independent assortment: Mendel's law stating that the presence of particular "characters" (alleles) of one trait will not affect the expression of genes of another trait.

principle of segregation: Mendel's law stating that for any given trait, members of a pair of "characters" (alleles) separate (segregate) from each other during the formation of gametes, so that only one copy (one gene) is passed on from each parent.

Proconsul: Early and best-known Miocene **hominoid** from Africa.

prognathic: Forward protrusion of the lower face.

prokaryotes: Organisms that lack a nucleus surrounding the genetic material; members of kingdom Monera.

pronograde: Designates animals in which the backbone is parallel to the ground (quadrupedal).

prophase: First phase of cell division, after DNA replication, in which chromosomes condense and become visible and the cell prepares to divide.

Propliopithecidae: Extinct primate family from the Oligocene of Africa (found in Egypt in the Fayum); early catarrhines.

Prosimii: One of the two suborders of Order Primates in the traditional classification scheme; includes tarsiers, lemurs, and lorises.

protein: Molecules with a working or structural function in the body; made up of one or more polypeptides (strings of amino acids).

protein synthesis: Process by which proteins are assembled from amino acids according to the sequences of bases in a DNA gene.

proximal: Means closer to the attachment of limb to trunk of body (nearer the hip or the shoulder).

Punnett square: Mathematical tool used to predict probabilities of various offspring depending upon parental genotypes.

Purgatorius: Member of extinct mammalian group Plesiadapiformes from the Paleocene; found in North America.

R

race: A term traditionally used to distinguish biological groupings among people from various regions on the basis of a small number of characteristics.

recessive: An allele that is expressed only when inherited by both parents in the homozygous condition.

replication (DNA replication): The process of duplicating genetic material prior to cell division; ensures that all cells have the full complement of DNA making up the chromosomes.

Rh blood group: A blood type system coded for by alleles at a locus on chromosome; two primary alleles determine blood type (Rh$^+$, Rh$^-$); Rh$^+$ individuals produce antigens on the surface of their red blood cells.

Rh incompatibility: Immune response of a mother to her developing fetus if the Rh$-$ mother begins to produce antibodies in response to antigens on her Rh$+$ fetus' red blood cells; can result in potentially fatal anemia.

ribonucleic acid (RNA): A nucleic acid in the form of a long, linear molecule composed of four kinds of bases and sugar and phosphate molecules.

ribose: Type of sugar molecule found in RNA.

ribosomal RNA (rRNA): Type of RNA that associates with various proteins to form ribosomes, which "read" the mRNA strand during protein synthesis.

ribosomes: Small structures composed of proteins and RNA.

robust australopith: Group of early hominids with massive jaws, teeth, and chewing musculature; includes *Australopithecus robusts*, *A. boisei*, and *A. aethiopicus*.

Rooneyia: Member of extinct superfamily Omomyoidea from North America.

rugose: Rough area on bone at the site of muscle attachment.

S

Sahelanthropus tchadensis: Recent fossil discovery from Central Africa (Chad); some interpret this fossil as the earliest known hominid to split from the ape line.

scan sampling: A method in which behavior for all animals (or a particular set of animals) is recorded simultaneously at predetermined time intervals.

science: Activity that seeks to explain (natural) phenomena; employs the steps of the **scientific method**.

scientific method: Rigorous procedure that is used to identify the most probable explanation for natural phenomena.

sectorial P$_3$: Lower premolar tooth just posterior to the diastema, sharpened as the upper canine hones against it.

segregation analysis: The process of testing various genetic hypotheses to determine which of several modes of inheritance is responsible for producing specific patterns in a familial line.

selective advantage: Greater propensity of individuals with the form best adapted to a specific environment to reproduce, passing on that trait in higher frequency to the next generation.

selective pressure: Environmental factors that influence reproductive success of individuals.

sesamoid bone: Bones that form within tendons of joints (e.g., patella).

sex chromosomes: Chromosomes responsible, via their gene products, for determining the sex of an individual; X and Y chromosomes.

sex-linked trait: A trait coded-for by a gene on a sex chromosome.

sexual dimorphism: Differences in size or other characteristics (besides primary or secondary sexual characteristics) in males and females of the same species.

short bones: Category of bone that includes the blocky, often cube-shaped bones of wrist and ankle, and sesamoid bones.

silent mutation: Substitution mutation whereby a nucleotide is mistakenly replaced by another, but the same amino acid is coded for.

simian shelf: A thickened area on the internal aspect of the mandible, serves as a buttress for chewing forces.

simple traits: Also termed **Mendelian traits;** determined by alleles at a single gene locus.

single base substitution mutation: Mistaken replacement of one nucleotide for another, different nucleotide.

sister chromatids: Two identical chromatids attached at the centromere.

Sivapithecus: Miocene **hominoid** from Asia; extinct relative of orangutan.

somatic cells: Cells making up the structural composition of the body; all cells other than gametes; possess the diploid chromosome number.

species: A group of individuals that can potentially interbreed and produce fertile offspring (biological definition of species).

sperm cells: Gametes present in males, originating in the testes.

spongy (cancellous) bone: Type of bone containing many large spaces; concentrated primarily within the ends of long bones; filled with mostly red marrow.

stance phase: Phase of **bipedalism** in which the foot is in contact with the substrate and the weight is supported by the foot.

stop codon (terminating triplet): The sequence of bases making up three types of codons (UGA, UAA, and UAG) that determine the termination of protein synthesis.

Strepsirhini: Primate suborder that includes the lemur and loris groups.

striding gait: Unique gait characteristic of human **bipedal** locomotion.

Subphylum Vertebrata: Group of organisms within the Phylum Chordata that share numerous features, the most important of which is a vertebral column and spinal cord.

sugar molecule: Component of DNA and RNA that, together with phosphate molecules, makes up the "backbone" of the strands.

superficial: Designates a position near the body's surface.

superior: Refers to portion of the body located closer to the top of the head.

sutures: Margins of skull bones as they abut each other.

swing phase: Phase of **bipedalism** in which the foot comes off the substrate and is being repositioned for the next stance phase; leg comes forward and around toward the center (adducts).

T

Tarsiiformes: Infraorder of haplorhines consisting of tarsiers.

taxon (pl: taxa): A group of organisms belonging to a particular group at a particular level within the biological classification scheme.

telophase: Final phase of cell division, in which the nuclear membrane begins forming around chromosomes at each pole of original cell.

terminating triplet: *See* **stop codon**

terrestrial: Ground-living.

Tetonius: Member of extinct superfamily Omomyoidea from North America.

tetrad: A pair of homologous chromosomes in their doubled state, during the **crossing over** that occurs early in meiosis.

theory: A statement of relationships that rests upon some firm basis; based on confirmed/corroborated hypotheses.

thymine: One of the four bases in DNA; not found in RNA; chemically similar to **uracil**.

tissue: Group of identical cells forming organs.

trait: A feature or characteristic determined either by the inherited properties of an organism or by a combination of inherited and environmental factors.

transcription: The first step of protein synthesis in which mRNA is synthesized, using a DNA segment (a gene) as a template; occurs in the nucleus.

transfer RNA (tRNA): Type of RNA whose function is to transport amino acids to their appropriate place along the mRNA strand during protein synthesis.

transitional forms: *See* **"archaic"** *Homo sapiens*

translation: The second step of protein synthesis in which mRNA codons are "read" by ribosomes, and "translated" into an amino acid sequence; occurs in the cytoplasm.

transverse plane: Imaginary plane dividing body into upper and lower parts.

trisomy: Situation in which an extra chromosome is present.

Trisomy 21: An extra chromosome 21, which causes **Down syndrome**.

U

universal donors: Individuals with type O blood because their blood can be donated to type A and type B individuals without provoking an immune response.

universal recipients: Individuals with Type AB blood who can receive all blood types because their blood serum has neither anti-A nor anti-B antibodies with which to attack antigens of blood cells of a different type.

Upper Paleolithic tools: Describes a group of several tool kits associated with early anatomically modern humans in Europe.

uracil: One of the four bases in RNA; not found in DNA; chemically similar to **thymine**.

V

ventral: Designates position on body closer to the belly; term used more frequently for quadrupeds.

X

X chromosome: Female sex chromosome.

X-linked dominant: Trait coded-for by dominant allele on X chromosome; expressed whenever present.

X-linked recessive: Trait coded-for by recessive allele on X chromosome; always expressed in males; must be in homozygous condition for expression in females.

X-linked: Trait coded for by alleles on the X chromosome.

Y

Y chromosome: Male sex chromosome, relating mostly to male sexual development.

Y5 molar cusp pattern: Characteristic Y-shape formed by valleys between molar cusps in apes and humans.

Z

zygote: Fertilized egg formed by union of male and female gametes.

Photo Credits

American 3B

Casts used for photography:
- Fetal skull . . . . p. 103 (Photo 7.6), p. 105 (Photo 7.11), p. 108 (lower right), p. 241 (A)
- Articulated skeleton . . . . p. 115 (Photo 7.15), p. 117 (Photo 7.19, 7.20), p. 120

Copyright 3B Scientific, Hamburg, Germany. www.a3Bs.com. Used with permission.

Bones Clones

Casts used for photography:
- Asian male skull. . . . . p. 162 (Photo 8.8A), p. 166 (Skull 2)
- African male skull . . . . p. 162 (Photo 8.6A), p. 166 (Skull 3)
- Comparative maxilla set . . . . p. 162 (Photo 8.6B, 8.7B, 8.8B), p.166 (Dental arcade), p. 259 (lower right)
- Night monkey (*Aotus trivirgatus*) . . . . p. 190 (C)
- Mandrill skull . . . . p. 195 (D)
- *Aegyptopithecus* skull . . . . p. 221 (Photo 12.1), p. 226 (A and B)
- *Proconsul* skull Photo . . . . p. 221 (Photo 12.2), p. 227
- *Sivapithecus* . . . . p. 222 (Photo 12.4), p. 228 (A and B)
- Gorilla hand unassembled . . . . p. 238 (Photo 13.1B)
- *Australopithecus afarensis* . . . . p. 247 (A-D, upper)
- Lucy pelvis and femur . . . . p. 245–246
- *Australopithecus aethiopicus* . . . . p. 247 (B, lower right), p. 248 (upper and middle right)
- *Homo erectus* – Peking Man . . . . p. 255 (Photo 14.2A)
- *Homo ergaster* . . . . p. 255 (Photo 14.2B), p. 259 (A – D)
- *Homo heidelbergensis* . . . . p. 261 (Photo 14.4), p. 266
- Homo neanderthalensis . . . . p. 262 (Photo 14.5A)

Cast © Bone Clones, Inc. Used with Permission.

Photos used from Bone Clones website:
- Modern human adult female pelvis . . . . p. 150 (Pelvis 1)
- 10-year-old child skull . . . . p. 157 (Dentition A)
- 5-year-old child skull . . . . p. 157 (Dentition B)
- Modern human Asian female skull . . . . p. 150 (Skull 3)
- Human European male skull . . . . p. 149 (Skull 2)
- *Australopithecus africanus*, Taung Child . . . . . p. 250
- Set of 6 Neanderthal Mousterian Tools . . . . . . p. 262 (Photo 14.6)
- Fossil Hominid bi-facial hand-axe . . . . p. 255 (Photo 14.3)
- *Homo habilis* skull (KNM-ER 1813) . . . . p. 254 (Photo 14.1A)
- *Homo rudolfensis* skull (KNM-ER 1470) . . . . . p. 254 (Photo 14.1B)

Cast © Bone Clones, Inc. Used with Permission.

Chetham's Library

- Consul photo (Photo 12.3) . . . . p. 221

Copyright © Chetham's Library, Manchester, United Kingdom. Used with permission.

Cleveland Museum of Natural History

Casts used for photography:
- Chimpanzee pelvis . . . . p. 242 (B)
- Chimpanzee femur . . . . p. 242 (B)
- Male aye-aye . . . . p. 190 (D)
- Male capuchin . . . . p. 195 (B), p. 225 (lower right)
- Male ring-tailed lemur . . . . p. 190 (B) (lower section), p. 196 (B), p. 223–224 (lower right)
- Male tarsier . . . . p. 171 (Photo 9.1), p. 173 (C), p. 193(Photo 10.1), p. 195 (C), p. 225 (upper right)

Copyright © The Cleveland Museum of Natural History.

Somso

Casts used for photography:

- Neanderthal reconstruction .... p. 262 (Photo 14.5B), p. 267 A-C (upper)
- *Homo sapiens sapiens* – Predmöst .... p. 262 (Photo 14.7), p. 267 A-C (lower)
- *Australopithecus africanus* – Sterkfontien ..... p. 247 (A, lower left), p. 248 (upper and middle left, lower), p. 258 (A, upper)
- *Homo habilis* .... p. 258 (A-D)
- Male gorilla skull .... p. 240 (Photo 13.7), p. 196 (A), p. 229 (lower A and B)
- Male chimpanzee skull .... p. 226 (lower right), p. 228 (upper left), p. 239 (Photo 13.2-13.4), p. 240 (Photo 13.5-13.6)
- Young chimpanzee skull .... p. 241 (B)
- Disarticulated plastic human skeleton .... p. 105 (Photo 7.10), p. 114 (Photo 7.13, 7.14), p. 116 (Photo 7.18), p. 133 (Photo 7.33), p. 134 (Photo 7.34), p. 119 (C, D), p. 136 (both), p. 242 (lower)

Used by permission of Somso Modelle.

Index